Ethnic Minority Women's Writing in France

After the Empire: The Francophone World and Postcolonial France

Series Editor: Valérie K. Orlando, University of Maryland

Advisory Board: Robert Bernasconi, Memphis University; Claire H. Griffiths, University of Chester, UK; Alec Hargreaves, Florida State University; Chima Korieh, Rowan University; Mildred Mortimer, University of Colorado, Boulder; Obioma Nnaemeka, Indiana University; Alison Rice, University of Notre Dame; Kamal Salhi, University of Leeds; Tracy D. Sharpley-Whiting, Vanderbilt University; Nwachukwu Frank Ukadike, Tulane University

Recent Titles

Ethnic Minority Women's Writing in France: Publishing Practices and Identity Formation, 1998–2005 by Claire Mouflard

Theory, Aesthetics, and Politics in the Francophone World: Filiations Past and Future by Rajeshwari S. Vallury

Refiguring Les Années Noires: Literary Representations of the Nazi Occupation by Kathy Comfort

Paris and the Marginalized Author: Treachery, Alienation, Queerness, and Exile by Valérie K. Orlando and Pamela A. Pears

French Orientalist Literature in Algeria, 1845–1882: Colonial Hauntings by Sage Goellner

Corporeal Archipelagos: Writing the Body in Francophone Oceanian Women's Literature by Julia Frengs

Spaces of Creation: Transculturality and Feminine Expression in Francophone Literature by Allison Connolly

Women Writers of Gabon: Literature and Herstory by Cheryl Toman

Backwoodsmen as Ecocritical Motif in French Canadian Literature: Connecting Worlds in the Wilds by Anne Rehill

Intertextual Weaving in the Work of Linda Lê: Imagining the Ideal Reader by Alexandra Kurmann

Front Cover Iconography and Algerian Women's Writing: Heuristic Implications of the Recto-Verso Effect by Pamela A. Pears

The Algerian War in French-Language Comics: Postcolonial Memory, History, and Subjectivity by Jennifer Howell

Writing through the Visual and Virtual: Inscribing Language, Literature, and Culture in Francophone Africa and the Caribbean by Ousseina D. Alidou and Renée Larrier

State Power, Stigmatization, and Youth Resistance Culture in the French Banlieues: Uncanny Citizenship by Hervé Tchumkam

Violence in Caribbean Literature: Stories of Stones and Blood by Véronique Maisier

Ethnic Minority Women's Writing in France

Publishing Practices and Identity Formation, 1998–2005

Claire Mouflard

LEXINGTON BOOKS
Lanham • Boulder • New York • London

Published by Lexington Books
An imprint of The Rowman & Littlefield Publishing Group, Inc.
4501 Forbes Boulevard, Suite 200, Lanham, Maryland 20706
www.rowman.com

6 Tinworth Street, London SE11 5AL, United Kingdom

Copyright © 2021 The Rowman & Littlefield Publishing Group, Inc.

Nora Hamdi, *La Couleur dans les mains* © Editions Leo Scheer – Paris 2011, Tous droits reserves.

Dans l'enfer des tournantes by Samira Bellil © 2002, Editions Denoel

All rights reserved. No part of this book may be reproduced in any form or by any electronic or mechanical means, including information storage and retrieval systems, without written permission from the publisher, except by a reviewer who may quote passages in a review.

British Library Cataloguing in Publication Information Available

Library of Congress Cataloging-in-Publication Data

Names: Mouflard, Claire, 1982- author.
Title: Ethnic minority women's writing in France : publishing practices and identity formation, 1998-2005 / Claire Mouflard.
Description: Lanham : Lexington Books, [2020] | Series: After the empire : the francophone world and postcolonial France | Includes bibliographical references and index.
Identifiers: LCCN 2020039662 (print) | LCCN 2020039663 (ebook) | ISBN 9781498587297 (cloth) | ISBN 9781498587310 (pbk) | ISBN 9781498587303 (epub)
Subjects: LCSH: French literature—Women authors—History and criticism. | French literature—Minority authors—History and criticism. | French literature—21st century—History and criticism. | Identity politics in literature. | Identity (Psychology) in literature. | Literature and society—France—History—21st century. | France—Ethnic relations—History—21st century.
Classification: LCC PQ149 .M68 2020 (print) | LCC PQ149 (ebook) | DDC 840.9/9287—dc23
LC record available at https://lccn.loc.gov/2020039662
LC ebook record available at https://lccn.loc.gov/2020039663

To my parents.

Contents

List of Figures	ix
Acknowledgments	xi
Introduction: The "Black-Blanc-Beur" Utopia and the Autobiographical Response	1
1 Utopia, Paratexts, and Publishers	13
2 "Beur," "*Banlieue* Victims," and "*Intégrées*": Samira Bellil, Nina Bouraoui, Nora Hamdi	41
3 "Black," "Afro-French," and "*Évoluées*": Calixthe Beyala, Bessora, Fatou Diome	79
4 Franco-Vietnamese Literature: The Unspoken Making of Anna Moï and Linda Lê	115
Conclusion: Beyond "Black-Blanc-Beur": Negotiating Labels and "*littérature-monde*"	155
Appendix	161
Bibliography	165
Index	175
About the Author	179

List of Figures

Figure 1.1	Front Cover of *Femme nue, femme noire* by Calixthe Beyala, Published by Éditions Albin Michel (2003)	32
Figure 1.2	Back Cover of *Femme nue, femme noire* by Calixthe Beyala, Published by Éditions Albin Michel (2003)	33
Figure 2.1	Front Cover of *Dans l'enfer des tournantes* by Samira Bellil, Published by Éditions Denoël (2002)	58
Figure 2.2	Front Cover of *Dans l'enfer des tournantes* by Samira Bellil, Published by Gallimard (Folio, 2003)	60
Figure 2.3	Front Cover of *La couleur dans les mains* by Nora Hamdi, Published by Éditions Léo Scheer (2011)	75
Figure 4.1	Front Cover of *Riz noir* by Anna Moï, Published by Gallimard (Folio, 2006)	123
Figure 4.2	Front Cover of *Parfum de pagode* by Anna Moï, Published by Éditions de l'Aube (2004)	131
Figure 4.3	Front Cover of *Parfum de pagode* by Anna Moï, Published by Éditions de l'Aube (L'Aube Poche, 2007)	132

Acknowledgments

This research started at the University of Washington where I completed my dissertation under the guidance of Richard Watts and Bénédicte Boisseron, who were both fantastic mentors. My extended gratitude goes to Bénédicte for her unwavering support through the years, from my days at the University of Montana where we met in 2005, to today. In Seattle, I greatly benefited from the support of my cohort and colleagues, in particular Lisa Connell, Amal Eqeiq, Delphine Gras, and Hedwige Meyer. My sincere and eternal thanks go to my copyeditor and longtime friend, reader, and supporter from the University of Washington, Jacinthe Assaad. I would also like to thank my colleagues at Union College where I first began to transform my dissertation into this book, for their conversations, support, and encouragements: Charles Batson, Deidre Hill Butler, Tommaso Gazzarri, Christine Henseler, and Cheikh Ndiaye. My greatest thanks go to Hamilton College which granted me the funds and junior sabbatical leave necessary for the research I conducted in France, as well as my travels to key conferences where I received precious feedback from my colleagues in the field. I would like to acknowledge the strong support and encouragements I received from my colleagues at Hamilton College, Martine Guyot-Bender, Roberta Krueger, and Cheryl Morgan through the various stages of this book. Last but not least, for their encouragements, love, and support, I am eternally grateful to my wife Deidre, my longtime friend Lisa, and all my family members and friends, in France and the United States.

Introduction
The "Black-Blanc-Beur" Utopia and the Autobiographical Response

On the eve of the twenty-first FIFA World Cup tournament, all eyes were on the French men's national team, "les Bleus" (a nickname given in reference to the color of their jerseys), as 2018 marked the twentieth anniversary of France winning the 1998 World Cup. The 2018 team was coached by former captain Didier Deschamps, who in 1998 was instrumental in turning the "Bleus" into famed *champions du monde* (world champions). At Deschamps' side in 1998, players Lilian Thuram, Emmanuel Petit, and Zinedine Zidane quickly achieved tremendous fame by scoring decisive goals in both the semifinal and final games. That night, these players became the faces of the "Black-Blanc-Beur" slogan popularized by the media during the 1998 tournament.[1] The phrase, originally used to connote multiethnic delinquent groups from the *banlieue* (the French projects) in the early 1990s,[2] was repurposed by the media to promote an idealized version of life in France for ethnic minorities, particularly for second-generation *male* immigrants. Athleticism was portrayed as a path to integration, with the French press presenting the World Cup win as proof of the assimilation of "non-Blanc" players within the French Republic's order.[3]

As Yvan Gastaut exposes in *Le métissage par le foot: l'intégration, mais jusqu'à où?* French newspapers presented the "Black-Blanc-Beur" victory as a historical event, one that sparked "une communion nationale sans précédent depuis la fin de la Seconde Guerre mondiale" ("a national harmony unprecedented since the end of the Second World War") (Gastaut 2008, 50). And yet, as Zidane was hailed as "l'icône de l'intégration" by *Libération* (40), the male integration model promoted by "Black-Blanc-Beur" contributed to a nation-building narrative which ignored the reality of ethnic minority *women* in France. Despite opposing voices in the sociocultural and literary contexts, such as Fadela Amara's in the Ni Putes Ni Soumises movement, the mainstream media regularly exploited the identities and lives of "non-Blanc" women in France. From the heavy mediatization of *banlieue* rape and the public victimization of young *banlieue* women in the early 2000s, to the 2004 ban on the Muslim veil,[4] women of North-African, Sub-Saharan, and Caribbean descent were simultaneously excluded from, yet made instrumental to the "Black-Blanc-Beur" nation-building exercise.

These identity formation processes by the media did not however abruptly start after the 1998 win. During the 1996 Olympic Games in Atlanta, Guadeloupian track athlete Marie-José Pérec's image was also exploited by the press. As with the 1998 team, claims made by the media contributed to the national discussion around race, gender, and—ultimately—the athlete's servitude to the French nation. In *Sport and Society in Global France: Nations, Migrations, Corporations*, Cathal Kilcline exposes how Pérec's image and athletic performance served different purposes: on the one hand, the American media saw in Pérec a symbol of the rise of the formerly colonized and enslaved black population; on the other hand, the French media regularly decried Pérec's departure from France to a Los Angeles-based athletic center, interpreting it as disloyalty to the nation (Kilcline 2019, 2–3). Kilcline writes: "The sense that the [French] nation had somehow been jilted by Pérec's transatlantic relocation was facilitated by her reputation as a 'diva' . . . and the sexual allure she evidently held for many commentators from sporting and non-sporting milieus" (2). The sexual stereotypes emphasized by the media were clearly linked to Pérec's ethnicity, as well as to racial and gender-based hierarchies inherited from the colonial era.

The mediatic persecution of Marie-Josée Pérec in 1996 coincided with French-Cameroonian author Calixthe Beyala's public trial and condemnation for plagiarism. In both instances, a black woman was publicly shamed for disobeying the "rules of the game," before being acclaimed shortly thereafter in a *mise-en-scène* of public repentance: Beyala won the Grand Prix du Roman de l'Académie Française a few months after her condemnation, and Pérec won two gold medals for France at the '96 Olympic Games. Both women eventually earned momentary praise from the media and the French public. Yet the '98 win and its idealization of male, immigrant yet integrated "Bleu" athleticism caused an even more striking vilification of ethnic minority women in the public discourse. In turn, ethnic minority women writers discussed and disputed the utopia of a perfectly integrated French society in their narratives.

In *Le ventre de l'Atlantique*, French-Senegalese author Fatou Diome directly addressed the excessive glorification of male athleticism as a symbol of integration in France. In her semiautobiographical narrative, Diome engaged with the dangers of the "Black-Blanc-Beur" utopia, ultimately revealing the inherent falseness of the slogan's image of immigration. Through the voice of her narrator Salie, Diome wrote: "Quant à leur politique d'intégration, elle vaut tout au plus pour leur équipe nationale de football . . . *Blacks, Blancs, Beurs,* si ça allait de soi dans la société française, on n'aurait pas besoin d'en faire un slogan" (As for their integration policy, it only applies to their national football team . . . *Blacks, Blancs, Beurs*—if French society was truly integrated, they wouldn't need to invent a slogan) (Diome 2003, 178/125). In her novel, Diome built on the sociocultural implications of the French team's victory in order to reveal the discrepancies between the media's representation of multicultural bliss and the reality of life in France for a black woman in the early 2000s. Diome was in fact one of several female authors whose autobiographical and autofictional accounts crystallized into a corpus of counter-discourses opposing the idealized narrative of "Black-Blanc-Beur" multiculturalism.

The present book examines the works of ethnic minority women writers who shed light on the reality of immigrant life between late 1990s and early 2000s France: Bessora who lifted the veil on the French immigration process in *53 cm*, Nora Hamdi who portrayed *banlieue* women's resistance to France's continuing ethnic hierarchies in *Des poupées et des anges*, and Samira Bellil who provided her testimony of gang rape in *Dans l'enfer des tournantes*. This book also investigates the works of politically engaged authors who directly addressed the hypocrisy of the institutions toward immigration and integration: Calixthe Beyala in her anti-racist manifesto *Lettre d'une Afro-française à ses compatriotes*, and Fatou Diome in *La préférence nationale et autres nouvelles* and *Le ventre de l'Atlantique*. Finally, this study addresses the works of authors who, while disregarded by the media, investigated their own identity formation processes within France's literary sphere: Anna Moï who reflected on her self-labeling process in *Espéranto, désespéranto: la francophonie sans les Français*, and Linda Lê who established her literary lineage in *Le complexe de Caliban*.

The autobiographies and autofictions selected for this study problematize the idealistic representation of immigrant male athleticism and its sociocultural consequences on the identity formation processes of second and third-generation immigrants in France. These narratives address gender, ethnic, and national identity constructs in the public sphere (in the media, institutional, and literary realms), as well as in their self-definition processes as ethnic minority women authors who write in French yet continue to see themselves and their oeuvres demoted to the *francophone* category of French-speaking (but not entirely "French") literature. In addition to offering textual analyses of these narratives, this book reveals the pervasive influence that select metropolitan publishing houses exert on these authors and their works through the use of identity formation practices, which range from the choice of strategic paratextual and marketing elements, to direct text editing. In turn, these practices have either hindered or encouraged the author's self-definition and self-categorization process.

Each author problematizes in their own way the idealistic immigrant representations encouraged by the "Black-Blanc-Beur" World Cup win and subsequent slogan. Together, they offer broader pictures of second-generation immigrant life and self-identity formation practices than the ones promoted by French institutions through the postcolonial era. The works under study in this book were selected because they were all published between the years 1998 and 2005, and they all address—openly (Bellil, Bessora, Beyala, Diome, and Hamdi) or more subtly (Bouraoui, Lê, and Moï)—the identity politics of the postcolonial French era. In particular, they reveal the impacts of these politics on their own identification as authors writing in the French language in the metropolitan literary realm. All texts are self-reflections on the process of writing in French as an author of French colonial ancestry (North-African, Sub-Saharan, Southeast Asian), as well as reflections on the role of contemporary French institutions (education, the media, publishing, the literary sphere) in the delineation of one's public and private identity.

This book ultimately reveals that the notable absence of the Franco-Vietnamese identity from the "Black-Blanc-Beur" utopia enabled authors such as Linda Lê and Anna Moï to establish themselves outside of the "Black-Blanc-Beur" paradigm in a way that allowed them to find and reclaim their voices as authors *de langue française* (writing in the French language). In comparison, although the aforementioned "Black" and "Beur" authors are also known for being *de langue française*, their first signifier on the metropolitan literary market remains one of Otherness and exoticism, a reminder of France's colonial past which resurfaced during the "Black-Blanc-Beur" years. In spite of the literary labels and other essentializing packaging and marketing artifacts developed by their publishers, and in spite of the exclusionary identity politics that defined the 1998–2005 era, all the women writers in this book have challenged the "Black-Blanc-Beur" utopia and encouraged the next generation of women writers to follow suit.

The works studied in this book were published at a time of heavy commodification of the "non-Blanc" identity in France: while men were being valued for their athletic feats under the supposedly egalitarian "Bleu" French jersey, women were publicly condemned, either because they donned the Muslim veil or, like Calixthe Beyala, because they exposed the French institutional hypocrisy regarding France's colonial past. The immediate institutional punishment for these acts (the 2004 ban on religious symbols in public schools, Beyala's condemnation for plagiarism, and subsequent marketing as a pariah), when compared to the instant glorification of the men's national soccer team are revealing of what Marc Augé has recently termed "un culte totémique" (a totemic cult) in his 2019 publication *Match retour: anthropologie de la revanche et autres textes* (12). For Augé, in sports as in politics, those who do not adequately participate in the "cult" find themselves excluded and punished, as "[l']appartenance totémique se mérite" (totemic belonging must be earned) (13). In their texts, the authors studied here actively denounce the commodification of bodies and identities, as well as the cult-like aspect of "Black-Blanc-Beur" identity politics. Each author demonstrates that their expulsion from the "cult" (or their perennial exclusion from it) is actually part and parcel of the neocolonial construction of the "Black-Blanc-Beur" utopia. This book therefore seeks to encourage further discussion on that era's gendering of immigration politics through the glorification of a male athletic ideal, sustained in part by the literary industry's fabrication of subservient female ideals of integration.

CONTEXT

The dates chosen for this study, 1998–2005, frame the period from the French men's soccer team's victory in the World Cup tournament (July 12, 1998) to the *banlieue* riots of October and November 2005. These two symbolic events serve as bookends to the phenomenon that I term the "'Black-Blanc-Beur' utopia," as it began with the glorified win of a supposedly multicultural French team and ended with revealing manifestations of the social fracture that subsists in metropolitan France, one that could not be healed by the "Black-Blanc-Beur" propaganda. These seven years between 1998 and 2005 encompass the end of President Jacques Chirac's first (seven-year) mandate and the beginning of his second (five-year) one, which he won by a historical margin against his second-round opponent, Front National leader Jean-Marie Le Pen. Beyond the rise of nationalistic extremisms in France characterized by Le Pen being voted into the second round of the presidential race in 2002, Chirac's presidency was marked by the 2004 headscarf ban and debate on *laïcité* in French public schools, the 2005 *banlieue* riots, and—last but not least—right-wing politician Nicolas Sarkozy's ascent to power, first as Minister of the Interior and then as the new President after his 2007 election win against socialist candidate Ségolène Royal. Sarkozy's xenophobic acts included, among others, the closing of the Sangatte Red Cross refugee center in Calais, and his incendiary comments regarding the uprising of the *banlieue* youth in 2005. These events, forming a pattern of increased political fear-mongering and overtly expressed nostalgia for colonial France, seriously affected the operations of the metropolitan literary industry during the years 1998–2005, notably in the ways it defined authorial identities and literary genres for postcolonial immigrant, bicultural, and binational authors. The research for this book is therefore based at the intersection of national identity politics, gender norms, immigrant identities, and the publishing industry between 1998 and 2005.

ETHNIC MINORITY WOMEN'S AUTOBIOGRAPHIES: PROBLEMATIZING "NON-UNITARY" IDENTITIES

In her study of autobiographies written by Gisèle Halimi, Julia Kristeva, Assia Djebar, and Hélène Cixous, entitled *Shifting Subjectivity in Contemporary Francophone Women's Autobiography* (2011), Natalie Edwards contends that although "[t]he writers belong to very different cultural backgrounds . . . they are united by their desire to inscribe their 'I' in a way that refutes unitary autobiography and highlights the problems inherent in writing non-unitary selfhood. Writing an individual '*I*' that is representative of one distinct identity is not possible for them" (Edwards 2011, 10). Edwards highlights the fact that the genre of autobiography has long been perceived as reflecting a unitary (or unified) self, and that, consequently, "[m]any marginalized and dispossessed groups thus lay beyond the scope of these necessary requirements, and women are just one example" (1). The fragmented identities of the four authors studied by Edwards resemble those portrayed in the semi- to full autobiographical works examined in the following chapters of this book; their identity formation processes are inspired by their multifaceted cultural and ethnic backgrounds which cannot reasonably be encapsulated within a single term, or slogan. This book aims to demonstrate that, like the women in Edwards' study, authors like Bellil, Bessora, and Lê each produced "non-unitary" autobiographies at a time when the unitary identity of a perfectly integrated male "Black" or "Beur" was heavily promoted in the public arena.

Between 1998 and 2005, French media outlets promoted a unified discourse of "Black-Blanc-Beur" (male) multiculturalism, one which on the surface called for the celebration of cultural as well as ethnic differences, yet was also evidently controlled by the French institutions. This utopic version of French multiculturalism, one of male athletic accomplishment and of all-around successful postcolonial integration, prompted the women authors studied here to write from an autobiographical perspective in order to counter the utter lack of accurate representation of second-generation immigrant life in late 1990s and early 2000s France. As Edwards underlines in her own study:

> Despite the fact that they all write in French, the women thus grew up in different parts of the world and had a specific relationship to the idea of the nation

in general and to the idea of the French nation in particular. This renders their autobiographical writing all the more interesting since they are forced to handle this in some way: by repressing it, by fictionalizing it, by dramatizing it, or by attempting to understand it and its impact upon their identity. (11)

The women whose works are examined here all use the autobiographical or autofictional genre to challenge institutionalized notions of ethnicity and gender constructs as they relate to national and cultural identity in a postcolonial world—particularly at the turn of the century, in "Black-Blanc-Beur" France. In addition, the authors studied in this book come from a variety of backgrounds: Beyala and Diome are first-generation immigrants to France, as are Moï and Lê; Bellil and Bouraoui were born in Algeria but partially raised in France; Hamdi was born in France; Bessora was born in Belgium, the daughter of a Gabonese man and a Swiss woman, yet she resides and publishes in France. These variations thus bring to the present study a range of multifaceted perspectives on the ethnic minority female authorial identity in 1990s–2000s France.

Françoise Lionnet asserts in *Autobiographical Voices: Race, Gender, Self-Portraiture* that comparative studies of francophone women's autobiographies reveal a "growing interest in highlighting *alternative* patterns of resistance to cultural and political hegemony" as well as these women's opposition "to all rigid, essentializing approaches to questions of race, class, or gender" (xii). Lionnet also denounces the censorship imposed on these women's voices following the criticism of their male counterparts that shunned them as "unenlightened, apolitical, and at best embarrassing sisters because the confessional nature of some of their narratives does not offer ready-made solutions to the problems of racism in their respective countries" (xii). Finally, Lionnet writes that her focus on francophone women's literature is anchored in the strong belief that their voices are and have been problematizing hegemonic power constructs in the postcolonial world. Herself an author from Mauritius, Lionnet writes: "We who have been oppressed and silenced . . . will never be tempted by the illusions of leadership, will never be deluded into thinking that we can represent anyone but ourselves. That is why we have much to contribute to a global understanding of affirmative and egalitarian principles" (6). The authors whose works are examined here follow in the footsteps of authors studied by Lionnet, among whom Maryse Condé, Zora Neale Hurston and Maya Angelou, and represent a new generation of ethnic minority women who have used their talent with the word to pen anticolonial, antiracist, and anti-hegemonic manifestoes which still read true to this day. In its examination of selected autobiographies and autofictions written by ethnic minority women in metropolitan France during the specific 1998–2005 period, this book aims to shed light on these anticolonial, antiracist, and anti-hegemonic discourses, as well as on the metropolitan publishing industry's role as it either aided or hindered the circulation of these texts.

CHAPTER OVERVIEW

Chapter 1, entitled "Utopia, Paratexts, and Publishers," serves as an introduction to the notions used throughout this book, such as the function of the colonial and postcolonial paratexts according to the works of Gérard Genette and Richard Watts, and the methods pertaining to the making and marketing of books by their publishers in metropolitan France. The second aim of this introductory chapter is to establish the rationale for this study: the 1998 "Black-Blanc-Beur" utopia was modeled after the ideal of a successful *male* immigration confined to the domain of sports, to which, in contrast, a series of semi- to full autobiographical works written in French by women authors *issues de l'immigration* (with an immigrant background) appeared as counterpoints to the widely portrayed male immigrant experience. In turn, these autobiographical and autofictional works along with their authors were fashioned according to gendered and colonial marketing practices by both their publishers and the media. Eventually, women of Southeastern Asian descent (particularly Vietnamese women) were left out of the "Black-Blanc-Beur" equation. Interviews recorded with select authors and editors in 2019, along with research conducted at Caen's IMEC (Institut Mémoires de l'édition contemporaine) reveal the extent of the ethnic and gender-based editing and marketing practices of the "Black-Blanc-Beur" utopia years.

Chapter 2, "'Beur,' '*Banlieue* Victims,' and '*Intégrées*': Samira Bellil, Nina Bouraoui, Nora Hamdi," positions three female authors in contrast with Zinédine Zidane ("Zizou"), the French soccer team's superstar player whose portrait was projected onto the Arc de Triomphe after the Bleus' victory in 1998. This chapter first details how the promotion of Zizou's *intégré* male identity for the *beur* generation effectively compartmentalized women of North-African descent into a sub-discourse, from which writing in the semi or full autobiographical mode emerged to help certain authors create a public identity that differed from common stereotypes. The research of this chapter centers on the works of three female authors who were at one time or another between 1998 and 2005 officially branded as "Beur," with an additional implicit label of *banlieue* or *intégrée* as expressed in the paratext of their published works. This chapter therefore investigates the marketing practices of selected publishing houses (Denoël, Folio, Stock, Au Diable Vauvert, and Léo Scheer) and their authors' rapport with the paratext in which they were framed, as expressed in their narratives, interviews, and additional essays.

Chapter 3, "'Black,' 'Afro-French,' and '*Évoluées*': Calixthe Beyala, Bessora, Fatou Diome," compares the marketing practices surrounding the published works of three authors who incarnate different facets of the "Black" literary identity spectrum at the turn of the millennium.[5] While the term "Black" in "Black-Blanc-Beur" was meant to erase the colonial history and racism that were undeniably attached to the term *noir* all the while giving "Black" an urban, therefore supposedly integrated connotation, its meaning and defining features varied greatly from its attachment to a male soccer persona such as Lilian Thuram to its labeling of politically vocal authors such as Calixthe Beyala, Bessora, and Fatou Diome. Just as "Black" became a symbol of success after Thuram's two winning goals in France's semifinal against Croatia, as well as a symbol of successful integration, "Black" in the literary context became an implicit label that signified female rebellion and a lack of conformity to the République's ideals.[6] In this chapter, I compare Beyala's tokenization by her publisher, the media, and the Académie Française, to Bessora's work and publishing history as Bessora incarnates a global and multifaceted black identity, as opposed to the fabricated, fixed, and sexualized "Black" identity imposed on her by the French literary authorities. This chapter concludes with a study of Fatou Diome's use of the epitext (interviews and essays) as peripheral commentaries to her oeuvre: in this instance, *La préférence nationale et autres Nouvelles* and *Le ventre de l'Atlantique*.

Chapter 4, "Franco-Vietnamese Literature: The Unspoken Making of Anna Moï and Linda Lê," is dedicated to two of the writers excluded from the "Black-Blanc-Beur" slogan and who nevertheless succeeded in anchoring themselves in the French literature realm: Franco-Vietnamese women writers Linda Lê and Anna Moï. As this concluding chapter reveals, Southeastern Asian identities are not completely absent from the French postcolonial discourse, specifically in the metropolitan publishing industry, but they are often only visible in iterations that openly contribute to the framing of authorial identities within a nostalgic colonial context, a fabricated space of Orientalism and subservience to the French literary institutions. While francophone writers of Southeastern Asian descent remain largely invisible, if not completely absent, from main catalogs of publishing houses such as Gallimard, Stock, or Albin Michel, some appear to have found a home and made a career with smaller, yet significantly prolific publishing houses such the Éditions de L'Aube (Moï) and the Éditions Christian Bourgois (Lê). This chapter thus concludes with a study of Linda Lê's work with Christian Bourgois between the years 1998 and 2005, in terms of paratextual and marketing practices as well as narrative strategies in relation to the question of her own postcolonial and authorial identity. In *Le complexe de Caliban*, similarly to Bouraoui's *Garçon manqué* (chapter 2), Bessora's *53 cm* (chapter 3), and Anna Moï's *Espéranto, désespéranto: La francophonie sans les Français* (chapter 4), Lê reflects on the process of writing, especially writing in French, as a third identitarian space that is neither French nor "Other" and which enables her to exist beyond any type of colonial or postcolonial paradigm. In this chapter, I demonstrate that the exclusion of women writers such as Moï and Lê from the "Black-Blanc-Beur" paradigm has benefited these authors in affording them a space in which to settle within another domain of French literature, one not quite institutionally French nor francophone.

The present study does not claim to be exhaustive, nor is it meant to classify the selected ethnic minority women writers and their works according to specific (official or unofficial) labels. Rather, this hybrid examination of autobiographical and autofictional narratives, of paratextual elements and marketing practices, and of interviews granted by select authors and editors, humbly seeks to shed light on the phenomena of authorial identity formation and the creation of literary subcategories in the metropolitan literary sphere during a specific time period. In turn, the study of these labeling processes is meant to highlight the intrinsic relationship between the media and identity politics France, as well as their impact on the literary and publishing industries.

NOTES

1. Thuram was turned into a signifier connoting a global "Black" identity, Petit represented a rather traditional "Blanc," white "French" identity, and Zidane was hailed as the ideal "Beur"—a term which refers to French citizens whose parents emigrated from the Maghreb.

2. "Initialement, rappelle le chercheur [Gastaut], [l'expression] n'a rien à voir avec le football mais s'utilise, au début des années 1990, pour évoquer une forme de petite délinquance dans les quartiers dits sensibles . . . En clair, le *"black-blanc-beur"* du début des années 1990, et notamment après les émeutes de banlieue de 1992, raconte une forme de communauté de destin, perçue comme négative par ceux qui utilisent l'expression." (The researcher [Gastaut] recalls that, initially, [the expression] has nothing to do with soccer but is used, in the early 1990s, to evoke a form of petty crime in neighborhoods known as disadvantaged . . . In sum, the *black-blanc-beur* of the early 1990s, and notably after the 1992 *banlieue* riots, speaks of a community bound by fate, [and] perceived negatively by those who use the expression.) (Leprince 2018, par. 5).

3. Here and throughout this study, the term "non-Blanc" refers to ethnic minority French citizens (men and women) during the period of inquiry, 1998-2005, whose identity differs from the "Blanc" (seen as originally "French") of the "Black-Blanc-Beur" slogan.

4. In March 2004, the French parliament enacted a law that prohibits students from wearing religious signs in public schools. Derek Davis explains: "While the law is broadly applicable on its face . . . the unstated but clear aim of the law, if the French media is any guide, is to prohibit female Muslim students from wearing the hijab, or headscarf" (Davis 2004, 221).

5. The term *évoluée* is used here in the same sense and context as in Dominic Thomas' chapter entitled "The 'Marie NDiaye Affair,' or the Coming of a Postcolonial *évoluée*" (Thomas 2013).

6. According to Etienne Achille and Lydie Moudileno in *Mythologies Postcoloniales: Pour une décolonisation du quotidien*, the role of defending the integration process in France was "assigned" to Thuram after 1998. Thuram progressively emancipated himself from this role through various publications (most notably his *Manifeste pour l'égalité* in 2012), thus leading scholars in postcolonial studies to consider him an "*organic* postcolonial intellectual" (Achille and Moudileno 2018, 101–106).

Chapter 1

Utopia, Paratexts, and Publishers

In the past twenty years, what I term the "Black-Blanc-Beur" utopia—a forced, faulty, and incomplete ideal of integration—has waned to the point that it is now considered by many to be only a vestige of the past. In fact, in the weeks leading to the start of the 2018 World Cup, several news outlets in France and abroad had emphasized that the "Black-Blanc-Beur" ideal of 1998 had been, after all, nothing but a myth (AFP 2018).[1] In *Affreux, riches et méchants? Un autre regard sur les Bleus*, Stéphane Béaud explains that the element that truly unified the 1998 men's national soccer team was in fact not its apparent multiethnic origins, but rather the shared values of its members who had all grown up in blue collar families, regardless of their parents' geographical origins. Béaud contends that the team represented the values of their own parents, which were in turn transmitted to the public: "un *ethos* sportif et social . . . le sens du collectif, une certaine forme d'humilité, le respect des anciens, l'amour du maillot tricolore et de la patrie" (an athletic and social *ethos* . . . a sense of community, a certain form of humility, the respect of their elders, the love of the tricolor jersey and of the nation) (Béaud 2014, 49). Despite these commonalities, the men of the 1998 team represented for the French media "une aubaine" (a godsend) as Yvan Gastaut emphasizes in *Le métissage par le foot*, an opportunity to represent "l'aspect constructif de l'apport des immigrés à la société française" (the constructive aspect of what immigrants bring to French society) (Gastaut 2008, 38). As *métissage* (ethnic mixing) quickly became a "terme en vogue" (fashionable term) during the '98 World Cup, the players' multiethnic origins were publicly emphasized as "atout[s] majeur[s]" (major assets) in the team's victory and, by extension, in the country's progress toward a more global understanding of diversity (37). This progress was however uneven and often challenged by official and unofficial acts of racism, highlighting the faults of the "Black-Blanc-Beur" utopia.

THE MAKING OF THE "BLACK-BLANC-BEUR" UTOPIA AND THE PARATEXTUAL RESPONSE

In his study simply entitled *Utopia*, Merlin Coverley articulates the Greek root and primary meaning of the term "utopia" as "good place" but also "no place": "*Utopia* is, of course, the name Sir Thomas More created for his book of 1516. But More's title combines two Greek neologisms, *outopia*, meaning no-place, and *eutopia*, meaning good-place, to create a word that is also a pun, and a place that is simultaneously good and non-existent" (Coverley 2010, 9–10). The term "utopia" is a key concept used in this book along the terms of the definition outlined by Coverley. The idealized "Black-Blanc-Beur" France that was portrayed and promoted through the national men's soccer team's victory in the 1998 World Cup is one that did not exist at that time, nor did it ever exist at any time in postcolonial French history. However, the promotion of a peaceful and egalitarian republic has become—and, as outlined as early as in More's sixteenth century text, has always been—a political tool largely used by governing forces in order to appease the population and, simultaneously, divert their attention from the political power's actual plans and actions.

The reference to Thomas More's *Utopia* is one to keep in mind in the context of the present study. In *Utopia*, More imagined an island where all members of society lived equally but had to follow a certain set of rules in order to maintain the balance of the utopian regime. John Carey in *The Faber Book of Utopias* wrote: "It is a land of happy, healthy, public-spirited communists. Money and private property are extinct. Anyone can enter any house at any time: doors are never locked [but] . . . In Utopia there is no frivolity and little freedom. Clothing is uniform . . . You need a permit to travel, and must go in a group. If you travel without a permit, you are arrested as a runaway and severely punished" (Carey 1999, 39–40). In "Utopia and its Discontents," Edward Rothstein highlights the constant desire of individuals to strive for something better (a better place, a better government, better living conditions . . .) as well as the inevitable political entanglements that characterize the creation and pursuits of utopian places or, more commonly, of utopian political regimes. For Rothstein, the combination of political interests and the human search for the perfect place can either encourage social progress, or, as underlined by Carey, allow the utopian society to fall into totalitarianism. Rothstein explains:

> Utopia is not an impossible place, or at any rate, it is generally not *supposed* to be. It is a place that can conceivably exist—and, in the teller's view, a place that *should* exist. At any rate, however out of reach, most utopias are meant to be pursued. Utopias represent an ideal toward which the mundane world must

reach. They are examples to be worked for. Utopianism creates a political program, giving direction and meaning to the idea of progress; progress is always on the way to some notion of utopia. (Rothstein 2003, 3)

In addition, Rothstein warns of the dangers of utopia, noting: "The last century's worst horrors—including Nazi Germany, the Soviet regime, the Maoist Cultural Revolution—grew out of utopian visions. With such examples in mind, the philosopher Isaiah Berlin argued that utopianism leads not to freedom but to tyranny" (5). In a sense, the conceptual structure of the "Black-Blanc-Beur" utopia led to tyranny and totalitarianism as the "idea of progress" (Rothstein) which characterized the "Black-Blanc-Beur" years and slogan was essentially one of exclusion as opposed to inclusion. The "Black-Blanc-Beur" ideal imagined first and second-generation immigrants visibly renouncing their particularities in favor of a superficially multicultural yet quintessentially French republican ideal, one in which only a few predefined traits would be valued as part of the nation's imagined sociocultural homogeneity.

The utopia of a multicultural and multiethnic society that could completely forgo France's colonial past and violent history of subjugation, enslavement, and humiliation in the colonies, is one that resembles the utopian colonial society that was outlined in Hannah Arendt's *Origins of Totalitarianism*. In her second volume entitled *Imperialism*, Arendt argues that French colonial forces had essentially based their colonial power overseas on the treatment of the local populations as both brothers and subjects. She writes:

> The French, in contrast to the British and all other nations in Europe, actually tried in recent times to combine *ius* with *imperium* and to build an empire in the old Roman sense. They alone at least attempted to develop the body politic of the nation into an imperial political structure . . . they wanted to incorporate overseas possessions into the national body by treating the conquered people as "both . . . brothers and . . . subjects" . . . The result of this daring enterprise was a particularly brutal exploitation of overseas possessions for the sake of the nation. (Arendt 1951, 129)

This colonization and subjugation model, based on a promised utopian structure of equality between the ruling nation and its subjects, is a model that was effectively reproduced in the discourse of the 1998 "Black-Blanc-Beur" utopia. The perceived and propagated images of equality between "Blacks" (French citizens of Caribbean and Sub-Saharan descent), "Beurs" (French citizens of North African descent), and "Blancs" (the so-called *Français de souche*, French citizens who supposedly do not bear any genetic trait of non-French ascendance, this concept itself being somewhat of a utopia), similarly and inevitably—as outlined by Rothstein—led to tyranny and civil unrest (the *banlieue* riots of 2005), a symptom of the impossibility of the proposed egalitarian "Black-Blanc-Beur" model.

In effect, this proposed "Black-Blanc-Beur" model lacked and actually excluded French citizens of Southeastern Asian descent. To simply accept that their exclusion from the slogan was based on there being no player of Asian descent on the 1998 men's national soccer team would amount to accepting the discursive and identitarian totalitarianism that surrounded the "Black-Blanc-Beur" era. In reality, the populations that were most visibly portrayed in the media as causing unrest during the 1990s in France were of North African and Sub-Saharan descent, which explains the 1998 media focus on regulating the public image of "Blacks" and "Beurs." Beyond the numerous terrorist attacks led by the GIA (Groupe Islamique Armé) on the French territory during the Algerian Civil War (1991–2002), the political discourse on immigration at that time was also geared toward—or rather against—citizens of Sub-Saharan descent. In a 1991 discourse (the "Discours d'Orléans") made when he was the mayor of Paris, Jacques Chirac infamously mentioned "le bruit et l'odeur," the "noise and smell" of immigrants from the African continent. Chirac explained:

> Notre problème, ce n'est pas les étrangers, c'est qu'il y a overdose. C'est peut-être vrai qu'il n'y a pas plus d'étrangers qu'avant la guerre, mais ce n'est pas les mêmes et ça fait une différence. Il est certain que d'avoir des Espagnols, des Polonais et des Portugais travaillant chez nous, ça pose moins de problèmes que d'avoir des musulmans et des Noirs.
>
> (Foreigners are not the problem: our problem is that there is an overdose. It may be true that there are not more foreigners here today than there were before the war, but they are not the same and that makes a difference. Certainly, having Spaniards, Polish and Portuguese people working in our country is less problematic than having Muslim and Black people here.) (Chirac 1991, par. 1)

In order to rectify this faux-pas, Chirac eventually profited from the men's soccer team's win in 1998, and built his politics of immigration on a completely utopian vision of equality between the so-called *Français de souche*, and the formerly colonized and their children.

It then quickly became clear that Chirac's adherence to the "Black-Blanc-Beur" slogan was not exactly sincere, but rather strategic in order to quiet the civil unrest between France's "Blancs" on one side, and the "Blacks" and "Beurs" on the other. During the final match of the World Cup, Chirac was filmed in the presidential tribune mouthing the names of the players as they were announced on the field: Chirac was however mocked for his lack of knowledge regarding the players' names and accused of profiting from the team's success in order to improve his own political ratings. During the traditional July 14th televised interview that year, immediately following the victory of the "Black-Blanc-Beur" team, Chirac was asked by two journalists if the "Black-Blanc-Beur" slogan reflected the government's intentions to curb racism and promote integration. Chirac did not directly address these pointed questions, but instead praised a "France multicolore" and spoke of a "peuple qui a besoin de se retrouver ensemble, et de se retrouver autour d'une idée qui le rend fier de lui-même" (people that needs to gather, and to bond over an idea that makes it proud of itself) (INA 1998, 2:10). The shift in Chirac's discourse concerning the "Blacks" and the "Beurs" was evidently politically motivated, and the president was extremely mindful of the potential that lay in the "Black-Blanc-Beur" utopia.

The "Black-Blanc-Beur" slogan and its potential were concurrently appropriated by the publishing industry in their marketing of (perceived as) "Black" and "Beur" authors after the 1998 win. In fact, in this study, I argue that the 1998 launch of the popular phrase "Black-Blanc-Beur" encouraged some of the most influential French metropolitan publishers to create alternative literature categories in reaction to this newly phrased utopic notion of French multiculturalism, all the while leaving authors of Southeastern Asian descent entirely out of the equation. In so doing, publishing houses reproduced colonial stereotypes and further divisions between the "Blanc" (or perceived as "Blanc") authors and "Other" authors from the former colonial empire, specifically from Sub-Saharan Africa and the Maghreb. These post-1998 publishing practices particularly affected ethnic minority women writers both in the marketing of their autobiographical works and, concurrently, in the formation of their literary identities.

Francophone Asian literatures were visibly excluded from the "Black-Blanc-Beur" paradigm and its consequential shift in metropolitan publishing practices, which enabled authors such as Linda Lê and Anna Moï to establish themselves outside of the millennium's reductive multicultural utopia, with the help of minor, yet established, publishing houses: namely, the Éditions Christian Bourgois and the Éditions de l'Aube. As will be further exposed in chapter 4, Lê took great care to stay away from essentialist labels from the beginning of her writing career, a choice facilitated by her professional relationship with the Éditions Christian Bourgois which have published all of Lê's oeuvres in their *littérature française* ("French literature") collection. On the other hand, Anna Moï suffered from similar marketing practices developed during the "Black-Blanc-Beur" era in the case of "Black" and "Beur" authors, yet managed to voice her own detachment from neocolonial labels, notably in her memoir, *Espéranto, désespéranto: la francophonie sans les Français* published with Gallimard in 2006.

We first need to define the paratext as well as its function in the commercialization of a book. In essence, the paratext of a printed production is composed of a series of elements that are meant to represent the text in pictorial form (such as the artwork on the front cover or a photo of the author on the back cover), introduce the narrative along with the author's identity (on the dust jacket or back cover, a short biography and bibliography of the author, sometimes the previous literary prizes he or she might have received), and frame the text within a particular historical, sociocultural, or political context (in the manner of prefaces and postfaces written by the author, the editor, or an external introducer). In *Seuils*, translated as *Paratexts: Thresholds of Interpretation*, French theorist Gérard Genette explains that paratextual elements have a specific function in the publication process of a book, and that they are strategically chosen by the publishing houses. Genette thus states in his introduction:

> Cette frange [le paratexte], en effet, toujours porteuse d'un commentaire auctorial, ou plus ou moins légitimé par l'auteur, constitue, entre texte et hors-texte, une zone non seulement de transition, mais de transaction: lieu privilégié d'une pragmatique et d'une stratégie, d'une action sur le public au service, bien ou mal compris et accompli, d'un meilleur accueil du texte et d'une lecture plus pertinente— plus pertinente, s'entend, aux yeux de l'auteur et de ses alliés.
>
> (Indeed, this fringe [the paratext], always the conveyor of a commentary that is authorial or more or less legitimated by the author, constitutes a zone between text and off-text, a zone not only of transition but also of *transaction*: a privileged place of a pragmatics and a strategy, of an influence on the public, an influence that—whether well or poorly understood and achieved—is at the service of a better reception for the text and a more pertinent reading of it [more pertinent, of course, in the eyes of the author and his allies].) (Genette 1987/1997, 1/1)

The idea for this book is based on the application of the aforementioned concepts in the case of ethnic minority women writing in French and publishing in the Metropole. I argue that the "*transaction*" mentioned by Genette in the case of the authors selected for this study is one that heavily relies on colonial stereotypes relating to the author's perceived race, gender, and sexuality.

When compared with the publications of nonimmigrant metropolitan authors, the publications of francophone women writers from Africa, the Caribbean, and the Maghreb are decidedly marked in terms of gender and race, and presented to the French metropolitan reading audience in specific forms of packaging. This packaging—the physical paratext—frames the narrative and often denotes a broader political, sociocultural, and postcolonial discourse than would originally be anticipated. In the case of francophone women writers of African descent, these paratextual clues are fashioned by publishing houses to attract audiences into what Graham Huggan has termed a "postcolonial exotic" realm (in *The Postcolonial Exotic: Marketing the Margins*), one that undeniably reproduces gender and racial stereotypes created during the colonial era for commercial purposes, and one in which "postcolonialism" (the intellectual discourse) and "postcoloniality" (the commercial discourse) have thus become inseparable:

> Postcolonialism, understood this way, becomes an anti-colonial intellectualism that reads and valorises the signs of social struggle in the faultlines of literary and cultural texts . . . Postcoloniality, put another way, is a value-regulating mechanism within the global late-capitalist system of commodity exchange . . . the point that needs to be stressed here is that postcolonialism *is bound up with* postcoloniality—that in the overwhelmingly commercial context of late twentieth-century commodity culture, postcolonialism and its rhetoric of resistance have themselves become consumer products. (Huggan 2006, 6)

Under these terms, postcolonial publications in France, beyond their mere nature as "narratives" or "autobiographies," *possess* but are also almost always *affixed* an additional cultural and ideological value that has been strategically formatted by the metropolitan literary institutions (the publishing houses or the Académie Française) in order to broadly characterize the desired state of the Republic to these texts' targeted audience. In reviewing the studied authors' reactions to the "branding" of their literary productions and personae for a specific audience through the use of gendered, ethnic, or neutral paratextual elements, this book seeks to determine the nature of the discursive power relations that bind authors to their texts and also to their publishing houses, as well as the manner in which each author chooses to navigate these relations.

POWER AND PUBLISHING IN CONTEMPORARY FRANCE

The publishing world in metropolitan France has long been directed by French white men. In its power structure and history, the French publishing sphere actually mirrors the social, cultural, ethnic, and linguistic constructs that have continually ostracized nonwhite colonized and postcolonial authors from the center—namely, the *littérature française* realm. Jean-Yves Mollier notes in his article "L'histoire de l'édition: une histoire à vocation globalisante" that the history of French publishing is essentially "[l'][h]istoire d'un homme, le fondateur le plus souvent, mais aussi le repreneur dans bien des cas, et d'une famille ou d'une dynastie" ([the] history of a man, most often the founder, but also the buyer in many cases, and of a family or a dynasty) (Mollier 1996, 329). Mollier emphasizes in this article that the financial aspect of every decision made by the directors of French publishing houses supersedes the book in and of itself (and, inevitably, authors and their authority over their texts):

> Parce que le créateur est un chef d'entreprise . . . la dimension économique est fondamentale dans la prise en compte de la construction, du développement, de la réussite ou de l'échec de la société. Par son ancrage dans son environnement, le patron est aussi un personnage public dont le rôle politique, la fonction sociale, le rayonnement culturel ne peuvent être négligés.

> (Because the creator is the head of a business . . . the economic scope is a fundamental element in our consideration of the construction, development, success or failure of a company. Because he is anchored in his environment, the director is also a public figure whose political role, social function, and cultural influence cannot be ignored.) (Mollier 1996, 329)

In this section, I consider the interactions between the paratextual decisions made by selected publishing houses (which are studied further in the following chapters) and the financial, cultural, and political background in which these decisions are made: that of the "Black-Blanc-Beur" utopia. The research for this chapter is supplemented with the examination of authentic documents made available to me at the IMEC in Caen, Normandy in June 2019, and with phone and email interviews performed in 2019.

The 1998–2005 period reveals itself to be the site of resurgent colonial publishing standards, which were essentializing and objectifying and affected both the book and its author. These strategic marketing decisions essentially prevented a certain number of "non-Blanc" authors writing in French from ever being considered as belonging to the sacrosanct realm of *littérature française*, or from having the same purview over their oeuvre as any other "Blanc"—or perceived as "Blanc"—French-speaking author. In this sense, publishing practices of the "Black-Blanc-Beur" years as they are studied in the following chapters find themselves at odds with the supposedly inclusive nature of the era. In truth, the resurgence of colonial modes of thinking about Otherness in France during the Chirac years were reflected in the largely ostracizing publishing practices of both major and minor publishing houses in metropolitan France.

In *Packaging Post/Coloniality: The Manufacture of Literary Identity in the Francophone World*, Richard Watts provides an overview of colonial publishing practices. Watts explains that the colonial entity in charge of approving or refusing an author's publication effectively became the paratextual voice to the text, thus affirming France's hegemony in the linguistic and cultural realms in the colonies. Watts writes:

> In the earliest works of colonial subjects using their newly acquired literacy in French and, more to the point, recent mastery of French cultural forms (namely, the novel), the paratext often functions as a marker of colonial ownership. In the preface of a colonial administrator, the dedication by an author to a colonial governor, and the reduction of indigenous culture to a visual cliché in the book cover's illustration, the authority over the text and the cultures it represents passes from its expected possessor, the author, to the predominant voice in the paratext, that of the colonizer. (Watts 2005, 5)

The following chapters of this book seek to highlight the "visual cliché[s]" used to reduce the testimonies and novels of a selection of non-Blanc women authors to ahistorical, exotic products, all the while reinforcing the colonial constructs of the publishing realm as outlined by Watts. From the colonial era to the "Black-Blanc-Beur" years, one can easily pinpoint the strategic choices of certain editors as they seek to comfort their potential reader in their colonial and neocolonial constructs of Frenchness and Otherness, with the evident goal of financially benefiting from these essentialist constructs. As a matter of fact, in addition to the notions of cultural power and appropriation by the institutions, the financial aspect of publishing decisions is one that was and still is intrinsically tied to the colonial endeavor.

In *Édition, presse et pouvoir en France au XXème siècle*, Jean-Yves Mollier reviews the power relations, financial transactions, strategic associations, and at times betrayals that built the metropolitan literary publishing realm. From the early days of Gallimard and Flammarion in the nineteenth century to 2008 (which marks the end of his study), Mollier reveals that books have always ultimately been commodities, and even more so in the early twenty-first century when giant media conglomerates in France and North America entered the market and purchased their way into the publishing realm. In his last chapter entitled "À l'heure des groupes de communication planétaires" ("In the era of international media conglomerates"), Mollier explains that, after the fusion of AOL and Time Warner in 1998 in the United States, the domination of newly merged and financially powerful media companies marked the beginning of a new era, one that André Schiffrin would eventually nickname "l'édition sans éditeurs" (publishing without publishing houses) in his own work, *The Business of Books: How the International Conglomerates Took Over Publishing and Changed the Way We Read* (Mollier 2008, 395).

In 1998, an until then relatively unknown French businessman comes to the forefront of the publishing and entertainment realm: Jean-Marie Messier, former counselor of right-wing politician Edouard Balladur, chairman of the Compagnie Générale des Eaux (the General Water Company) and head of the financial group Vivendi, purchases the publishing group Havas, later renamed Vivendi Universal Publishing (VUP). Mollier explains the financial and political extent of this acquisition ("208 milliards de chiffre d'affaires," "208 billion in revenue") as a first step for Messier on his way to becoming the main owner of media outlets in France and North America at the beginning of the century:

> Deux ans plus tard, c'est une acquisition autrement plus considérable qui frappe les observateurs de stupeur lorsqu'ils apprennent, en juin 2000, que Vivendi, allié à Canal Plus, va acheter un groupe canadien spécialisé dans les alcools, Seagram, parce que dans son portefeuille figure Universal, c'est-à-dire les studios d'Hollywood, et, en sus du cinéma, tout ce qui concerne Universal Musique.
>
> (Two years later, another quite formidable acquisition of a different nature stupefies the public when, in June 2000, Vivendi, in an alliance with Canal Plus, is about to purchase a Canadian group which is specialized in alcohol, Seagram, because its portfolio includes Universal, meaning Hollywood studios and, in addition to the film industry, everything under the Universal Music umbrella.) (400–401)

Following the Seagram acquisition, Vivendi moved its headquarters to New York City in 2000 and rebranded as VUP. However, a short two years after, Vivendi's shares crumbled on the stock market and Messier, "l'homme qui s'était rêvé en grand maître de la communication mondiale" (the man who had imagined himself as the grand master of world communication), lost his empire (402).

The Vivendi domination in the realms of French and North American media lasted four years, and it is no coincidence that these four years intersect with the research and argument at hand in this book. It is indeed essential, for the purpose of this research, to consider the financial interests that the publishing realm attracted during the 1998–2008 period, as they are outlined in Mollier's extensive research. During the "Black-Blanc-Beur" years, the economic, political, and identitarian lines that defined the metropolitan publishing market continually intersected as to produce a perfect image of a modern, multicultural, and ultimately utopic France.

The fact that a single French businessman and former politician was behind the largest media acquisition in the twentieth century is significantly characteristic of a structure in which, at the time, the book and its author had equally become "hot" commodities. In order to avoid another monopoly of the publishing realm as that of VUP, which crashed and burned in such little time, the European Commission lead an investigation from 2002 to 2004 with the aim to secure a more stable structure and market for French publishing (405). In 2004, Ernest-Antoine Seillière, head of Wendel Investissement, agreed to purchase a considerable share of the former VUP group at the rather low price of 180 million euros (407). By 2008, his original investment had more than doubled (365 million euros), prompting Mollier to note that: "le livre est bien un produit comme les autres, et que l'on n'attend pas de lui autre chose que ce que l'on demande au pétrole, à la chimie, à l'automobile ou à un objet de consummation courante" (a book is a product like any other product, and that we do not expect anything else from it than we do from gasoline, chemistry, the automobile industry, or any other object of daily consumption) (408).

Publications under the rule of France's "one percent" were not necessarily "animés par cette seule ambition" (moved by this sole ambition), which would have been exclusively financial (408). In fact, another form of capital had been turned into a strong and effective currency in the publishing realm and on the political stage: that of a supposed cultural and multiethnic utopia, an identitarian currency which, if packaged and marketed strategically, could ultimately provide financial gains and publishing fame to the editor. Publishers were not the only ones to notice the potential for this type of cultural—and eventually financial—revenue following France's victory in 1998, as entrepreneurs from all realms attempted to ride the wave of this new multiculturalism *à la française*, as Laurent Dubois explained in *Soccer Empire: the World Cup and the Future of France*:

> Politicians, journalists, and intellectuals rushed to celebrate the victory, often proclaiming that it signaled the dawn of a new era in French political and social life. The team, they declared enthusiastically, represented the possibilities of the collaboration of white and black, immigrant and native born. It signaled the birth of a new French identity that, like the French flag, brought together three colors: black, white, and *beur*—the last a term describing the children of North African immigrants. It showed France what it could be: a nation free from racial divisions and conflict, a nation that gained strength from its diversity. (Dubois 2010, 3)

Dubois also speaks of "utopianism" in the years following the World Cup victory of 1998, pointing to the fatal end of this multicultural new France ideal in the *banlieue* riots of 2005 (3). He even notes later in his study that "the hope that Zidane and his teammates could smash racism and create a world without prejudice rapidly came to seem fantastical" (166). In the sphere of metropolitan publishing, the utopian "Black-Blanc-Beur" identity was turned into a neocolonial currency used to promote racial and gender stereotypes. In a stark opposition to the supposed multiculturalism it praised, the "Black-Blanc-Beur" movement encouraged publishers to reinforce existing hierarchies while implementing implicit ones that were aligned with the sociocultural climate (tensions in the *banlieue*, debates on *laïcité* and the Muslim veil, etc.) and, concurrently, the reader's potential interest at the time.

Not all publishing houses chose to use the same paratextual tools and marketing strategies during the "Black-Blanc-Beur" era, as the present study seeks to demonstrate—yet, major and minor publishers often function along a similar set of guidelines when it comes to marketing an ethnic minority woman writer and her texts. Whether it is Gallimard and its inclusion of certain authors perceived as "noir" in its *Continents Noirs* series, or Le Serpent à Plumes and its decision to attach a sensual front cover illustration to an otherwise dark tale of immigration, all the publishing houses examined in this study—except for Christian Bourgois whose practices are presented separately in chapter 4—have evidently partaken into stereotypical marketing practices at the time of the "Black-Blanc-Beur" utopia, both in terms of gender and perceived ethnic markers (of the text and/or author).

PUBLISHING PRACTICES OF THE "BLACK-BLANC-BEUR" UTOPIA

In 2008, Julia Waters published an article entitled "From *Continents Noirs* to *Collection Blanche*: From Other to Same? The Case of Ananda Devi," in which she relates and questions the move of Mauritian writer Devi from Gallimard's *Continents Noirs* ("Black Continents") series to the publisher's "White" series, *la Blanche*, its French literature collection named in reference to its neutral, cream-colored packaging. Between 2001 and 2003, Devi published four novels in Gallimard's *Continents Noirs* series: *Pagli*, *Soupirs*, *La vie de Joséphin le fou*, and *Le long désir*. All four novels bear the following labels on the publisher's website:

Sous-catégories: Littérature française > Poésie / Littérature étrangère > Africaines - Francophones
Pays: Maurice (île)
Époque: XXe-XXIe siècle

(Subcategories: French literature > Poetry / Foreign literature > African—Francophone
Country: Mauritius (island)
Era: twentieth–twenty-first century) (Gallimard, "Ananda Devi" 2019)

The question of how an author's work can be classified as both French literature and foreign literature is exactly at the core of the present study. Another question which arises from these subcategories is how or rather why Mauritius should be considered "African": Mauritius is located off the coast of the Reunion Island (a French overseas department) in the Indian Ocean, and was under French colonial rule from 1715 to 1814. If Mauritius is not exactly African nor French, and if its people have not been living according to French colonial or postcolonial standards for well over two hundred years, what makes Devi's literature both "French" and "African" yet tied to the so-called Black Continents in the eyes of Gallimard?

It is of course essential to note that Devi's publications in the *Continents Noirs* collection perfectly coincide with the "Black-Blanc-Beur" years. In fact, we could easily infer that Devi's works were classified as *Continents Noirs* precisely because of the focus on "Black" and "Beur" versus "Blanc" identities at the turn of the twenty-first century: because Devi is neither "Beur" nor "Blanche," she would have, at the time, only qualified for "Black" publishing practices (see chapter 3). In her article, Waters asks similar questions to the ones posed in this book:

> What compromises are entailed, for a non-metropolitan francophone writer, when choosing (or being chosen) to publish in France and for a predominantly French readership? . . . On what terms, inclusive or exclusionary, are non-metropolitan writers of French expression selected and promoted by their French publishers: as "French" or as "francophone," as same or as other? (Waters 2008, 55)

In her own study, Waters examines two of Devi's novels published in *Continents Noirs*, and two in the Blanche collection, in both their narrative and paratextual form. Ultimately, Waters highlights the author's nonnegotiable authority over her text, asserting that "Devi seeks subversively to establish different relations between author, text, and reader from those constructed by Gallimard's paratextual presentation and so to resist classification as 'other' or 'exotic'" (57).

Waters' conclusions about Devi's identity formation process echo those drawn in the present study. However, because Devi's narratives are not in direct dialogue with the political ramifications of the "Black-Blanc-Beur" utopia unlike, for example, Bessora's *53 cm*, Fatou Diome's *Le ventre de l'Atlantique*, or Nina Bouraoui's *Garçon manqué*, they are not included in this study which focuses on autobiographical reactions to the false multicultural political discourse of the early 2000s. Nevertheless, Devi's move from *Continents Noirs* to the Blanche collection connotes a questioning and possible shifting of labels at the time of the "Black-Blanc-Beur" utopia—shifts that were spurred on by the author herself. This shift is in turn comparable to Bessora's move to alternative publishing houses after the publication of *Cueillez-moi jolis Messieurs...* (2007) and *Et si Dieu me demande dites-Lui que je dors* (2008) in Gallimard's *Continents Noirs* series.

While the *raison d'être* of *Continents Noirs* is discussed further in chapter 3 (as both a colonial and postcolonial label, and in relation with Bessora's two publications in the series), it is essential to consider the time of its creation along with its production aspect in this opening chapter, as emphasized by Waters: "The creation of a series dedicated solely to francophone literature from Africa and its diaspora has been widely criticized for its essentialist divisiveness. As Bernard Loupias asked at the time of the creation of the series, 'pourquoi, en l'an 2000, ghettoïser à nouveau ces littératures?'" ('why, in the year 2000, would these literatures be ghettoized again?') (58–59). Waters further underlines the polarizing aspect of the series between France and Africa, particularly in its strategic use of the postface which encourages the reader to experience the text as a certain return to nature.[2] On Gallimard's choice to include a quote by white French ethnographer Michel Leiris at the beginning of each novel in the *Continents Noirs* series, "L'Afrique—qui fit—refit—et qui fera" (The Africa that did—redid—and will do), Waters justifiably concludes:

> Choosing a quotation from Leiris as the epigraph to the *Continents Noirs* series thus implicitly establishes a position of spectatorial distance between European reader and African text. Value and meaning are ascribed to the francophone African novel and writer as a result of the recognition granted them by Leiris's essentially Eurocentric, ethnographic gaze. (60)

In this sense, the addition of Leiris' words before each volume published in the collection could, and perhaps should, be considered as the equivalent of a colonial administrator approving of the natives' literature for publication, and expressing his validation through a preface as described by Watts (2005, 5).

Similarly, Odile Cazenave and Patricia Célérier in *Contemporary Francophone African Writers and the Burden of Commitment* point to the ghettoization and simultaneous racialization of the *Continents Noirs* series:

If they open up possibilities for publication and constitute spaces for experimentation, both aesthetic and editorial, these series regroup their writers according to their perceived origins. This may be construed as a form of *racialization*, problematically reminiscent of France's colonial epistemology and anthropological categorization. (Cazenave and Célérier 2011, 154–155)

This question of racialization is also evoked by Waters as she investigates the paratexts of Devi's later works published in Gallimard's Blanche collection. Her study of the paratext reveals that, while Devi's novels were eventually deemed "good enough" to exit the *Continents Noirs* series and join the French literature Blanche collection, they continued to be marked with explicit labels of otherness, such as the author's birthplace, or a list of literary prizes awarded to Devi—prizes which were solely created for francophone authors (Waters 2008, 71).

In this sense, Gallimard continued to racialize Devi within the Blanche collection, the practice in itself a not-so-subtle nod to the colonial equation of race and literary talent. As Waters justifiable underlines:

> Nowhere [on the publisher's website and printed productions] is a definition offered of what is considered to constitute 'la littérature française', with which *La Collection Blanche* is so insistently associated. Yet the recurrent references to history, origins, purity, tradition, excellence and centrality, in the portrayal of the collection's pivotal role in the development of the twentieth-century French canon, provide us with the essential components of such a definition, the neo-colonialist implications of which are particularly striking when considering the position of non-metropolitan writers within the collection and within its conception of "French" literature. (66)

Waters' conclusion on Devi's integration within the Blanche collection echoes the questions in the present study: will a nonwhite author writing in French ever see their works labeled by major metropolitan publishers like Gallimard as French literature, and presented without any allusion to their geographical ancestry? In addition, in relation to the era that concerns us in this study, the fact that Devi's integration within the Blanche collection occurred immediately after the 2005 *banlieue* riots—hence the end of the "Black-Blanc-Beur" utopia years—could be considered as signaling yet another strategic move made by Gallimard in order to rectify its former ghettoization of a nonwhite author. However, Gallimard's publishing of Bessora's *Cueillez-moi jolis Messieurs. . .* and *Et si Dieu me demande dites-Lui que je dors* in the *Continents Noirs* series reinforces the publishing house's ostracizing, ghettoizing, and racializing policies in terms of publishing nonwhite authors well after 2005.

Bessora's recent comments (recorded during a 2019 unpublished interview with the author) on her publishers' paratextual choices in the early 2000s encapsulate the issues of identity and authority which are at stake for ethnic minority women who write in French and publish in metropolitan France. In her interview, Bessora discussed her works published with Gallimard in the *Continents Noirs* series, and also emphasized her reactions to the paratextual choices made by her other publishers, Le Serpent à Plumes and La Margouline. Regarding her inclusion within the *Continents Noirs* collection, Bessora first noted that to classify her and her oeuvres in *Continents Noirs* or, if it had happened, in the Blanche collection, would have been to legitimize only half of her identity—she was born in Belgium of a Gabonese father and a Swiss mother—and termed it a "demi-escroquerie" (half-fraud) (Bessora 2019).

Bessora remarked that the main characters of *Cueillez-moi jolis Messieurs . . .* (published in *Continents Noirs*) and of *La dynastie des boîteux* (published by Le Serpent à Plumes) have been "reclassified" by the media as black characters because of racial stereotypes, and because of the fact that Bessora herself is black:

Pour me faire entrer dans l'une ou l'autre case, il y a parfois de petits arrangements: certains de mes personnages ont ainsi pu être requalifiés dans des médias ou lors d'échanges publics. Par exemple, puisque Claire (*Cueillez-moi jolis Messieurs*) est séropositive et que j'en suis l'auteure, Claire est présupposée noire. Puisque Jane I (*La dynastie des boîteux*) est l'ancêtre de métis, et que j'en suis l'auteure, elle est présupposée noire. Ces personnages blancs ont pu ainsi devenir des stéréotypes noirs, pour coller à des cadres préétablis ou à des idées préconçues.

(To have me fit under one label or the other [black or white], adjustments sometimes have to be made: some of my characters have therefore been reclassified in the media or during public conversations. For example, since Claire [*Cueillez-moi jolis Messieurs*] is HIV-positive, and since I am the author, it is assumed that Claire is black. Since Jane I (*La dynastie des boîteux*) is the ancestor of mixed-race people, and since I am the author, it is assumed that Jane is black. These white characters have therefore become black stereotypes, in order to adhere to preestablished frameworks or preconceived ideas.) (Bessora 2019)

Gallimard's decision to classify *Cueillez-moi jolis Messieurs. . .* in the *Continents Noirs* collection is quite problematic considering Bessora's comments. In fact, the narrative of *Cueillez-moi* is set in Paris, and the main character is indeed a white woman named Claire whose life is saved by a Gabonese author, Juliette. Juliette, in turn, is said to have written only one book, *Le Fantôme amnésique* (*The Amnesiac Phantom*) (Bessora 2007, 34), a clear reference to Michel Leiris' own *L'Afrique fantôme* (*Phantom Africa*)— and to the quote that precedes *Cueillez-moi* and all other novels published in *Continents Noirs*.

Gallimard was not the first publisher to mark Bessora's works as other than *littérature française* through the use of differential marketing practices. Bessora's first novel *53 cm* (published in 1999 with Le Serpent à Plumes) was assigned paratextual clues which, at the time, reduced the intricate first-person narrative of an African woman in Paris struggling with immigration services to what Bessora termed in her interview a "cul racoleur" (touting ass). At the time of publication, the author did not question the front cover image which depicted a black woman's naked back, as she thought it encapsulated the narrator's complex identity: Zara, a self-professed *griotte* (a traditional African storyteller), and an anthropologist who considers Paris as her field of study, thus reversing the assumed Eurocentrism of the French capital. Bessora explained in her interview:

> Non, je n'ai pas été consultée, mais j'ai trouvé la couverture intéressante à l'époque car j'y voyais le flou qui caractérisait Zara. Mais c'était peut-être du douzième degré... il semble que la couverture n'ait pas été perçue de cette manière. On y a vu surtout un cul racoleur. Peut-être aurait-il fallu une illustration qui exprime la déshumanisation ou la figure du paria. La folie aussi. Et cette couverture a peut-être manqué d'un trait qui rende à la fois la légèreté et l'ironie cruelle du texte.

> (No, I was not consulted [for the choice of the front cover image], but I thought the front cover was interesting at the time because in it I could see the vagueness that characterized Zara. But perhaps it was a dozen-degree thought . . . it seems that the front cover was not perceived that way. People mostly saw an eye-catching and touting ass. Maybe there should have been an illustration that expressed dehumanization or the character of the pariah. Madness as well. And this cover perhaps also lacked a trait that would have represented the lightness and cruel irony of the text.) (Bessora 2019)

As a result of this discrepancy between the text and its front cover illustration, Bessora's involvement in the production aspect of her oeuvres has increased. She states, "J'essaie désormais de m'impliquer dans la maquette graphique de mes romans " (I now try to be involved in the graphic mock-ups of my novels), further explaining that she handpicked the front-cover illustration for her novel *Le testament de Nicolas* (La Margouline 2016): a drawing by Egon Schiele which, to her, "a semblé bien illustrer la folie destructrice du héros" (accurately characterized the destructive madness of the hero), a young Islamist terrorist who dies while detonating a bomb in Paris (Bessora 2019).

One of the authors studied in this book, Calixthe Beyala, has seen the front cover illustrations attached to her oeuvres vary of the years, in particular after she was publicly condemned for plagiarism in 1996. Where Bessora noted that the front cover of *53 cm* had been considered by many as simply representing a "touting ass," the same reasoning could be applied to the front cover of *Femme nue, femme noire*, Beyala's novel published in 2003 by Albin Michel and reproduced in 2005 as a Folio: both editions of the novel bore on their front cover the photograph of a naked black woman looking at the camera. It is essential to note here that while Albin Michel and Gallimard are two of the most productive publishing houses in Paris, Le Serpent à Plumes, a historically Parisian yet more recent and minor publisher than the aforementioned two, also produced essentializing and reductive front cover illustrations, as evidenced with Bessora's *53 cm*. In this sense, both major and minor publishers in metropolitan France used racializing and sexualizing marketing practices at the turn of the millennium.

EDITORS, COVER ARTISTS, AND MARKETING PRACTICES

In an article published in the French magazine *L'Express* in 2016 and entitled "Édition: la bataille des quatrièmes de couverture" ("Publishing: the battle of the back covers"), journalist Delphine Peras establishes the various dynamics and relationships that exist between authors and their editors, the latter being the ones responsible for choosing the written paratextual elements of a novel's back cover. Peras interviewed several editors from various metropolitan publishing houses, including Seuil, Albin Michel, Gallimard, and Actes Sud. In the article, Jean-Marie Laclavetine, an editor at Gallimard, expresses the variables with which each editor has to work in order to compose the text of a novel's back cover, and whether or not the process is done in dialogue with the author: "Certains ont une idée précise, d'autres sont désemparés . . . J'ai fait des propositions à Jean-Baptiste del Amo et à Leïla Slimani à partir de mes notes de lecture. J'ai entièrement rédigé la quatrième de couverture d'Antoine Bello sans qu'il la retouche. C'est très variable" (Some [authors] have a clear idea, others are distraught . . . I made suggestions to Jean-Baptiste del Amo and Leïla Slimani from my reading notes. I composed the back cover in its entirety for Antoine Bello without him making any modifications. It varies a lot) (Peras 2016, par. 17). Regardless of its author(s), the written paratext on the back cover functions as a quick advertisement whose main goal is to attract the reader's attention, or as Peras suggests, "capter un lecteur volatile, impatient, plus sensible aux commentaires de ses pairs sur Internet qu'aux sirènes éditoriales" (capture a fickle and impatient reader, who is more sensitive to his peers' comments on the internet than to the publisher's siren song) (par. 4). In fact, Peras and Laclavetine's reflections are aligned with Mollier's 2008 conclusion which stated that, in the end, the book is nothing more than another object of consumption ("a book is a product like any other product" [Mollier 2008, 408]).

During the course of this research, I have reached out to several editors at the publishing houses mentioned in this book and have seldom received positive answers, if any at all. I was able to make the most fruitful discoveries regarding their editing and publishing practices thanks to author, design, and editing files that were made available to me at the IMEC, the national repository for contemporary French publishing archives, with the previous authorization of both Albin Michel and Christian Bourgois.[3] I consulted Albin Michel's author file for Calixthe Beyala as well as edited manuscripts of her novels *Amours sauvages* (1999), *Les arbres en parlent encore* (2002), *La plantation* (2005), and *L'homme qui m'offrait le ciel* (2007). I also had the opportunity to consult the "dossiers de fabrication" ("design files") for several of Linda Lê's publications, including for *Les trois parques* (1997), *Les aubes* (2001), *Le complexe de Caliban* (2005), and *In memoriam* (2007). Early conclusions will demonstrate that Albin Michel and Christian Bourgois exercise a much different type of control regarding the editing and marketing of their authors' works as they occupy different positions in the French publishing realm.

Beyala published *Amours sauvages* with Albin Michel one year after the French soccer team's World Cup win and the advent of the "Black-Blanc-Beur" slogan. Only three years before this publication, Beyala had been condemned for plagiarism in her novel *Le petit prince de Belleville* but she had nonetheless received the Grand Prix du roman de l'Académie française for *Les honneurs perdus* in 1996. *Amours sauvages* was marketed by Albin Michel in a way that exemplifies the adjustment operated by the publisher in the marketing of Beyala's oeuvre following her condemnation for plagiarism. Beyala's subsequent publication of *Femme nue, femme noire* with Albin Michel in 2003 visibly belongs to the same implicit series as *Amours sauvages* in terms of front cover art, paratextual back cover elements, and general marketing. The front cover image of *Amours sauvages* portrays the face of a black woman partially hiding behind her own hand so that only her eyes are visible and directed at the camera. Published a few years later, *Femme nue, femme noire* also bears the image of a black woman on its front cover, only this time she is naked and partially hiding her body behind a large bouquet of flowers.

Figure 1.1 Front Cover of *Femme nue, femme noire* by Calixthe Beyala, Published by Éditions Albin Michel (2003).

The image chosen for *Amours sauvages* in 1999 does not exactly correspond to its storyline, nor to the description written by the publisher for one of its marketing flyers. Indeed, the first words on the flyer are "Eve-Marie, une grosse Africaine fessue, mafflue et sympathique, également appelée « Melle Bonne Surprise » car elle n'est guère farouche, exerce divers boulots plus ou moins avouables chez M. Trente pour cent (un Français cupide qui prend 30% sur tout)" (Eve-Marie, a fat African woman with a big butt, chubby, and friendly, also nicknamed "Miss Good Surprise" because she is not exactly shy, holds several more or less respectable jobs at M. Thirty per cent's [a greedy French man who takes 30% on everything]) (Albin Michel "Amours

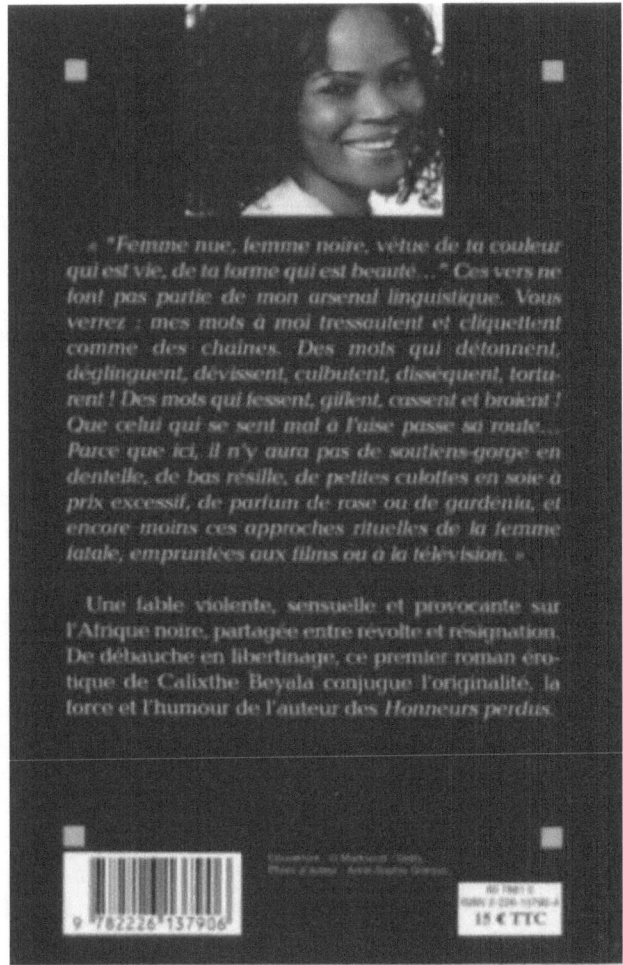

Figure 1.2 Back Cover of *Femme nue, femme noire* by Calixthe Beyala, Published by Éditions Albin Michel (2003).

Sauvages" 1999, par. 1). This overtly sexualized and racialized description of the narrative is counterbalanced by the summary's ending sentence: "Sur le thème de la mixité, l'auteur prend une position forte et surprenante: les mariages mixtes sont pour la plupart voués à l'échec" (On the theme of diversity, the author assumes a strong and surprising position: mixed marriages are for the most part bound to fail) (par. 4). Albin Michel's position regarding Beyala's views on diversity and mixed marriages as supposedly transpiring through this 1999 narrative is representative of the "Black-Blanc-Beur" slogan of the time in which the three identities were solidly separated.

In the words of the publisher, if diversity exists, the "mixing" of categories can never be met with success—a thought that emblematizes the neocolonial classification process of literature post-1998 as exemplified in this book's research.

In fact, in an article entitled "Rencontre. Calixthe Beyala: l'éloge du métissage" (and included in the author's file), the unnamed journalist and Beyala herself directly contradict the official marketing flyer produced that same year by Albin Michel:

> Pour l'auteur, l'intégration à la française est une utopie, dans le sens où l'on veut qu'elle soit une assimilation: « Personne ne peut oublier son éducation et sa culture ». Son livre est, en fait, une sorte d' « éloge du métissage »: « Le métissage est essentiel, qu'il soit génétique ou culturel, sinon on meurt », ajoute Calixthe Beyala, qui est cosignataire, avec 699 autres Noirs vivant en France, d'un recours gracieux contre le gouvernement français, pour demander une représentation plus forte des gens de couleur dans la politique, l'économie et les médias: « On en parle ailleurs qu'en France. C'est comme si on voulait étouffer cette démarche », souligne l'écrivain, qui vit en France depuis quinze ans.
>
> (For the author, integration as it was designed by the French is utopic since it is meant to be an assimilation: "No one can forget their education or culture." Her book is actually a sort of "praise for interracial mixing": "Interracial mixing is essential, whether it is genetic or cultural, otherwise we die," adds Calixthe Beyala, who cosigned, with 699 other Black people living in France, a non-contentious plea against the French government advocating for stronger representation of people of color in politics, business, and the media: "It is being talked about in countries other than France. It is as if they wanted to suppress this step," highlights the author, who has lived in France for fifteen years.)
> (*France Dimanche* 1999, par. 3)

Beyala's words in this interview are in stark opposition with Albin Michel's statement that the author portrays mixed marriages in *Amours sauvages* as "for the most part bound to fail" (Albin Michel "Amours Sauvages" 1999, par. 4). *Amours sauvages*'s opening quote, written by Beyala herself, is significant of this discrepancy between the author's intentions and her publisher's: "Plus je deviens une femme libre, plus je suis prisonnière" (The more I become a free woman, the more I am a prisoner) (Beyala 1999, 7). Truly, the more Beyala continued to publish with Albin Michel, the more she and her oeuvre became constricted by the publisher's paratextual and epitextual codes.

The publisher's influence on how the text is meant to be received by potential readers does not begin at the marketing stage, but rather at the editing stage. The manuscript that was loaned to the IMEC by Albin Michel for *Amours sauvages* contains numerous editing notes that are for the most part edits on the French language, spelling, and punctuation. In addition to these rather traditional edits on form, a certain number of editing notes have directly affected the novel's narrative in and of itself. For example, with a metropolitan reader in mind, the unnamed editor for *Amours sauvages* expanded the author's depiction of one of the characters' illegal migration from Cameroon to France. The names of the countries that were originally listed were modified as follows: the sentence "Elle avait traversé la Lybie, via le Nigeria, le Maroc . . ." (She had crossed Libya, via Nigeria, Morocco . . .) was replaced with "Elle avait traversé le Mali via le Niger et le Nigeria, [puis] le Maroc. . ." (She had crossed Mali via Niger and Nigeria, Morocco . . .) in order to depict a more direct trajectory through Western Africa (Albin Michel 1999, 25). Additional edits were made to the author's geography throughout the text: the name of a church was modified in order to fit the narrative's Belleville location ("Notre-Dame-de-Lorette" in the ninth arrondissement became "Notre-Dame-de-la-Croix," located in the twentieth)—eventually, the printed version simply read " l'église," "the church," and the Saint-Michel metro station's name was added in order to place the characters closer to their next stop of Odéon (Beyala 1999, 103, 134). These edits appear to be relatively small, simply connecting the narrative's geographic locations together for a metropolitan reader, especially one familiar with the Parisian geography. Yet, the constant correction of an author's geography can also be seen as a thinly veiled colonial editing practice in which Beyala's spatial conception of France and Africa are to be corrected in order to match a supposedly universal knowledge of geography.

Another significant narrative edit appears later in the novel when the narrator reveals that she is indeed an author (not just a prostitute as advertised in Albin Michel's marketing materials), one who wishes to be published and who sends her manuscript to a selection of Parisian publishing houses. After she receives her first rejection from a fictitious "A.A. Grand éditeur de France" (A.A. Great editor of France), Eve-Marie's friend Flora-Flore tells her—in the original version—that it is "merveilleux" (wonderful) that "A.A" found her manuscript to have an "immense intérêt" (great interest) (Beyala 1999, 145). Interestingly, Albin Michel's editor added the following sentence to Flora-Flore's original comment: "C'est magnifique qu'ils aient pris la peine de te répondre. Sûr qu'ils vont te publier le jour où ils auront un programme moins chargé" (It's fantastic they took the time to write you back. I'm sure they will publish your work once their schedules clear up) (Albin Michel 1999, 145). Here, Flora-Flore's longer comment gives the reader a more positive outlook onto the fictitious A.A.'s selection process and communication practices with authors. The editor's choice to add a note of elation and hopefulness to Flora-Flore's words to the narrator appears as a clear means to an end to positively characterize this fictitious A.A. editor (a possible ersatz of A.M.—Albin Michel), so as to highlight their possible responsiveness to unknown and unproven African women writers.

While the author file loaned by Albin Michel comprised several documents including press articles relating the political tensions of the time and correspondence with several bookstores and festivals regarding Beyala's professional travels, there was no indication (correspondence or other) that the author had approved or discussed any of the editing modifications made to her manuscript, or the choice of the front cover photograph for *Amours sauvages*. This was not the case in the files that were released by Christian Bourgois regarding the fabrication of Linda Lê's published works, as well as her responses to the editor's notes. The author and design files for Lê revealed that the main editor for her works was Malek Alloula, the famed Algerian author turned editor in the late 1960s. As an example, regarding Lê's 2007 publication *In memoriam*, Alloula was asked to check the back cover's summary that Lê had written herself in order to make sure it aligned with the rest of the text which he had previously corrected. Malek was indeed noted as a "correcteur" and not an "editeur" in all correspondence regarding Lê's oeuvre. The design file for *In memoriam* thus revealed a different relationship between the author, her publisher, and her "corrector" than Beyala's with Albin Michel (Christian Bourgois 2007).

The design and production files for both authors also demonstrated that the difference in output numbers between the two publishers was quite remarkable: while Albin Michel was able to produce 12675 first edition copies of *Le petit prince de Belleville* and 13126 copies of *Maman a un amant* (Albin Michel 1994), Christian Bourgois produced at most 5000 copies for some of Lê's novels (*Calomnies* in 1993 and *Les dits d'un idiots* in 1995), with most of her works being produced at 3000 or 4000 first editions (Christian Bourgois 1993, 1995). Albin Michel's large output undoubtedly reflects its reputation, history, and financial place in the metropolitan publishing market as this publisher is able to produce almost three times as many copies for a first edition than Christian Bourgois. However, the market of annual literary prizes influences all publishers, major and minor alike: it allows them to increase their book productions as they attempt to disseminate them to the largest possible number of readers in hopes to win a prize. Thus 10031 copies of Linda Lê's *Cronos* were eventually produced as it received the Prix Wepler Fondation La Poste in 2010, and 18208 copies of *Lame de fond* were printed in 2012 as it was nominated for the Prix Goncourt and the Prix Goncourt des Lycéens (Christian Bourgois 2010, 2012).

Overall, the relationship between Lê and her publisher seems to be more transparent than Beyala's with Albin Michel as numerous emails which were included in the author's design files revealed that Lê had been consulted and had approved several paratextual elements over the years, such as the front cover image for *Calomnies* (1993) and the back cover's text for *Cronos* (2010). Again, these discussions which involve Lê in the design of the final product are deeply contrasted with the discrepancy noted earlier between Beyala's statements on mixed marriages and her publisher's description of *Amours sauvages* in its marketing flyer. The remaining chapters of this book seek to demonstrate that, during the "Black-Blanc-Beur" years, larger publishers such as Albin Michel and Gallimard marketed a certain image of ethnic minority women writers, one that would appear to be inclusive of their authors' various ethnic ancestries yet one that would ultimately reveal the publishers' strategic marketing practices and financial drive. The narratives written by "Black" and "Beur" women writers were particularly manipulated according to colonial gender biases, as were the paratexts attached to their oeuvres.

Although the public media did not pay much attention to francophone authors of Southeastern Asian origin during the "Black-Blanc-Beur" years, preferring to focus on stereotypical representations of *banlieue* gangs and their victims and on African immigration, essentialist marketing practices similar to those affecting Beyala were used by both major and minor publishers in the case of one of the Franco-Vietnamese authors selected for this study, Anna Moï. Chapter 4 offers a longer reflection on Gallimard's paratextual presentation of Moï and of her text *Riz noir* (2004), as well as the Éditions de l'Aube's characterization of the author in *L'écho des rizières* (2001) and *Parfum de pagode* (2003), Moï's first publications in metropolitan France. While the front cover illustration for *Parfum de pagode* portrays a group of people sitting in a fisherman's boat at a distance, *L'écho des rizières* bears on its front cover a photograph of Anna Moï herself. When asked if their authors were ever consulted in the image selection in the production of their oeuvres, Jean Viard and Marion Hennebert, who cofounded the Éditions de l'Aube, explained during their individual phone interviews that it is indeed the publisher who selects the front cover illustrations and who designs the back cover (Viard and Hennebert 2019). However, Hennebert highlighted that, at l'Aube, and specifically in the case of Anna Moï, the author is kept informed of these paratextual decisions and final form of the book. Similarly to Linda Lê with Christian Bourgois, Anna Moï was therefore consulted in the production of her works published with the Éditions de l'Aube.

The typically Asian and specifically Vietnamese front cover illustrations that adorn the first and subsequent editions of her works with l'Aube (as described and analyzed in chapter 4) effectively precluded Moï from being visually perceived as *littérature française*. In fact, Moï's works with l'Aube were published in a "Le Viêt-Nam" catalog which the publisher no longer carries (see chapter 4 for further discussion of this catalog with Jean Viard). Regarding the illustrations chosen in relation with the works of Franco-Vietnamese authors, Viard noted that "il faut reconnaître que la ligne vietnamienne a toujours été surchargée en photos féminines" (it is important to acknowledge that the Vietnamese field has always been overloaded with feminine photographs) (Viard 2019). Marion Hennebert later noted that, while the Éditions de l'Aube had worked with illustrator Marcelino Truong for the design of a number of book covers in the now defunct "Le Viêt-Nam" collection, Truong's sexually suggestive designs remain the exception rather than the rule. In fact, while Truong produced a drawing of a sleeping naked woman for the front cover of female author Dương Thu Hương's *Histoire d'amour racontée avant l'aube* (2003 edition), he also designed an illustration of a naked woman bathing for the front cover of male author Chu Lai's *Rue des soldats* (2003)—thus breaking the bind between the author's gender identity and the gendering of the novel—yet confirming Viard's note on the excessive presence of "feminine" front cover illustrations (Hennebert 2019). Ultimately, both Viard and Hennebert's comments corroborate the present study's argument on differential marketing practices: a number of nonwhite women writers and their oeuvres were and are still publicized differently precisely because of their gender, thus contributing to the perpetuation of gendered colonial stereotypes (such as the subjugated yet sexually suggestive *Indochinoise*, as drawn on Duong Thu Huong's *Histoire d'amour racontée avant l'aube*, or, more recently, as photographed on the front cover of Loo Hui Phang's *L'Imprudence* published by Actes Sud).

As literature has increasingly been reduced to the status of "a product like any other product" (Mollier 2008, 408), and as authors themselves have been turned into products, a number of publishing houses like l'Aube, Albin Michel and Gallimard have at one time or another resorted to marketing techniques that promote the circulation of ethnic and gendered stereotypes in contemporary France—whatever "sells." In fact, Jean Viard recalled an encounter with President Jacques Chirac at the annual Salon du Livre (the national book fair) in Paris, stating that "il faut être honnête, la seule chose qui l'a arrêté [sur notre stand], c'est les couvertures de la série 'Vietnam'" (honestly, the only thing that caught his attention [on our bookstand] were the front covers of the 'Vietnam' series) (Viard 2019). The unsolicited mention of Chirac's reaction to the stereotypical images of Vietnam displayed by L'Aube during his presidential mandate directly connected Jean Viard's thoughts on differential marketing practices with the marked return of colonial thought during the "Black-Blanc-Beur" years. The following chapters will demonstrate that very few oeuvres written by ethnic minority women in the early 2000s were publicized in a neutral fashion and that, in some cases, the absence of colonial imagery or subtext was itself also part of a marketing strategy: that of selling a utopic idea of integration.

CONCLUSION

The "Black-Blanc-Beur" World Cup victory and utopian discourse on multiculturalism that ensued occurred at an opportune time in France, a time when divisiveness and extremism were on the rise in society and politics alike. The various institutions which capitalized on the slogan actively worked to circulate a utopic vision of integration which did not reflect a new concept, but rather one dating back to the practices of the French colonial empire, especially in literature. The book, its author, and the lives of many ethnic minority women were used as neocolonial commodities to which strategically prefabricated "Black" and "Beur" values were assigned. These new values were built on colonial-era gender-based and ethnic stereotypes which denoted either rebellion or compliance to the French republican model. In their paratextual form, these "Black" and "Beur" literary markers served to offset and confirm the literary superiority of "Blanc" *littérature française*. Though excluded from the "Black-Blanc-Beur" motto, the postcolonial Vietnamese identity and literature written in French were also marketed using visual colonial stereotypes. These markers often confined Franco-Vietnamese authors and their works within the limits of Orientalism, thus seldom encouraging potential readers to imagine these identities or narratives as existing outside of the colonial realm.

In their paratextual, editing, and marketing practices, several publishing houses specifically worked to promote antiquated images of Otherness and femininity in France. The renewed ghettoization of ethnic minority women's writing after 1998 was equally practiced by publishing giants such as Gallimard and Albin Michel, as it was by minor yet regarded publishers such as l'Aube (despite their visible sensitivity and genuine desire to promote Franco-Vietnamese literature in France, as is further expressed in chapter 4). Linda Lê is among the very few female authors who benefited from a transparent relationship with their editor and publisher, a rather rare occurrence which allowed them a different perspective on their self-definition process as ethnic minority women writers in France. Bessora's comments in her 2019 interview corroborates the publishing houses' habitual lack of transparency, a practice which has now encouraged her to be involved in the marketing and paratextual decisions surrounding her publications.

NOTES

1. French historian Emmanuel Blanchard noted in "En 1998 comme en 2018, le discours d'une France "Black-Blanc-Beur" reste un mythe" that the "Black-Blanc-Beur" utopia arose at a time of significant social and cultural tensions in France (Blanchard 2018, par. 4). Politicians and the media alike were able to ride the wave of the "multicultural" French team's World Cup win and manipulate the reality of immigrant life in France (as well as the reality of multiculturalism in the realm of soccer) in order to assuage tensions in the nation (par. 2). According to Blanchard, it is due to chance rather than deliberate action on the part of French coach Didier Deschamps that the 2018 team included a "Beur" player after all (par. 9).

2. "The general postface, whose function is to offer an explanation, definition and justification for the series, is littered with disturbing racial stereotypes that would not seem out-of-place in a colonial era, 'exotic' text" (Waters 2008, 59).

3. This section and its conclusions were made possible by research done at the IMEC in late June 2019. The on-site research allowed for a study of a selection of Calixthe Beyala's manuscripts and editor notes, and a file relating Christian Bourgois' marketing decisions about Linda Lê's novels. This consequently gave us an insight into the marketing practices of these two publishers in Paris in the late 1990s and the early 2000s, and into the differential publishing practices affecting female authors of Sub-Saharan and Southeastern Asian origin at the time.

Chapter 2

"Beur," "*Banlieue* Victims," and "*Intégrées*"

Samira Bellil, Nina Bouraoui, Nora Hamdi

"ALGERIAN," "ARAB," "BEUR," AND "*BANLIEUE*": ZIZOU AND HIS OTHERS

When the French men's soccer team won the World Cup final on July 12, 1998, one player in particular was instantly portrayed as a hero: Zinedine Zidane, affectionately nicknamed "Zizou." *The star midfield attacker born in Marseilles of Algerian parents in 1972 scored two of the three winning goals against the opposing Brazilian team (Emmanuel Petit scored the third goal).* Zidane immediately became the face of the "Beur" in the "Black-Blanc-Beur" slogan, his portrait projected that night onto the Arc de Triomphe along with messages that read "Merci Zizou," "Zizou, on t'aime," "Zidane Président," and "Champion du Monde." On the night of France's World Cup victory, Zizou was instantly turned into the "perfect" representative of successful postcolonial immigration and, more importantly at the time, integration in France.

In 1998, France was still reeling from a number of terrorist attacks committed on French soil by the GIA (Armed Islamic Group) as part of the Algerian Civil War. The Algerian terrorist organization was responsible for the hijacking of an Air France flight in Marseilles on December 24, 1994, and for a murderous attack in the Saint-Michel RER station in Paris on July 25, 1995. For weeks after the Saint-Michel attack, the face of twenty-four-year-old French-Algerian Khaled Kelkal, believed to be the perpetrator of the bombing, was widely broadcasted onto television screens and in national newspapers. After a lengthy televised assault by the French police on the apartment where Kelkal was hiding, the young man was killed on live television on September 29, 1995. Therefore, Zidane's scoring of two decisive goals in the World Cup final of 1998 not only brought victory to the team, but it also refocused the public's attention on the possible successful integration of the "Beurs" within the French République's ideals.

The idealized "Beur" identity which surfaced with Zidane in 1998 suffered a first blow in 2001 during a soccer game opposing France and Algeria. Natalie Etoke recounts the match in her article "Black Blanc Beur: Ma France à moi":

> L'euphorie footballistique *black blanc beur* a cependant disparu en 2001 au cours d'un match opposant la France à l'Algérie. La Marseillaise a été sifflée. Par la suite, des mouvements de violence ont obligé les autorités officielles à interrompre la rencontre. Au terme d'un événement censé réconcilier et célébrer l'amitié entre les deux pays, l'heure était plutôt à la réflexion.
>
> (The *black blanc beur* soccer euphoria nevertheless vanished in 2001 during a game between France and Algeria. The Marseillaise [France's national anthem] was booed. Later, violent acts forced official authorities to stop the game. At the end of an event that was meant to reconcile the two countries and celebrate their friendship had come a time of reflection.) (Etoke 2009, 157)

In *Soccer Empire*, Laurent Dubois underlines that, before the brawl erupted onto the field, Zizou had not been treated by fans as a French player but rather as a player representing Algeria on the field: "The French team had been greeted with hostility from the start of the match, when some of the fans of the Algerian team hissed and booed during the playing of the "Marseillaise," as well as booing the names of the French players—except that of Zidane" (Dubois 2010, 178). That night, Algerian-born supporters and their descendants refused to consider Zizou a French player, or a fabricated "Beur" ideal of integration, which revealed the star athlete's true function as a pawn in a highly political game.[1]

In his 1997 study entitled *Immigration and Identity in Beur Fiction: Voices from the North African Community in France*, Alec Hargreaves established that "Beur" had become a common denominator for French citizens who had genetic or familial ties to the Maghreb French-speaking countries of Morocco, Algeria, and Tunisia.[2] Before "Beur," the most commonly used term was "Arab," which was often thought to only mean "Algerian." In "Perceptions of Ethnic Difference in Post-War France," Hargreaves clarified:

> Few people realized that many North Africans were Berbers, not Arabs, or that the number of immigrants originating in Morocco and Tunisia was rapidly catching up with those from Algeria. In everyday language, immigrants were equated with people of color: most were assumed to be Algerians and by the

same token Muslims, and all were exposed to prejudice and discrimination rooted in the long-standing distrust of immigrant "outsiders" that was now compounded by the bitter legacy of the colonial system and its bloody end in Algeria. (Hargreaves 1997, 13)

The long and violent history of France and its former colony, Algeria, is at the origin of this collective misunderstanding concerning the identity of men and women whose lineage ties them to North Africa. Hargreaves, using a testimony from Moroccan author Tahar Ben Jelloun, underlines that, nevertheless, the *Français de souche* (French people whose ancestry is supposedly completely French) show a certain ability and willingness to classify North-Africans according to class, basing their judgment on the degree of education of immigrants, which then either qualifies them as "immigrants" (not educated) or "étrangers" (educated).[3] This point is actually crucial in understanding how the publishing industry has managed to craft and market an "integrated" (per Hargreaves, "étranger") identity for the three women writers studied in this chapter (Samira Bellil, Nina Bouraoui, Nora Hamdi), an image which stems from an essentially racist and classist process of identity formation, one that mirrors the tools employed by the media to portray Zidane as the ideal "Beur" man.

The term "Beur" had been in use in France for almost two decades when it was appropriated by the media and assigned to the "Black-Blanc-Beur" slogan. Hargreaves explains:

During the early 1980s, a new designation for second-generation Maghrebis entered circulation: *Beurs*. This term had originally been adopted by young Maghrebis in the *banlieues* of Paris who were tired of the pejorative connotations attached to majority ethnic usage of the word *Arabe* . . . By the late 1980s, however, it had become widely used by the mass media, principally in contexts highlighting problems associated with stereotypical ideas of "immigration" and the *banlieues*. The negative stereotypes attached in this way to the *Beur* label led to its rejection by most of those to whom it was applied. (Hargreaves 2001, 15)

The "Beur" label as it is described here by Hargreaves evokes its double function as an ethnic and socio-geographical marker: in fact, after 1998, "Beur" was still used to connote the French *banlieue*'s need for institutional policing and general assistance as part and parcel of the idealized "Beur" identity of the "Black-Blanc-Beur" utopia. The ideal "Beur" identity was indeed split into two subcategories which complemented each other and represented both men and women: one was an ideal of integration that did not incite fear in the general public, in a word the utopic end goal which the institutional policing of the other "Beur," notably the one from the *banlieue*, was supposed to achieve. These two facets of the "Beur" identity coexisted in the media and the publishing industry until the *banlieue* riots of 2005 and the visible end of the "Black-Blanc-Beur" utopia. In women's literature, several strategies were employed by publishers after 1998 to publicize a compliant image of Maghrebian women and their works: compliance was either portrayed through a visible Westernization process and a lack of othering labels (for Nina Bouraoui and, later, Nora Hamdi, the "*intégrées*"), or through an infantilizing process which relegated the author to a "ward of the state" status, one who needed a translator, as well as an emotional and institutional support system in order to be published (Samira Bellil, the "*banlieue* victim").

To be clear, one would never encounter these fabricated "*intégrée*" or "*banlieue* victim" labels in a bookstore during the "Black-Blanc-Beur" utopia years: in lieu of blatant labeling, it is through the form and visual composition of the book cover (whether it includes a photograph of the author, whether it is adorned with a band listing the author's literary prizes, etc.) that the marketing of an approachable Other yet approved literature was performed on the metropolitan literary market. These paratextual markers were however in deep disconnect with the narratives themselves, which portrayed the bicultural lives of second-generation Maghrebian women in France. The three authors who were chosen for this chapter represent three different facets of the female French-Maghrebian identity: Samira Bellil was born of Algerian immigrant parents outside of Paris and suffered from sexual violence in a nearby Parisian *banlieue*; Nina Bouraoui grew up in Algeria before moving to France, the daughter of an Algerian diplomat and a French woman; Nora Hamdi, the daughter of Algerian immigrant parents, grew up in a blue-collar *banlieue* before moving to Paris proper to study the arts and become a painter and a writer.

Throughout their careers, the authors studied in this chapter along with their oeuvres have been classified by the literary institutions according to various labels that were meant to reflect their "non-Blanc" status: "francophone," "Maghreb," "Beur," "*banlieue*," "second-generation immigrant," but never simply "French"—or at least, not in their very first publications. In her 1998 article entitled "Beurette suis et beurette ne veux pas toujours être: entretien d'été avec Tassadit Imache," Frédérique Chevillot aptly reminds her reader that the term "beur," a label once accepted in literary studies as highlighting the cultural wealth of this bicultural generation, should in fact be problematized as it has been coopted to now (in 1998) stigmatize "beur" authors as minorities existing outside the realm of *littérature française* (Chevillot 1998, 632). In her interview with Chevillot, French-Algerian author Tassadit Imache recounts that, when her first novel *Une fille sans histoire* was published in 1989, her publisher, Calmann-Lévy, did not categorize it as "beur" and neither did the literary critics of the time. In fact, its paratextual clues were very subtle in the manner of Gallimard's *La Blanche* collection: the author's name and the novel's title appeared at the top of a plain white cover, with Calmann-Lévy's stamp at the bottom, under the word "roman" (novel). It is only after *Une fille sans histoire* received the Prix Radio-Beur in 1990—which, Imache explains, Calmann-Lévy was careful to not print on the text's commercial band as to avoid any classification of Imache or her oeuvre as "beur"—that the public began to forcefully determine her work and her identity as "beur," and to ask her whether or not she accepted these terms (637).[4] Imache, in her answers, along with Chevillot in her analysis, both confirm that "beur" (and its feminine form *beurette*) were terms which the media applied onto the identity and works of authors like Imache, whether or not these authors agreed with such denominational practices.

Chevillot's interview with Imache was published in March 1998, a few months before the victory of the "Black-Blanc-Beur" soccer team in July of the same year. It thus appears that the term "beur" had been revived and used by the media prior to the World Cup. According to Imache's interview answers to Chevillot, the effect of the circulation of the term "beur" appears to have been threefold: to instill a sense of nostalgia for a time when the institutions still had a possible role to play in the integration of former colonial subjects from the Maghreb; to hinder the success of these novelists whose works should have otherwise remained labelless; to compartmentalize these authors and their works into subcategories that served to publicly support the idea of a multicultural France, but in actuality confined them in a realm separate from that of *littérature française*. My use of the term "Beur" in this chapter therefore seeks to reflect the *faux* healing process regarding the "beur" identity question in France around and after 1998, especially in the case of women's literature.

Between Victimization and Self-Definition:
Banlieue **Women and Literary Journalism**

In the early 2000s, *banlieue* women were consistently portrayed as victims in the media coverage of the "tournantes" (gang rapes) phenomenon. This public victimization prevented them from expressing the socioeconomic hardships they faced as women marked socially, culturally, and geographically as *banlieue*. In response to a lack of discursive space in which to voice their truth and discontent, a number of *banlieue* women found solace in the social movement Ni Putes Ni Soumises (NPNS) founded by Fadela Amara in 2003.[5] In *Taking French Feminism to the Streets: Fadela Amara and the Rise of Ni*

Putes Ni Soumises, Brittany Murray and Diane Perpich report Amara's words as she expressed the "hidden" reality of *banlieue* women:

> We are fed up with unemployment and poverty .... Women are the first victims of unemployment, financial insecurity, reduced hours and underemployment .... Without even going so far as to demand domestic parity, we cannot ignore the appalling climate that prevails in many families in the *quartiers*. Everything is a power relation, everything comes down to violence or psychological pressure. (Murray and Perpich 2011, 27–28)

The following section examines Fadela Amara's *Ni putes ni soumises* (co-written with journalist Sylvia Zappi) and Samira Bellil's *Dans l'enfer des tournantes* (co-written with journalist Josée Stoquart), and addresses the external forces that influenced the editing and marketing of their testimonies.[6] These forces take the form of editors, journalists, and publishers who worked to fashion a certain image of Amara and Bellil, one that would fit the narrative of an integrated multicultural France, and attempt to constrain their testimonies to a space of institutional servitude and dependence.

Fadela Amara

Perhaps because of her age, or because her personal story differed from Bellil's (she was not a victim of sexual assault, but rather witnessed excessive police brutality in her *banlieue* growing up), Fadela Amara was not portrayed as a victim by the media.[7] Amara took action in creating the Ni Putes Ni Soumises movement with a small group of *banlieue* women, thereby negating the presupposed idea that "Beur" and especially *banlieue* women need the French institutions to defend them (Amara 2003/2006, 5/35). In *Ni Putes Ni Soumises*, Amara revealed her own version of the *banlieue* and the sexual violence that is inflicted on women while being completely disregarded by the institutions. Amara's words were altered by a journalist "collaborator" (or co-author), following the style of literary journalism. *Ni Putes Ni Soumises* bears the mark of this dual authorship on its front cover: "avec la collaboration de Sylvia Zappi" (with Sylvia Zappi) (Amara 2003/2006, front cover). While the "Black-Blanc-Beur" utopia era promoted a male ideal of "Beur" integration, the genre of literary journalism played a critical role in creating a subcategory to the "Beur" identity, that of female *banlieue* victims. To that end, the journalists who "collaborated" in the writing process of testimonies like Amara's or Bellil's appear to have acted as agents of a larger "Black-Blanc-Beur" institutional utopia.

In "Journalisme narratif: proposition de définition, entre narratologie et éthique," Marie Vanoost tentatively defines literary journalism in the following terms:

> Ce modèle journalistique particulier produit des récits hybrides, aux frontières du journalisme et de la littérature. Il se manifeste aujourd'hui dans la sphère journalistique francophone, où il s'inscrit en filiation avec le grand reportage, tout en s'affichant comme inspiré du *narrative journalism* américain.
>
> (This particular journalistic model produces hybrid narratives, on the border between journalism and literature. Today it manifests itself in the francophone journalistic sphere, where it inscribes itself in connection with international reporting, all the while presenting itself as drawing its inspiration from American *narrative journalism*.) (Vanoost 2013, 141)

Literary journalism, which Vanoost defines as a "hybrid" genre, allowed certain journalists during the "Black-Blanc-Beur" years to do more than transcribe the testimonies of the *banlieue* women they had interviewed or collaborated with: in effect, these "co-authors" or "collaborators" intervened within the text itself in order to give their own insiders' knowledge, oftentimes through comments and transitions which truly reflected the ideological tensions of the time. These narrative manipulations were either overt, as with Stoquart's interventions in the writing and editing of Bellil's text which she explains in her own introduction to the text, or, on other occasions, they were not openly discussed, as was the case with Sylvia Zappi's involvement in *Ni Putes Ni Soumises*.

Zappi is a French journalist who regularly publishes in *Le Monde* on the topic of politics in general, and the *banlieues* in particular. Her page on the *Le Monde* website introduced her, up to the earlier part of 2019, as "[c]hargée des banlieues dans le quotidien et anime un blog avec un regard sur ces périphéries qui racontent un autre quotidien que celui de la capitale" (In charge of *banlieue* daily reporting and moderates a blog with a perspective on these peripheries that tell another story on its inhabitants' daily lives than that of the capital [Paris]) (Le Monde 2019). In a 2016 *Les Inrockuptibles* article titled "Qui est Sylvia Zappi, la voix des banlieues au 'Monde'?" and focusing on Zappi's latest publication (*La maison des vulnérables*, Seuil 2016), Zappi is described as a feminist who began to fight for women's and students' rights in the 1980s before turning to the topics of immigration and the *banlieues* (Marlier 2016, par. 5, 12). Beyond any doubt, Zappi's pedigree as a journalist and an activist made her a natural ally to Amara's cause—but the extent of her contributions or alterations to Amara's text is unknown. The audience formation process for a social manifesto such as Amara's was one that would determine the visibility of the movement and the *banlieue* women it represented in circles outside of the *banlieue* itself, the circulation of the text in such spheres rendered possible by Zappi's editing of its "violent *banlieue*" marker into a "*banlieue* victim" narrative—one comparable to Bellil's after Stoquart's modifications. As Hargreaves argued in "Testimony, Co-Authorship, and Dispossession among Women of Maghrebi Origin in France": "Cuny, Zappi, Ponchelet, and Stoquart are all French journalists who were evidently hired to turn the texts of these novice authors into more marketable commodities than they might otherwise have been" (Hargreaves 2006, 47).

Considering the argument that these journalists formatted the author's original text in order to please a certain audience, one should not forget the time period in which the two works that concern us were produced: the turn of the millennium, meaning, the heart of the "Black-Blanc-Beur" utopia, before the 2005 *banlieue* riots and the undeniable broadcasted reality of France's social and racial fracture. Unlike Stoquart who provided a preface to Bellil's work explaining the editing work she had performed on the text (also explained in the main text by Bellil herself), Zappi and Amara were not as forthcoming in *Ni Putes Ni Soumises* regarding what parts of the text (if any, or all) were edited by the journalist. Without these precisions, the reader is left looking for clues in the text which might reveal an adaptation of Amara's original intent in order to reflect the "Black-Blanc-Beur" utopia of the early 2000s, as well as the formation of an archetypal female "*banlieue* victim."

Early on in her text, Amara gives her reader a timeline of her early involvement with militant activism in her *banlieue* near Clermont-Ferrand, which ultimately led her to become an active member of SOS Racisme in 1984. She writes:

> C'est donc sur le petit écran que j'ai vu apparaître SOS Racisme qui, à la différence du mouvement beur, représentait un vrai métissage. Ça me faisait plaisir de voir des Blancs, des Blacks et des Rebeus ensemble, qui revendiquaient le droit de vivre dans une société d'égalité et de fraternité.
>
> (So I first saw SOS Racisme on the little screen: in contrast to the Beur movement, it displayed a real ethnic diversity. I was delighted to see Blancs, Blacks, and Rebeus [the slang, "verlan" word for "Beur"] together, all demanding the right to live in a society of equality and fraternity.) (Amara 2003/2006, 28/57)

The "Beur movement" is mentioned by Amara in this passage in reference to the 1983 "Marche pour l'égalité et contre le racisme"—renamed by the media as "Marche des Beurs"—and the second "Marche des Beurs" in 1984, which was not as successful because the group was divided between the Beurs who wanted to be recognized as integrated by the French Republic, and those who wanted to live as "maghrébin[s] autonome[s]" (autonomous Maghrebian[s]) (28/57). Amara's use of the terms "Blancs," "Blacks," and "Rebeus" in her reminiscing of her early days of activism in 1984 is revealing of her narrative being ingrained in the "Black-Blanc-Beur" years and its utopia of multiculturalism, which she herself assigns to the 1984 context when she speaks of "un vrai métissage" (real ethnic diversity). Further, Amara's rejection of the "mouvement beur" (Beur movement) and its ultimate failure in 1984 serves to reinforce the "Black-Blanc-Beur" utopia within which the "Beur" ideal is one of compliance and respect for the French Republic (as exemplified by Zizou in 1998), rather than one demanding social change.

In her attempt to define the progression of sexual violence against women in the *banlieues* in the 1990s, Amara outlines two factors: one inherited from the immigrant family structure, and one from the "outside world," that is, France beyond the limits of the *banlieues*. According to Amara, while boys are praised and treated much more favorably than girls by their immigrant parents at home (41/67–68), they suffer from an "absence de reconnaissance extérieure" (absence of outside recognition) (42/68) when moving beyond the limits of their "quartier" or "cité" in order to look for work or simply enjoy a night out. Faced with increased scrutiny and racism during the 1990s, Amara contends that these boys turned their angst and anger toward the girls in their neighborhoods, since it was the only geographical space where they could exercise any form of power (42/68). The archetype of the angry, violent and irreverent young *banlieue* man of immigrant descent is, at the time of the text's publication in 2003, still positioned against the ideal model of the integrated "Beur" represented by Zidane.[8]

The men are however not the only ones painted with such a broad brush in Amara's text. On the behavior of girls in the *banlieue,* Amara comments that there are only three types of girls: those who cannot handle the discrepancy between the control that is imposed on them at home and life outside of their *banlieue,* who "dérapent en tombant dans la prostitution ou la toxicomanie" (slip into prostitution or drugs) (44/70), those who choose to imitate the *banlieue* men's violence in forming girl gangs, and who are "parfois pires que les hommes, car quand elles agressent, elles peuvent se montrer beaucoup plus dures et sadiques" (sometimes worse than the young men, because they can be tougher and more sadistic than males) (45/70). The third type of behavior according to Amara is "la transparence" (invisibility), a mode of being adopted by girls who only ever walk through the *banlieue* to get to their classes, who "n'ont qu'une chose en tête: réussir leurs études pour s'échapper de la cité" (have only one thing in mind: complete their education and get out of the projects (45/71).

It is difficult to assess whether there were more than the three above-mentioned types of girls living in the *banlieue* in 2003, just as there were only two types of resistance outlined by the author, "[c]elles qui portent le voile" ([t]hose who wear the headscarf) (47/73), and "[c]elles qui résistent au quotidien" ([t]hose who offer daily resistance) (49/75). However, these broad categories, statements, and dare we say stereotypes, might as well have been the product of journalist Sylvia Zappi's editing process, as her role was in many ways similar to Stoquart's in the editing of Bellil's *Dans l'enfer des tournantes*. As Hargreaves noted in "Testimony, Co-Authorship, and Dispossession among Women of Maghrebi Origin in France": "[The authors'] personal testimony is all too easily ensnared in the public circulation of stereotypes inherited from the colonial period which to a large extent rob them of the ownership apparently displayed on the cover of their books" (Hargreaves 2006, 53). In using the genre of literary journalism, and thus providing the public with easy categorizations that confirm the media representations of *banlieue* men and women, Amara and Zappi strategically outlined preformatted identities for a readership that needed to be kept engulfed in the "Black-Blanc-Beur" utopia, two years before the *banlieue* uprisings of 2005. Violent men, submissive (veiled) and rebel (resisting) women functioned as archetypes offsetting the image of the perfect male "Beur," Zidane. In addition, in their choice to contain the discourse of male violence in relation to their rapport with their female *banlieue* victims, the authors avoided a much more timely discourse that should have been centered on the general *banlieue* discontent that was about to explode in 2005.

Samira Bellil

The context which surrounded Samira Bellil's release of *Dans l'enfer des tournantes* was extremely political and weighted in terms of gender and ethnic constructs, as explained in the section above. This context undoubtedly affected both the writing and the editing process of *Dans l'enfer*, as well as its publication and marketing. Bellil's autobiography was a testimonial from the *banlieue* and, as one of the testimonies requested by the NPNS movement, it was consequently turned into a political statement, and stigmatized by the media as a *banlieue* text.[9] At the time, the term "*banlieue*" in both the media and literature was no longer a sole reference to the projects which are located at the periphery of Paris and other major French cities. Rather, it had become a derogatory socioeconomic marker connoting various imagined *zones de non-droit* (lawless zones) in which chaos, violence, and the rejection of the French State by "non-Blanc" youths were portrayed as daily occurrences.

A *banlieue* literature category was established in the early years of the twenty-first century, notably around the persona of author Faïza Guène and the success of her 2004 novel *Kiffe Kiffe Demain*. While Dominic Thomas thought of *banlieue* writing as "post-Beur" stating that *banlieue* literature was "working towards articulating a trajectory in which social exclusion and injustice are denounced, in order to work productively and responsibly in seeking solutions" (Thomas 2008, 35), Kleppinger declared in *Branding the "Beur" Author: Minority Writing and the Media in France, 1983-2013* that, regarding *banlieue* literature, "by 2004, reader expectations of novels by authors of the North African population in France had solidified around themes of urban poverty and immigrant identity confusion" (Kleppinger 2019, 2). In "'Qui fait la France?': New Configurations of Frenchness in Contemporary Urban Fiction," Stève Puig contends that the term "*banlieue*" has become somewhat of an erroneous marker when discussing the literature that originates from the urban peripheries of metropolitan France. In fact, Puig argues that *banlieue* should only be used as a spatial marker, itself referring to a group of authors who are producing "urban literature" (Puig 2018, 19). Puig's reasoning is quite simple: while *beur* literature was concerned with the question of integration, and was almost exclusively written by authors whose lineage tied them to the Maghreb, urban literature deals with the aftermath of integration ("the new wave of writers consider themselves fully French culturally speaking and therefore demand to be treated as such"), and its writers "come from various backgrounds," ethnically and geographically speaking (20-21). Today, "urban literature" allows scholars to think of these authors and their texts not in terms of ethnicity, but in terms of socio-geography (21). "Urban literature" was however not a popular or even existing label at the turn of the twenty-first century: the term *banlieue* along with all the racial and gender-based stereotypes it connoted prevailed in the media as well as in literature.

As this section seeks to demonstrate, the specific way in which Bellil's testimony was packaged by the media and by its publishers produced as a sub-discourse which effectively worked to contain a certain image of *banlieue* inhabitants within a narrative of need, service to, and ambivalent defiance of the French Republic's ideals. This narrative, while complementary to the previous definition of the *banlieue* genre as explained by Kleppinger (which was characterized by "themes of urban poverty and immigrant identity confusion"), emphasized the "victim" aspect of the author's identity, in particular the female author, and her need for a form of "higher" help—to be provided to her by the French institutions. Despite many interviews during which she excelled at presenting her story as separate from the latent immigration debate, Bellil was effectively turned into a marker of victimhood within the "Beur" ideal of 1998: that of a symbolically helpless woman, in and of herself reminiscent of the role of the colonized as imagined and enforced by France's *mission civilisatrice*, both on a human and creative (literary) level. In fact, her collaborator Josée Stoquart's role and actions during the editing process dangerously imitated the colonial practices of literary patronage as they applied to the now-formerly colonized.

In *Packaging Post/Coloniality*, Richard Watts summarizes the relationship between colonial patrons and authors as embodied in the colonial paratext (in particular, the preface) as follows:

> In the earliest works of colonial subjects using their newly acquired literacy in French and, more to the point, recent mastery of French cultural forms (namely, the novel), the paratext often functions as a marker of colonial ownership. In the preface of a colonial administrator, the dedication by an author to a colonial governor, and the reduction of indigenous culture to a visual cliché in the book cover's illustration, the authority over the text and the cultures it represents passes from its expected possessor, the author, to the predominant voice in the paratext, that of the colonizer. (Watts 2005, 5)

This practice described by Watts is applicable to the literary journalism model presented in this chapter. In Bellil's case, both the author and the "patron" (Stoquart) openly discussed their roles in the writing process of *Dans l'enfer des tournantes* in the text itself. In the epilogue, Bellil notably recounts her first meeting with Stoquart, and their agreement on the editing process. Bellil writes: "Je lui ai montré quelques pages rapidement écrites en Belgique. Elle décida que c'était à moi seule d'écrire et qu'elle se chargerait de restructurer mes textes et d'en reprendre la forme" (I showed her pages I'd jotted down in Belgium. She decided that I should write it myself and that she'd take on the task of restructuring and reshaping it) (Bellil 2003/2008, 301/202). She then further explains the different steps of the editing process, at the end of which "tout avait été extirpé et écrit, clarifié par le regard de Josée, réfléchi de nouveau puis, enfin, digéré et intégré" (everything had been spat out and written down, clarified under Josée's eyes, reflected on anew ... finally digested and integrated) (Bellil 2003/2008, 302/202). The editing process evoked here by Bellil appears to be similar to a translation exercise of the author's original writing in French —which, to her editor, does not appear to have been suitable for publication since she set out to "restructure" and "reshape" it—into what Stoquart would have considered to be standard French, ultimately producing a more traditionally linear narrative.

Stoquart openly expresses in her preface to *Dans l'enfer* that the goal of "restructuring" Bellil's testimony into a more chronological text was to reach a certain readership at the time of publication—undoubtedly one who would not have been familiar with *banlieue* slang. She writes (a passage which was not included or translated in the North-American edition):

> Écrire avec l'objectif d'être lue, par moi à la séance suivante puis plus tard par un lecteur éventuel, l'a obligée à garder une certaine rigueur et à ne pas « se

lâcher » dans une expression spontanée. Le livre ne devait pas être un prolongement de sa thérapie. J'ai tâché, par mes confrontations, d'amener Samira à plus de concision et de cohérence. En collaborant à l'écriture pour la rendre plus accessible, j'espère avoir respecté au plus près la couleur du récit et la personnalité de Samira.

(Writing with the goal to be read, by me at our next meeting and later by a potential reader, forced [Samira Bellil] to exercise a certain rigor and to not "let loose" into spontaneous expression. The book was not meant to be an extension of her therapy. I tried, in confronting her, to bring Samira to more concision and more coherence. In collaborating on her writing in order to make it more accessible, I hope that I respected the narrative's tone and Samira's personality as much as possible.) (Stoquart 2003, 15)

In fact, Stoquart's modifications of the original text go far beyond the traditional editing process: as she would not allow Bellil to "'let loose' into spontaneous expression" and as she pushed her towards "more concision and more coherence," Stoquart effectively transformed the original testimony of a survivor of sexual assault into a more palatable and chronological read for the average French reader. This process, in and of itself, crosses the limits of the literary realm and encroaches into the political realm.

Literary journalism in this case allows Stoquart, the journalist, to act politically in her transformation of the text in order to characterize *banlieue* inhabitants as uneducated and helpless people who need the services of the white French elite and, in particular, its literary institutions, in order not to *have* a voice but to *transcribe* their story into a "readable" text of literature. In addition, as per Watts' previously-mentioned assessment in *Packaging Post/Coloniality*, Stoquart takes visible responsibility for Bellil's text as she adopts the role of a neocolonial literary patron: in her preface, she is vouching for the original author in publicly approving the final form of the text, submitted for publication after a process of "translation."

In "La banlieue comme théâtre colonial, ou la fracture sociale dans les quartiers," French sociologist Didier Lapeyronnie explores this intricate relationship of dependence created by the French institutions with the intention of keeping young *banlieue* men and women outside of society, and consequently outside of reality. He writes:

Le vécu de la discrimination et de la ségrégation, et peut-être plus encore le sentiment d'être défini par un déficit permanent de « civilisation » dans les discours du pouvoir . . . évoquent directement la « colonie » et donc, pour un nombre d'habitants issus de l'immigration, un « passé qui ne passe pas ».

(The reality of discrimination and segregation, and maybe even more the sentiment of being defined by a permanent lack of "civilization" in official discourse ... directly evoke the "colony" and as such, for many second-generation immigrants, a "past that is still very present.") (Lapeyronnie 2005, 210)

The resurgence of this colonial relationship between *the banlieue*'s inhabitants and the French institutions is, according to Lapeyronnie, heavily anchored in language. Lapeyronnie explains:

Les mots sont largement vécus comme un obstacle matériel et non comme un vecteur de communication ... Ils ont une épaisseur, et notamment une épaisseur sociale, qui les rend étrangers à l'individu, mais surtout hostiles puisque le sens leur est donné par une société qui exclut et « racialise ».

(Words are largely perceived as a physical obstacle and not as a means of communication ... They bear a thickness, notably a social thickness, which makes them seem foreign to the individual, but most of all hostile since they are given meaning by a society that excludes and "racializes.") (215)

In his research, Lapeyronnie finds that *banlieue* inhabitants are particularly distrustful of journalists who "enregistrent" ("record") their words, and "en les publiant, [ils] les retournent contre ceux qui les ont prononcés" (in publishing them, turn them against those who pronounced them) (215). Words are manipulated by journalists to create an image of the *banlieue* inhabitant who uttered them, "[i]ls finissent par couper de sa propre réalité, par s'interposer entre soi et soi comme l'image" (they ultimately cut oneself from their own reality, setting themselves between the self and the self as image) (215). Using Albert Memmi's *Portrait du colonisé*, Lapeyronnie concludes that the *banlieue* individual becomes estranged from himself through this process, concluding that "[a]u fond, il ne se comprend plus" ([i]n the end, he does not understand himself anymore) (216).

In the case of Samira Bellil, we know that the writing and editing process allowed her to free herself from the guilt and shame she felt after the assault. She wrote in her postface: "Son écoute, ses questions et ses réactions ont petit à petit changé ma vision de moi-même, infiltrée si longtemps par celle de mon entourage" ([Stoquart]'s way of listening, her questions, and her reactions gradually changed my self-image, corroded over the years by the people around me) (Bellil 2003/2008, 303/203). Later in the editing process, Stoquart had Bellil reread her words once they had been edited by the journalist, placed in chronological order and along a traditionally linear narrative. Stoquart in her preface also described this practice:

Lorsque les violences de son histoire furent extirpées de sa mémoire, imprimées, lues et relues, elle commença à se distancier de son passé et à se pacifier. Tout était dit, hurlé, pleuré. Tout était réfléchi, compris, intégré. Elle avait remis à leur juste place tous les morceaux de sa vie. Tout était trié, rangé, consigné. Il y avait enfin de la place pour autre chose.

(When the violent acts in her story were extracted from her memory, printed, read and reread, she began to distance herself from her past and to calm down. Everything had been said, yelled, and cried. Everything was processed, understood, integrated. She had put all the pieces of her life back where they truly belonged. Everything was sorted, classified, recorded. There finally was room for something else.) (Stoquart 2003, 16)

Once again, Stoquart's editing process clearly appears to have been designed along the lines of a traditionally linear narrative, as expressed in the terms "sorted, classified, recorded." The edited text in itself even becomes a metaphor for the author, as Bellil was guided in the process of "put[ting] all the pieces of her life back where they truly belonged," in a chronological order.

Along the lines of Lapeyronnie's arguments, Stoquart did manage to create a distance between Bellil herself, and herself as an image. In projecting the image of a reborn French citizen, free of the guilt and trauma of the sexual assaults to which she was subjected in the *banlieue*, Stoquart presents herself as Bellil's savior as she confirms when stating: "C'est une grande chance que de participer à la libération d'un être" (It's a great opportunity to be able to participate in a human being's liberation) (16). Yet, for Lapeyronnie, it is through their own language manipulations and creations—or "spontaneous expression" according to Stoquart—that *banlieue* inhabitants can project, materialize themselves in their own reality, one which is unencumbered by society's hostile linguistic practices. He explains: "Savoir les manipuler [les mots] est savoir leur donner un sens qui ne passe plus par la société, voire leur conférer un usage contre la société en les retournant littéralement" (To know how to manipulate [words] is to know how to give them a meaning that does not pass through society, even to give them a function to work against society, in literally turning them around) (Lapeyronnie 2005, 216). Words in standard French "ne le leur permettent pas [d'accéder à la réalité], comme l'image qu'ils supportent leur en interdit l'accès. Ils vivent « à côté » de la société réelle" (Do not allow them to [access reality], just as the image of them as created by those words forbids them to enter reality. They live "next to" real society) (216). Effectively, Stoquart's editing practices support a very obvious political agenda: to give Bellil total autonomy in "spontaneous expression" and to publish her original testimony would have materialized for the reading audience an actual *banlieue* woman who fought *against* the legal institutions who distrusted her and contributed to her continuing despair. But in producing a traditionally linear narrative, Stoquart effectively created the image of an ideal *banlieue* victim who was meant to be saved by the French institutions, in this case the institution of literature.

Dans l'enfer des tournantes was published by Denoël, a sizeable publishing house whose parent company is the well-established Gallimard. Bellil's testimony was published in 2002 as a "récit" (narrative)—not a "témoignage" (testimony)—in Denoël's "Documents" category, in the "Impacts" collection. The "Impacts" collection gathers essays written by French authors (*"littérature française"*) as well non-French authors (*"littérature étrangère"*) (Denoël, "Collection Impacts" 2019). Up until early 2019, *Dans l'enfer des tournantes* was still classified on Denoël's online catalogue as: "Theme: sociology, demography; Category > subcategory: Documents > sociology, anthropology, demography" (as of December 2019, Bellil's novel is no longer included in Denoël's online catalog) (Denoël, "Dans l'enfer" 2019). On the "Impacts" page related to these categories and subcategories, Bellil's testimony appears along other texts such as Latifa Zoubir's 2009 *Je m'appelle Latifa: une "intégration à la française"* and Jérôme Pierrat's 2006 *La mafia des cités: économie souterraine et crime organisé en banlieue* (Denoël, "Collection Impacts" 2019).

Zoubir, who was a spokesperson for Ni Putes Ni Soumises, denounces in her text the "French-style" integration model according to which one should shed all of their particularities linked to their immigrant background in order to be accepted as a member of French society—until it becomes clear that the French institutions are not inclined to integrate someone with an immigrant background (what Zoubir terms "un hypocrite et quotidien modèle d'exclusion," "a hypocritical daily model of exclusion") (Denoël, "Je m'appelle Latifa" 2019). Pierrat on the other hand denounces the "mafia" which he believes operates as a small minority in the *banlieue*, yet is responsible for the crime that spills out of the *banlieue* and into the city-center (what he terms "la criminalité issue des banlieues," "crime from the *banlieue*") (Denoël, "La mafia des cités" 2019). Denoël's conscious choice of positioning these two texts—which were published within the same decade as Bellil's *Dans l'enfer des tournantes*—next to Bellil's testimony continues to frame and territorialize her voice within the confines of, on one hand, an all-too common violent image of the *banlieue* and, on the other hand, the impossible integration of women of Maghrebian descent within French society.

The front cover of the 2002 original edition of Bellil's *Dans l'enfer des tournantes* bears a black-and-white photograph of the author as an adult, arms crossed over a jean jacket, hair untied, looking directly at the camera. Her name, Samira Bellil, is written in block letters on the top-right corner of the cover, and "Récit" (Narrative) is typed in smaller characters under the title in the middle of the page (Bellil 2002, front cover). In and of itself, this front cover is fairly neutral insofar as it does not emphasize any element of Bellil's identity through the typography of her name. The categorization of the text as a "récit," however, allows a potential reader to expect a traditionally linear and fairly chronological narrative, which seemed to have been Josée Stoquart's end goal in her editing practices of Bellil's original text.

In 2003, Denoël published a Folio of *Dans l'enfer des tournantes* with a much differently formatted front cover. On the Folio cover, a picture of a much younger, teenage Bellil dressed in a leather jacket and jeans, leaning against barbed wire and looking slightly down at the camera, gives the impression of a specifically territorialized *banlieue* text: with orange roof tiles visible on the lower right corner, it appears that Bellil is standing on a rooftop which, since Matthieu Kassovitz's famous rooftop scene in his 1995 film *La Haine*, has become known to be a common "hang-out" spot for *banlieue* youths in the French public imaginary. Knowing the popularity of Kassovitz' film at the time, the above-described cover modification signifies Denoël's attempt to appeal to a larger audience, one which would perhaps not only be comprised of women (to whom, supposedly, a story of female resilience and survival after sexual assault would appeal most), but also of younger men, both in and outside of the *banlieue*.

The 2003 Folio front cover also emphasizes Bellil's last name which is printed in much larger type than her first name, thus attracting the reader's attention to her immigrant background. Under the title, the mention "Postface inédite de l'auteur" (Newly released postface from the author) appears to be in stark opposition with the first edition's mention of "récit": in emphasizing the author's continuous participation in the writing and evolution of the text, Denoël is now marketing the "real" as opposed to what would have appeared as potential fiction under the title "récit" (Bellil 2003, front cover). This is confirmed in Bellil's second postface written in 2003 in which she meditates on the impact that *Dans l'enfer des tournantes* as well as her televised interviews have had on young *banlieue* men and women. She notably mentions a young man's words of praise regarding her first televised intervention on the topic of the *tournantes*, noting that she was "touched" by his compliments, especially as they came from "un de ceux que l'on stigmatise souvent trop vite" (one of those that are often too quickly stigmatized) (306/206). However, readers rarely start with the postface, and the 2003 red cover adorned with the photo of a younger and rebellious-looking Bellil standing on a rooftop seems to feed into the mediatic *banlieue* discourse of the time, one that emphasized its inhabitants' differences from the *Français de souche*, and one which contributed to the 2005 uprisings through its propagation of stereotypes.

Figure 2.1 Front Cover of *Dans l'enfer des tournantes* by Samira Bellil, Published by Éditions Denoël (2002).

Both the 2002 original edition and the 2003 Folio bear a subtitle printed on the title page inside the book: *Dans l'enfer des tournantes, avec le soutien et la collaboration de Josée Stoquart*, "with the support and the collaboration of Josée Stoquart." This assessment on the title page gives Stoquart credit not only for the editing of the text but also for her "saving" Bellil through her "soutien" (support) as is also mentioned in Stoquart's own preface. Both the 2002 and 2003 editions bear the mention "Ouvrage publié sous la direction de Guy Birenbaum" (published under the guidance of Guy Birenbaum) before the text begins. Birenbaum was at the time editor-in-chief of Denoël's "Impacts" collection. Bellil's original text was therefore edited twice, once by Stoquart and once by Birenbaum. There is one postface by Bellil in the 2002 original edition, and two at the end of the 2003 Folio (the original postface and the "newly released" one). The Folio did promise its reader on its front cover a "postface inédite de l'auteur," allowing Bellil to reflect even further on the publication and impact of her testimony on the metropolitan reading audience. Her first postface began with the words, "Je tiens à dire que tout ce que j'ai décrit dans ce livre est scrupuleusement exact. Je n'ai rien exagéré . . . Je sais ce dont je parle" (I need to say that everything I have described in this book is scrupulously correct. I have not exaggerated anything . . . I know what I am talking about) (Bellil 2003/2008, 279/204). The veracity of Bellil's testimony was certainly questioned, and she herself was accused of "exaggerating" the despicable sexual assaults to which she fell victim (279/204). The fact that Bellil had to reaffirm the truthfulness of her testimony in a postface to the book unequivocally shines lights on the problematic terming of her testimony as a "récit" in Denoël's first edition.

In 2007, Lyon-based publisher Decitre obtained the rights to reprint Bellil's *Dans l'enfer des tournantes* and, for the first time since its first publication in 2002, the text was marketed as a "témoignage," a "testimony." Published in Decitre's "Succès du livre" (Book success) collection, the front cover bears a color photograph of an adult Bellil sitting on a window sill cushion, framed in between the window drapes, and looking out into the distance. The author seems at the same time contemplative and at peace. The 2007 edition bears yet another subtitle: "Pour briser la loi du silence" (To break the law of silence) (Bellil 2007, front cover). As the 2005 *banlieue* riots had brought extreme media attention to the young *male* rioters, Decitre's decision to revive Bellil's memory three years after her untimely death is not only an homage to the author, but also a way for the publisher to refocus the French readership's attention on the violence which *banlieue* inhabitants have to face every day—in particular, women.

The reproduction of Bellil's work as a "témoignage" also served to counter the institutional discourse of Nicolas Sarkozy's government in 2007: with

Figure 2.2 Front Cover of *Dans l'enfer des tournantes* by Samira Bellil, Published by Gallimard (Folio, 2003).

the concurrent opening of a Ministère de l'Immigration, de l'Intégration, de l'Identité Nationale et du Développement Solidaire (Ministry of Immigration, Integration, National Identity and Co-Development) and of the Cité Nationale (later renamed Musée National) de l'Histoire de l'Immigration, Sarkozy aimed at redefining what it meant to be "French" as opposed to "Other" in relation to the recent *banlieue* riots. The institutions' attempts at controlling the national identity discourse were severely criticized by Edouard Glissant and Patrick Chamoiseau who declared in their manifesto *Quand les murs tombent:*

l'identité nationale hors-la-loi (*When the Walls Fall: Outlawed National Identity*) that "nulle part on ne rencontre de fixité identitaire" (there is no fixed identity anywhere) (Chamoiseau and Glissant 2007, 1).

In reality, this desire to define a "fixed" (French or Other) identity had emerged almost ten years prior with the advent of the "Black-Blanc-Beur" utopia, and not so coincidentally during the years of Sarkozy's mandate as Minister of the Interior to Jacques Chirac. While Bellil and other authors of Maghrebian descent were positioned as "*banlieue* victims" in the literary realm, an alternative selection of authors were portrayed as having successfully integrated within French culture. Nina Bouraoui is one of these authors who were marketed as "*intégrées*" by their publishers, notably with the use of neutral and/or Westernized paratextual elements. In her semi-autobiographical *Garçon manqué* (*Tomboy*) published in 2000, Bouraoui offered a revolutionary negotiation of the gender, sexual, and cultural identity constructs with which Franco-Maghrebian authors were contending at the time. The figure of the "tomboy" also appeared a few years later in Nora Hamdi's *Des poupées et des anges* (2004), offering an alternative to the "pute" and "soumise" stereotypes that continued to plague the lives and public representations of *banlieue* women. The authentic mode of expression used by both authors allowed them to produce alternative images of second-generation Maghrebian womanhood both in and outside of the *banlieue*;[10] however, their publishers' differential paratextual practices continued to constrain their public identity on the metropolitan literary market, despite the authors' efforts to define themselves and their works outside of existing essentialist labels.

TOMBOYS, "*INTÉGRÉES*," AND THE MOVE TOWARD PARATEXTUAL NEUTRALITY

Nina Bouraoui

Nina Bouraoui, born of an Algerian father and a French mother, spent her childhood between a newly independent Algeria and a France that was still reeling from its colonial army's defeat. Bouraoui's childhood as recounted in *Garçon manqué* and some of her later novels reads as a multifaceted questioning of her familial, national, gender, and sexual identity.[11] Bouraoui is the product of the history and political constructs of colonization and immigration in France, a country where she has now permanently settled and in which she writes, publishes and publicizes her oeuvres. Bouraoui is not a second-generation immigrant *per se*, nor has she ever lived in a *banlieue*, as she was raised as the daughter of a diplomat and grew up in an upper-middle class environment. Therefore, the commonly accepted signifiers of locale (*banlieue*) and history (the French colonization of Algeria, and the Algerian War of Independence) do not actually fit Bouraoui's identity: her geography is variable and not truly aligned with the sociocultural "Beur" label broadcasted by the French institutions after 1998.

In *Garçon manqué*, Bouraoui portrays the complex identity of her younger self, first in Algeria and then in Rennes, as she struggles with her gender, sexual, and cultural identity. Written in short sentences and mostly in the present tense, the first-person narrative reflects the author's childhood and teenage years, constantly in movement, and constantly questioning every aspect of her identity. Against the media's promotion of a monolithic "Beur" ideal of integration, and also against the stereotypical images of violent Muslim men in Algeria and in the *banlieue*, Bouraoui develops in *Garçon manqué* a multifaceted authorial identity which is not constrained by racial or gender constructs. Early on in her narrative, Bouraoui explains her desire to be "integrated" in Algeria (not in France) and to be considered one of the men. She presents herself in public as a boy (what she calls "le jeu," "the game") and writes: "Ma force n'est pas dans mon corps fragile. Elle est dans la volonté d'être une autre, intégrée au pays des hommes. Je joue contre moi" (My strength is not in my fragile body. It is in my desire to be other, passing in the world of men. I play against myself) (Bouraoui 2000/2007,17/9).

Bouraoui offers a different perspective on the female, bicultural Franco-Maghrebian identity as she questions the gender and ethnic constructs of the young, "fragile" girl from the Maghreb which had become customary in France's public discourse. Her desire to be seen as a man in Algeria is twofold: first, to reconcile her attraction to women (as is developed later in the narrative), and also to have freedom of movement, to blend in with the crowd of mostly men in the Algerian public space. Her status as a young biracial and binational girl in Algeria after the country's independence puts her at risk when she leaves the heavily guarded compound where other French-Algerian families reside. The autobiographical quality of this narrative, along with its interweaving of the notions of gender, race, history (colonial and postcolonial), and socio-geography, make *Garçon manqué* a strong response to the "Black-Blanc-Beur" utopia and "Beur" female archetypes of the early 2000s.

In the context of the arduously fluctuating definitions of "Beur" versus "*banlieue*," Nina Bouraoui, like Samira Bellil and Nora Hamdi, has had to make additional efforts in order to define herself and retain some of her personal self-identifying traits, especially during the post-1998 "Black-Blanc-Beur" period. Bouraoui was in 2000 and remains today in a constant process of self-definition in a metropolitan literary realm that has adopted her as an "*intégrée*," that is, accentuating her French qualities while simultaneously not denying (but also not accentuating) her North-African identity. Over the years, and beyond her identity as a French-Algerian and a global national, Bouraoui has become a symbol of successful integration, a symbol propagated and reinforced in the paratext attached to her published works. Ironically, and perhaps strategically, Bouraoui has always voiced her disregard for literary labels, preferring to focus instead on her narratives.

In "Vision, Voice, and the Female Body: Nina Bouraoui's Sites/Sights of Resistance," Adrienne Angelo contends Bouraoui's writings are indeed difficult to categorize as she herself does not exactly fit the traditional *beur* model: "Although it is tempting to categorize Bouraoui's fictions as an example of *beur* fiction, a bit of caution should be heeded, since . . . the author's identity is in constant flux and thus remains irreducible to any specific theoretical grouping" (Angelo 2010, 77). This association between the author herself and the text (and its content) has become customary among academics as much as general audiences. The error in continuing to associate an author with her text stems, as argued by Richard Watts, from the colonial era in terms of location and narrative expectations based on fabricated stereotypes.

Siobhan McIlvanney in "Double Vision: The Role of the Visual and the Visionary in Nina Bouraoui's 'La voyeuse interdite (Forbidden Vision)'" also attempts to "locate" Bouraoui somewhere along the already-set French-*beur* continuum, without being able to provide a definitive answer:

> Nina Bouraoui is a notoriously difficult writer to categorize autobiographically, in that, while born in France of an Algerian father and French mother, she spent her childhood in a variety of different countries, including Algeria, the United Arab Emirates, and Switzerland. Thus, she cannot easily be assimilated under the category of *beur* writers, writers of Maghrebi parentage born in France and brought up as French citizens. (McIlvanney 2004, 105–106)

In "Embodiement, Environment and the Reinvention of Self in Nina Bouraoui's Life-Writing," Helen Vassallo defines Bouraoui in the following terms, which appear to form the most accurate way to consider the author and her works:

> She is commonly considered a French author rather than a Maghrebi one, and has lived in France all of her adult life. Bouraoui has never returned to Algeria, although it is often alluded to in her oeuvre. Much of her writing is considered as autobiographical or autofictional, due to the preference for a first-person narrator and the similarities between her own life and recurring themes in her work, such as national identity, sexual identity, lesbian desire and the negotiation of subjectivity and identity. (Vassallo 2013, 141)

In fact, the main focus of Bouraoui's writing is not the condition of the ethnic Other in Paris. Angelo explains that the author's focus has been to express movement and fluidity from a female perspective in moving across the boundaries of gender, race, and geography (Angelo 2010, 93). Bouraoui's "nomadic writing," Angelo explains, "further suggests a precise development within Bouraoui's writing as she herself has moved from one culture to another, from one social sphere to another and from one literary form and narrative voice to another and suggests a particular strategy for viewing, speaking, and writing the visual and visualized female body in her works" (93).

In "Freedom from Oneself: Artistry and the Postcolonial Woman Artist in Nina Bouraoui's *La Voyeuse interdite*," Anna Kemp suggests that beyond the scope of Bouraoui's bicultural and feminist writing lays a true confirmation of the author's place in the mostly masculine realms of French and world literature. Bouraoui's *La voyeuse interdite* relates the story of a young Algerian girl, Fikria, whose marriage is being arranged by her father, as she herself remains locked in her room, observing from within those walls what goes on outside her window, powerless if not for her ability to tell her story.[12] Kemp explains: "Bouraoui's protagonist covets the impersonal and disembodied subject position of supposedly "masculine" artistic traditions. It is this position that postcolonial women writers are most often denied, not only by patriarchal narratives, but also by the reflexes of postcolonial criticism" (Kemp 2013, 237). In all her works, particularly *La voyeuse interdite*, Bouraoui masterly uses the fluid lines of ethnicity and sexuality in relation to the fixed institutions of culture, tradition and family, especially in the Algerian setting. In demonstrating the manner in which these traditional institutions cannot effectively control subjects in their entirety—the creative freedom of the main character as well as the author's voice—through vivid, physical descriptions, Bouraoui's testimonial is transformed into a manifesto that articulates the fluidity of artistic creation in postcolonial narratives. For Adrienne Angelo, Bouraoui expresses a "nomadic sense of identity" in *La voyeuse*, "a cross-cultural and cross-sexual transformation from woman seeing though not seen to woman seeing, desiring, and writing" (Angelo 2010, 79).

La voyeuse interdite was first published in 1991 in Gallimard's Blanche collection. After winning the Prix Inter the same year, *La voyeuse* was reedited and published in Gallimard's Folio collection in 1993. In the Folio, Gallimard affixed a stereotypically exotic image to the front cover, one that would simultaneously signal attractive Otherness to the reader and bind the identity of Bouraoui to that of Fikria, the imprisoned writer in the novel. As Pamela Pears justly notes in *Front Cover Iconography and Algerian Women's Writing: Heuristic Implications*: "The paratextual message of Bouraoui's *La voyeuse interdite* draws the reader in with the idea that this book is solely about women's oppression in Algeria. The front cover image attracts readers to the book, based on what they perceive to be its subject, even if there is a separate and equally powerful literary project happening" (Pears 2015, 98). Regarding the cover of the Folio itself, which portrays a woman's eyes peering from behind the slats of a wooden, orange blind, Pears pointedly comments:

> The placement of the orange band mimics the placement of a hijab and niqab. The book's title, *La voyeuse interdite*, the author's family name, *Bouraoui*, and the first line of the back cover's promotional blurb, "Dans les rues d'Alger . . ." [In the streets of Algiers. . .] all work along with the image to form an entryway paratext pointing the potential reader to the testimonial of an Algerian woman. The reader sees what could be a veiled woman, a Maghrebian sounding last name, and the geographical marker of Algiers, all indications associated with a testimonial such as the aforementioned *Mariée de force*. (99–100)

This first novel by Bouraoui was not the only one to be published by Gallimard. Bouraoui's *Poing mort* was first published in the Blanche collection in 1992, and again as a Folio in 1994. *Avant les hommes* (2007), a first-person narrative about a young *banlieue* man coming to terms with his homosexuality, was first published by Stock in its French literature, "Bleue" collection, before being republished as a Folio by Gallimard. None of these afore-mentioned reeditions were marked quite as remarkably as Bouraoui's first novel: her introduction into the realm of metropolitan French literature was and remains linked to the association of her identity as a woman and as an author with the stereotypical traits commonly (but incorrectly) attributed to a supposedly subdued Algerian woman.

After *La voyeuse interdite*, Bouraoui worked with the Éditions Stock, one of the main and most reputable publishing houses in metropolitan France. Stock's *littérature étrangère* collection is characterized by neutral dark red covers, while novels in "La Collection Bleue" (*littérature française*) bear dark blue covers. Bouraoui's works with Stock have all been published in "La Collection Bleue," from *Le jour du séisme* in 1996 to *Sauvage* in 2011. Since then, Bouraoui has collaborated with Flammarion for the publication of *Standard* (2014), and with JC Lattès for *Beaux rivages* (2016) and *Tous les hommes désirent naturellement savoir* (2018). As previously mentioned, in "Vision, Voice, and the Female Body," Adrienne Angelo examines Bouraoui's narratives and use of literary devices in *La voyeuse interdite*, *Garçon manqué* and *Poupée Bella*, establishing a pattern of movement, what she terms "a nomadic sense of authorial authority" and a "nomadic sense of identity that is unique to her work" (Angelo 2010, 78–79). Reading Angelo's research in parallel with a study of Bouraoui's evolving paratexts as created first by Gallimard, then by Stock, allows us to unveil a substantive dichotomy between the sense of female postcolonial metropolitan identity which Bouraoui seeks to convey within her works (one which reveals fluidity as opposed to the fixed poles of French/ Algerian, male/female, or even Blanc/ Beur) and the identity that is displayed and marketed on the book covers designed by these influential publishers. Although impossible to locate along the lines of established literary identities such as French, *beur*, or "writers of Maghrebi parentage born in France and brought up as French citizens" (McIlvanney 2004, 106), Bouraoui's publishers have made considerable efforts to provide her readers with a "quick" visual categorization of the author which has evolved over the years: while Gallimard presented her as decidedly Algerian in the paratext to *La voyeuse interdite*, Stock has visually presented her as an *intégrée* within the *littérature française* category.

Nina Bouraoui's successful career, which is unquestionably due to her talent as a writer, has been equally propelled by Stock's decision to publish her works under the label *littérature française* in their "Bleue" collection, which is characterized by its neutral packaging elements. Unlike Samira Bellil whose portrait was affixed directly on the front cover of her testimony, Bouraoui's is only present on a detachable band, her Otherness an attractive yet easily removable paratextual appendix.[13] This lack of permanent "Other" paratextual elements effectively showcases Bouraoui as an approved author of *littérature française* despite of, or in addition to the Otherness which remains visible in her last name and in the portrait printed on the band. As such, Bouraoui's identity and literature are fashioned to symbolize the ideal "Beur" who, like Zidane, has been vetted by the institutions (in her case, not athletic but literary) and whose compliance to the French rules of *écriture* (writing) has allowed her to be published by the renowned Éditions Stock. During the "Black-Blanc-Beur" years, this fabricated *intégrée* literary identity effectively contrasted the "*banlieue* victim" whose image was fine-tuned by the news and literary media in order to comfort a portion of the French public in their neocolonial values.

Bouraoui has, however, never conformed to the fabricated assumptions that come with the *intégrée* packaging of her oeuvres, as evidenced in both McIlvanney and Vassallo's discussions of the author's identity and possible literary classification. In fact, not only has Bouraoui not complied with the public's expectations of her and her writing (as they are linked to her ethnic background), she chose to address them directly in the narrative of *Garçon manqué*:

> Je suis indéfinie. C'est une guerre contre le monde. Je deviens inclassable. Je ne suis pas assez typée. « Tu n'es pas une Arabe comme les autres. » Je suis trop

typée. « Tu n'es pas française. » Je n'ai pas peur de moi. Ma force contre la haine. Mon silence est un combat. J'écrirai aussi pour ça. J'écrirai en français en portant un nom arabe. Ce sera une désertion. Mais quel camp devrais-je choisir? Quelle partie de moi brûler?

(I am nondescript. It's a war against the world. I become unclassifiable. I'm not ethnic enough: "You are not an Arab like other Arabs." I am too ethnic: "You are not French." I'm not afraid of myself. My strength defies hatred. My silence is a battle. I will also write because of this. My writing will be in French, while my last name remains Arab. It will be a desertion. But which camp should I choose? Which part of me should I burn?) (Bouraoui 2000/2007, 33/18)

In the same manner as Bouraoui, despite the eventual "*intégrée*" labeling of her oeuvres, Nora Hamdi has struggled with her dual French-Maghrebian identity both socially and culturally, as she expressed in her 2004 novel *Des poupées et des anges*. While the paratext to Hamdi's oeuvres has been equally manipulated as Bouraoui's, the two women's experiences are however different in that Hamdi was first marketed as a "*banlieue* victim" before being propelled out of the *banlieue* and into the central, integrated realm of Parisian publishing.

Nora Hamdi

Nora Hamdi, the daughter of first-generation Algerian immigrants, was born in Argenteuil, a Parisian *banlieue,* and grew up in nearby Sartrouville.[14] Both Argenteuil and Sartrouville are located Northwest of Paris and considered typically uneventful, blue-collar *banlieue* towns (as opposed to Northeastern *banlieue* towns such as Clichy-sous-Bois, which were regularly portrayed in the news as violent at the turn of the millennium). Hamdi attended night classes at the École des Beaux-Arts in Paris and was a painter for several years before turning to writing (*La couleur dans les mains*, published in 2011 with Léo Scheer, is semi-autobiographical). Her first published work, *Trois étoiles*, published with Au Diable Vauvert, took the form of a graphic novel which she composed with Virginie Despentes.

On the back cover of *Des poupées et des anges*, her biography indicates: "Née à Argenteuil, artiste autodidacte multisupport, graffeuse, peintre et réalisatrice, Nora Hamdi a publié un manga punk, *Trois étoiles*, au Diable Vauvert en 2002. *Des poupées et des anges*, lauréat du Prix Yves Navarre 2005, est son premier roman" (Born in Argenteuil, a self-taught multimedia artist, graffiti artist, painter and filmmaker, Nora Hamdi published a punk manga, *Trois étoiles,* with Au Diable Vauvert in 2002. *Des poupées et des anges*, winner of the Prix Yves Navarre 2005, is her first novel) (Hamdi 2004, back cover). In *Des poupées et des anges*, which was published a year before the *banlieue* riots, Hamdi portrays the mounting tensions and malaise of second-generation immigrants in the *banlieue*, all the while focusing on the coming-of-age of her first-person female narrator.

In *Des poupées*, the familial *mise-en-scène* is tinted with violence, and challenging of stereotypical gender roles. In *Des Poupées*, Hamdi's female characters become the voices of women like Samira Bellil whose testimonies have become exclusively sequestered inside the *"banlieue* victim" box, and outside the French literature realm. In Hamdi's novel, the family lives under the authority of the father. Physically violent and emotionally abusive to his wife and daughters, he is a construction worker who suffers a permanent injury and becomes paralyzed. Nora Hamdi's text is raw like Bellil's, embodying the reality of domestic violence in a highly detailed yet fast-paced narrative form:

> Dans l'épreuve de la douleur, jamais de ma vie je n'ai vu une femme en passer par autant de positions. À la verticale, à l'horizontale, par terre, sur le ventre, sur le dos, hématome en pleine face, trempée de peur, se cacher dans les chiottes, devant l'évier, ensanglantée, crâne ouvert . . . une énorme poignée de mèches dans les mains de mon père, la rage monter, genoux en sang, supplier, prier.
>
> (Throughout the painful ordeal, I have never seen a woman go through so many positions. Vertical, horizontal, on the floor, on her stomach, on her back, bruises on her face, drenched with sweat, hiding in the bathroom, in front of the sink, bleeding, open skull . . . a large fistful of her locks in my father's hands, rage boiling inside, bleeding knees, begging, praying.) (Hamdi 2004, 85)

The breathless punctuation in this episode recounted by the main character, Lya (the tomboy), is reminiscent of Bouraoui's narrative rhythm in *Garçon manqué*. The sense of authenticity that transpires in this first-person narration, punctuated with a sense of urgency in its retelling of a shockingly violent scene, echoes the mode of "spontaneous expression" (Stoquart 2003, 15) which Stoquart corrected in Bellil's original version of *Dans l'enfer*, in order to make her testimony more accessible to the average metropolitan reader.

In *Des poupées*, Hamdi's negotiation of gender and racial constructs in 2004 France is expressed through the duality between Lya and her older sister Chirine. In the narrative, Chirine's efforts to become a model are driven by her strong will to integrate the white French middle-class, and to leave her sister Lya who, in Chirine's opinion, has become compliant to her role of *"banlieue"* Other. Chirine embodies the dangers of the utopian integration model of "Black-Blanc-Beur":

while it is true that Chirine eventually becomes a model, marries a white French man, and moves to Paris proper, all these goals are achieved through countless plastic surgeries and other degrading physical practices, as well as her shunning her family entirely. In the voice of Chirine, Hamdi explains:

> Était-ce la faute de sa sœur si elle représentait tout ce qu'elle fuyait? Était-ce sa faute si cette fille du même sang qu'elle lui rappelait tout ce qu'elle n'avait cessé de gommer en elle? Ces traits qu'elle a tenté d'effacer à l'aide de la chirurgie, des nombreuses crèmes, des régimes, de nouvelles façons de parler, marcher, penser. Cachée sous des vêtements plus coûteux les uns que les autres. Non. . . C'était pas la faute de Lya, mais Chirine préférait devenir une étrangère.
>
> (Was it her sister's fault if she represented everything she was running away from? Was it her fault if this girl of the same blood reminded her of all the things she had been constantly eliminating in her own self? These traits she tried to erase with the help of plastic surgery, numerous creams, diets, new manners of speaking, walking, thinking. Hiding under the most expensive clothes. No. . . it wasn't Lya's fault, but Chirine would rather become a stranger.) (200-201)

In the end, Hamdi offers an alternative for the women who, like Lya, decide to stay in the *banlieue* but refuse to be victimized by other *banlieue* men or the institutions. Unlike Bouraoui's narrator in *Garçon manqué* whose tomboy identity was partially linked to her sexual identity, Lya's masculine demeanor is carefully developed through the narrative as a defense mechanism against the dangers of utopian thinking, as they take the physical form of her sister Chirine's actions.

Hamdi's *Des poupées et des anges*, opens with a quote from George Sand's 1846 *La mare au diable* as a foreword, specifically from its first section entitled "L'auteur au lecteur":

> En poignant la misère, si laide, si avilie, parfois si vicieuse et si criminelle, leur but est-il atteint et l'effet en est-il salutaire comme ils le voudraient? Nous n'osons pas nous prononcer là-dessus. On peut nous dire qu'en montrant ce gouffre creusé sous le sol fragile de l'opulence, ils effraient le mauvais riche . . . Nous confessons que nous ne comprenons pas trop comment on le réconciliera avec l'humanité qu'il méprise, comment on le rendra sensible aux douleurs du pauvre qu'il redoute . . .
>
> (When they depict poverty as being so hideous and degraded, and sometimes so corrupt and criminal, do they really achieve their purpose, and is the result as salutary as they claim? We won't venture to say. It may be argued that they

terrify the unjust rich man . . . Frankly, we can't understand how it will reconcile him to the human race he despises, or make him care about the sufferings of the poor wretch he dreads . . .) (Sand 2004, 5/88–89)

Hamdi's choice to preface her novel with a quote from the famed nineteenth-century French writer George Sand is symbolic of several of her narrative choices in *Des poupées*. George Sand was a male pseudonym used by female writer Amantine Aurore Lucile Dupin, who shocked her contemporary audience with her political views on marriage and the condition of women in French society, and her habit of dressing as a man. After her, several female authors took on male pseudonyms in order to be able to publish their works. For Nora Hamdi, Sand is a symbolic choice of personalized paratext both in terms of having to alter one's female identity in a conventional publishing market, and of her own character in *Des poupées*, Lya, a tomboy who chooses to dress as a boy. Hamdi's choice to include a quote from Sand's *The Devil's Pond* is equally revealing of her sociocultural intentions with the publication of *Des poupées* in 2004: as *The Devil's Pond* takes place in the countryside of the Berry region as opposed to the bustling city of Paris, the disregarded peasant population of Sand's narrative seems to mirror the immigrant families living in the ex-centered *banlieues* at the turn of the twentieth century. Hamdi's inclusion of Sand's work thus prefigures the strong parallels she will draw in her novel regarding social and geographical discrepancies in France in the early 2000s.

Furthermore, in choosing to quote Sand from her "Author to the Reader" section which, in and of itself, establishes a form of reading contract between the author and her reader beyond the manipulations that could later be executed by an eventual editor, Hamdi aligns herself with Sand's unwavering will to retain authority over her text. Finally, Hamdi establishes her female and "Other" presence in a male and white-dominated French literary sphere like Sand in the nineteenth century: that is, learning to own and manipulate France's literary conventions in order to reach a larger public with writings that question the French nation's social order. Ultimately, as *The Devil's Pond* is set in the Berry region, Hamdi's inclusion of a quote from Sand's text can also be seen as a recognition of her partnership with the Au Diable Vauvert publishing house, located in the Camargue area in the South of France, an homage to the French countryside—also ex-centered, both geographically and culturally, from the literary center of Paris.

The Au Diable Vauvert publishing house is described on its official website as "pop et urbaine mais installée en Camargue entre marais et costières" (pop and urban but set in Camargue, between marshes and coasts) (Au Diable, "Présentation" 2019). In 2004, for a relatively unknown author such as Nora Hamdi who could not have been vetted by institutional entities or literary prizes other than her one and only other publication (the graphic novel *Trois étoiles*), the choice to work with a minor publisher such as Au Diable Vauvert may not have been a choice at all. She did however publish one other novel with Au Diable Vauvert, *Plaqué or* (*Laminated Gold*) in 2005, another work featuring characters from the *banlieue*. *Plaqué or* follows the same type of narrative as *Des poupées*, featuring second-generation immigrant characters attempting to cross the sociocultural and geographical boundaries of their *banlieues* and family structures in order to "integrate" Parisian life. Au Diable Vauvert advertises *Plaqué or* as follows:

Dans une langue moderne, imagée et musicale, Nora Hamdi déroule les itinéraires parallèles de Seloula et Hédi, elle actrice intermittente, lui saxophoniste, deux enfants d'immigrés ayant tout à inventer de leur identité française. Séparés dès l'enfance, déracinés mais libres d'attache, ils traversent Paris, des quartiers privilégiés aux plus démunis, et portent sur leur destin un regard à la fois acerbe et drôle, sublimé par le désir et le talent de vivre.

(In a modern language, musical and full of imagery, Nora Hamdi unfolds the parallel itineraries of Seloula, a part-time actress, and Hédi, a saxophone player, both children of immigrant parents in need of creating an entire French identity for themselves. Separated during their childhood, uprooted but unattached, they travel across Paris, from privileged areas to the most impoverished neighborhoods, assessing their destiny with a simultaneously bitter and funny outlook, enhanced by their desire and talent to live.) (Au Diable, "Plaqué or" 2019)

On the novel's front cover, the words "Plaqué or" stand out in yellow capital letters, "or" occupying over a third of the front cover in its center. Below and above the title are hazy photographs of an urban skyline—possibly a Parisian *banlieue*. The top photograph is upside down, mirroring the one on the bottom, thus highlighting the narrative's many dualities: Paris and its *banlieue*, success and failure, its male and female characters, and so on.

In this sense, the same paratextual markers have been used by Au Diable Vauvert in the marketing of both *Des poupées* and *Plaqué or*: both front covers emphasize the geographical location of the narrative (the *banlieue*), as well as the malaise linked to that socioeconomical urban space. On *Des poupées*' front cover, a female teen is sitting on the floor of what seems to be an apartment, with scattered items spread around her (candles, roller-skates). The teen could be of immigrant origin although that is unclear. The front cover's typography is similar to *Plaqué or*'s: the title is typed in block letters and occupies half of the front cover, the word "Anges" itself occupying half the page as it is superimposed onto the rest of the title, and printed in pink (accentuating the notion of gender in Hamdi's narrative). Nora Hamdi's name is typed in a regular-sized font and in black on the upper left corner of the cover. On the upper right corner, what resembles shredded pieces of a typed journal have been added sparsely, perhaps in reference to the narrator's own journal, or in reference to the importance of the media in the general public's perception of the *banlieues* at the time.

The paratext for both novels accentuates Hamdi's immigrant background: the "self-made" aspect of her authorial persona (she is characterized as "autodictate," "self-taught," on the back cover of both novels) is presented in connection with a headshot of Hamdi wearing her hair long and naturally wavy, a photograph which is permanently affixed to the inside cover of her books. In this sense, Hamdi's narrative and authorial identities are packaged in the same way Bellil's were around the same timeframe: as a *banlieue* "Beur," not an *"intégrée"* like Bouraoui. She is however not presented as a "victim" like Bellil had been two years earlier in the Folio edition of *Dans l'enfer des tournantes*. In fact, she resembles the later iteration of Bellil as pictured on the 2007 front cover of her "témoignage" published by Decitre: Hamdi looks confident and determined, in a way mirroring the 2007 image of Bellil looking into the distance toward a brighter future than the one which the *banlieue* could offer.

These are Hamdi's only two narratives set in the *banlieue*. Her later novels, published with various publishing houses, treat of rather different topics. In return, the paratext of these later works shifted in order to broadcast a more "integrated" author and narrative, in fact revealing the same mechanisms that were applied to Nina Bouraoui's novels during the "Black-Blanc-Beur" utopia. However, Bouraoui was almost immediately characterized as an *"intégrée"* (notwithstanding the Folio edition of *La voyeuse interdite*) possibly because of her binational and bicultural background, while it took Hamdi's switching of locale in her narratives and her personal life in order to reach that realm, and finally enter the circle of the *"intégrées"* in 2011, a decade after Bouraoui. These differential publishing practices for Hamdi are indicative of the almost insurmountable leap that one has to perform in order to exit the ex-centered realm of *banlieue* literature when one has not had the "advantage" of having a French parent or a rather wealthy education, like Bouraoui.

As an example of these differential practices, Faïza Guène, born in the *banlieue* of Algerian immigrant parents, continues to be marketed as "Other." Her latest novel, *Millénium blues* is advertised by its publisher Fayard in the following terms: "Faïza Guène n'était pas censée devenir romancière à succès. Fille d'immigrés algériens, habitante des Quatre Chemins et du quartier des Courtillières à Pantin, le système scolaire lui réservait un autre destin. A la force de sa plume, la jeune femme s'est pourtant fait une place de choix dans le milieu littéraire" ("Faïza Guène was not supposed to become a successful novelist. The daughter of Algerian immigrants, and a resident of the Quatre Chemins and the Courtillières projects in Pantin, she was bound to a different future as determined by the education system. As a result of her own persistence in writing, the young woman nevertheless achieved a regarded position within the literary realm") (Fayard, "Millénium blues" 2019). In 2018, Guène continues to be labeled as a "victim" of the education system and of the predetermined fate that comes with being born in the *banlieue*. Even though Fayard recognizes the "regarded position" Guène finally achieved, the publisher brings more attention to the struggles and personal strength of the author who, like Bellil, has not truly become accepted within the French literature realm, but is rather tolerated by an otherwise undefined "literary realm." Guène, who thus continues to represent the *banlieue* because of her family history and socio-geographical origins, has yet to transition over to the realm of the "*intégrées*" in the publishing center of Paris.

Hamdi's 2011 publication, *La couleur dans les mains*, which is a semi-autobiographical, was produced in the same way Bouraoui's texts have been marketed by Stock for years. Similarly to Bouraoui, Hamdi's publishers for *La couleur* at Éditions Léo Scheer included a photograph of the author as a band to the book, as they do for all their authors. Hamdi's novel *Les enlacés*, published in 2010 with Léo Scheer, was in fact also printed under a plain white front cover, with a red band attached to the book featuring a headshot of Hamdi with her hair straightened. The visual paratext's function in 2010–2011 is dual: its temporary form further reinforces the immateriality of the author, and it conversely liberates the text from the stereotypes attributed to the author's image. Unlike Samira Bellil's headshots, directly affixed onto the front covers of her novels—therefore inescapable—Hamdi's portrait is detachable, so barely there for readers to be influenced in their reading of the text. Hamdi's band thus functions similarly to Bouraoui's with Stock as it allows the reader to not dwell on a possible "Other" identity, but rather to consider it just long enough in order to enter a Westernized narrative of immigration set in Paris. On the 2011 band's photo, Hamdi's hair is straightened and her complexion is ghostly, almost blanched in contrast to her naturally curly hair and olive complexion as seen in the 2004 *Des poupées* photograph chosen by Au Diable Vauvert. Her publisher's epitext regarding *La couleur* follows the same lines as the paratext chosen for the novel: the sole "revue de presse" that is included on Léo Scheer's webpage for *La couleur* links to an article entitled "Nora Hamdi: 'On peut réussir hors de la culture des cités'" ("Nora Hamdi: 'One can succeed outside of the *banlieue* culture'") published in the fashion magazine *Be* (Léo Scheer, "La couleur" 2019). As Hamdi's narratives have drifted from the reality and violence of *banlieue* life in *Des poupées et des anges* and *Plaqué or* towards the Parisian life of a painter who changes her name from "Yasmine Belhifa" to "Janine Beli" in order to obtain a lease on a Parisian studio in *La couleur dans les mains*, the paratext surrounding her works has visibly evolved into a more Westernized, institutionalized representation of the author.[15]

While the paratext chosen by the Au Diable Vauvert publishing house in 2004—2005 for *Des poupées* and *Plaqué or* appeared to somewhat align itself with the "*banlieue* victim" identity that was at the time at the forefront of the media with Samira Bellil and Fadela Amara's focus on *banlieue* violence, the paratextual elements to Hamdi's later novels published with Léo Scheer drastically shifted to portray an *intégrée* author, in the same manner as Bouraoui. However, while Bouraoui was portrayed as an *intégrée* during the "Black-Blanc-Beur" utopia, it took a few more years—and a change of publisher—for Hamdi to be portrayed as such. In truth, the geographical shift in Hamdi's narratives from the realm of the *banlieue* to that of bohemian, artistic downtown Paris in *Les enlacés* and *La couleur dans les mains* called for a more *intégré*, neutral form of paratext, in the vein of that attributed years earlier to Bouraoui. We can therefore assess that Hamdi's literary works during the "Black-Blanc-Beur" years served a purpose in reaffirming the "*banlieue* victim" facet of the "Beur" identity, and that she was only recognized as an *intégrée* author several years after the end of the "Black-Blanc-Beur" utopia, as she herself chose to no longer write about or be associated with the *banlieue*.

CONCLUSION

The "Beur" ideal which was promoted in the media through Zinedine Zidane's athletic success after the '98 World Cup aimed to reconcile the French public with the second-generation immigrants from the Maghreb, especially after the terrorist attacks perpetrated by the GIA on French soil. This idealized version of North-African integration within the French Republic's culture and values was in turn sustained by different aspects of the *female* "Beur" identity as publicized by the media and publishing industry: the "neither whore nor submissive" outspoken *banlieue* victim who, through demonstrated acts of allegiance to the French state and literary realm obtained closure from her violent past (Bellil); and the Westernized "*intégrée*," whose socio-geographical move from the periphery into the center translated into a public narrative of postcolonial success (Bouraoui, and later, Hamdi). Hamdi and Bouraoui's fabricated "*intégrée*" status in the French publishing realm

Figure 2.3 Front Cover of *La couleur dans les mains* by Nora Hamdi, Published by Éditions Léo Scheer (2011).

has allowed them to obtain a certain level of recognition, while continuing to publish narratives which problematize France's colonial history and its postcolonial institutions. As mentioned in this chapter, Nina Bouraoui's success continues to this day in both the literary and institutional realms. As for Hamdi, she recounted in her 2014 novel entitled *La maquisarde* the life of her mother as a resistance fighter within the Algerian war effort against France during the War of Independence (1954–1962). After *Des poupées et des anges* was turned into a movie starring Leïla Bekhti as Lya in 2008, a film adaptation of *La maquisarde* was shot in 2019, once again bringing Hamdi's literary works to a larger audience.

At the turn of the millennium, these women writers (Amara, Bellil, Bouraoui, and Hamdi) outlined the innate dangers and falseness of utopian thinking in terms of a fabricated "Beur" ideal of integration through their autobiographical or autofictional narratives. In spite of the various manipulations from which Bellil and her testimonial suffered at the hands of her own editor, her various publishers, and the French media, the young author accomplished what very few had accomplished before her: she was heard (and read), and she was able to obtain resolution and closure. Similarly, Bouraoui's ability to publish her autobiographical and autofictional narratives on the topics of biculturality, gender identity, and homosexuality, has been nothing short of revolutionary in a country that continues to grapple with these concepts. Finally, Hamdi's texts, although less known by the public and academics alike, illustrate the reality of many *banlieue* women who refuse to be treated as victims by the media, and who continue to challenge the socio-cultural and gender-based stigma of the female *banlieue* identity.

NOTES

1. The politicization of "non-Blanc" soccer players continued after 1998 and strongly resurfaced at the 2010 World Cup in South Africa. After Nicolas Anelka insulted head coach Raymond Domenech and was subsequently fired from the team, the "Bleus" went on strike and refused to attend their pre-game practices. In *Affreux, riches et méchants*, Stéphane Béaud explains that this event, portrayed in the French media as *banlieue* youths being ungrateful for the opportunity to represent France in the World Cup, was turned into such an "affaire d'état" (government matter) that President Sarkozy had to intervene, to save "l'honneur de la nation" (the nation's honor) (Béaud 2014, 8).

2. Hargreaves further explains: "Beur is a name popularly applied to the sons and daughters of North-African immigrants. A longer-established label is that of 'second-generation immigrant', but as most of those concerned were born in France, this is something of a misnomer, for they have never migrated from one country to another. In their daily lives, the Beurs have, however, been compelled to migrate constantly

between the secular culture of France and the traditions carried with them by their Muslim parents from across the Mediterranean" (Hargreaves 1997, 1).

3. Hargreaves writes: "In a relatively small number of cases, class can sometimes work to free individuals from the stigmatizing gaze of the majority ethnic "Other." Professional people of Third World origin are often exempted from the "immigrant worker" label despite the fact that they are migrants and—in the generic sense of the word—workers. When recognized as businesspeople, academics, or writers, migrants from Africa, the Middle East, or Asia are more likely to be seen as "foreigners" than as "immigrants," even when they match all the formal criteria by which immigrants are defined" (Hargreaves 1997, 14).

4. In her answers to Chevillot's questions, Imache expressed resistance against what she considered a ghettoization of her works along with those of her contemporaries (Chevillot 1998, 638). In addition, Imache recalled fighting her own editor's pressure to alter *Une fille sans histoire* in order to incorporate her own narrative of immigration (639).

5. The movement in itself was inspired by the publication of Bellil's testimony. In *Ni putes ni soumises*, Amara writes: "Cru, direct et douloureux, le témoignage de Samira avait fait l'effet d'une bombe en révélant cette réalité incroyable. Cette femme a été très seule dans sa bataille, mais elle est allée jusqu'au bout" (In revealing the facts, Samira's testimony—raw, direct and painful—acted like a bomb. She faced her struggle alone and told the whole story) (Amara 2003/2006, 7/36–37).

6. Parts of the research for this section were presented at the Women in French's annual conference in Tallahassee, Florida entitled "Le bruit des femmes," in a paper entitled "Préfaciers et traducteurs: le monde de l'édition et les manipulations du témoignage de la femme maghrébine en France (Josée Stoquart et David Thomson)" (February 8-10 2018).

7. Amara recounts how she realized at an early age "comment les flics pouvaient maltraiter des gens, simplement parce qu'ils étaient arabes" (I saw how the cops were able to mistreat people simply because they were Arabs) (Amara 2003/2006, 24/53).

8. The intention to paint young men from the *banlieues* with a broad brush was also present in *Dans l'enfer des tournantes* but not in Bellil's own words—rather, in journalist Josée Stoquart's preface to the text. Alec Hargreaves in his introduction to the English translation of the text (*To Hell and Back: The Life of Samira Bellil*) noted the discrepancy between Bellil and Stoquart's words on the role that Islam would have played in the upbringing of Bellil's attackers: "This did not prevent Stoquart from adding a preface to the book, in which she portrayed the sexual violence of young men in the banlieue as a consequence of them being caught between Islamic fundamentalism and the cheap pornography of Western consumer society. Bellil's narrative made no reference to Islamic fundamentalism, but Stoquart's representation of events in those terms was given widespread currency by journalists, many of whom may have seen in the preface a shortcut that saved them the trouble of reading Bellil's text" (xviii).

9. Amara explained: "We think that if women and young girls in the *quartiers* are given the opportunity to assert themselves by participating in collective actions, they

will play an important role in changing the *quartiers* . . . We think that silence and isolation are the principal sources of oppression" (Murray and Perpish 2011, 23).

10. *Des poupées* is not semi-autobiographical like Bouraoui's text—rather, it is an autofiction based not on the life of the author, but on what she observed growing up in the Paris *banlieue*.

11. Parts of the research for this section were presented at the American Comparative Literature Association's annual meeting in Seattle, WA (2015), which resulted in the publication of an article entitled "Évoluée or Intégrée: Black and Beur Publishing Practices in Contemporary Metropolitan French Women Writing."

12. "Retranchée derrière toutes sortes d'ouvertures, je regarde, j'ausculte, je dévisage pour rendre laid le sublime, sombre le soleil, banales les situations les plus complexes . . . je suis l'œil indiscret caché derrière vos enceintes, vos portes, vos trous de serrure afin de dérober un fragment de Vie qui ne m'appartiendra jamais!" (Hidden behind all manner of openings, I look, sound out, stare, in order to make the sublime ugly, the sun dark, the most complex situations ordinary . . . I am the indiscreet eye hidden behind your enclosures, your doors, your keyholes, in order to unearth a fragment of Life which will never belong to me!) (Bouraoui 1991/1995, 15–16/8)

13. In *Seuils*, Gérard Genette explains the function of the band as follows: "Le trait matériel commun de ces deux éléments [la jaquette et la bande] . . . est leur caractère amovible, et comme constitutivement éphémère, qui invite presque le lecteur à s'en débarrasser une fois remplie leur mission d'affiche, et éventuellement de protection . . . La jaquette et la bande portent de préférence des messages paratextuels que l'on souhaite eux-mêmes transitoires, à oublier après effet" (The material feature that these two elements [the dust jacket and the band] have in common . . . is their detachable character, as if they were constitutively ephemeral, almost inviting the reader to get rid of them after they have fulfilled their function as poster and possibly as protection . . . most likely the paratextual messages that appear on the jacket and band are also meant to be transitory, to be forgotten after making their impression) (Genette 1987/1997, 30/27).

14. Parts of the research for this section originate from the author's doctoral dissertation, *L'Autre en Mouvement: Representations of the Postcolonial Urban Other in Contemporary Metropolitan French Art, Literature and Cinema*.

15. In the opening pages of *La couleur dans les mains*, the narrator is encouraged by her real estate agent, a Jewish woman who had previously experienced discrimination in Paris, to change her name in order to not alert her new landlord as to her North-African origins. Hamdi writes: "J'évite le miroir au-dessus du lavabo, j'évite mon physique typé arabe, j'évite de penser à mon nom, typé arabe aussi, j'oublie que je viens de le troquer. Changer d'identité pour devenir parisienne n'était pas vraiment dans mes plans" (I avoid the mirror above the sink, I avoid my typically Arab physique, I avoid thinking about my name, also typically Arab, I forget that I just traded it. I had not exactly planned to change my identity in order to become Parisian) (Hamdi 2011, 14–15).

Chapter 3

"Black," "Afro-French," and *"Évoluées"*

Calixthe Beyala, Bessora, Fatou Diome

Up until 1996, the question of plagiarism in French literature had never been brought to the forefront of the French media in the way it was about to be exposed with the trial of Franco-Cameroonian author Calixthe Beyala and her 1992 novel, *Le petit prince de Belleville*. Published by the very established Éditions Albin Michel, the novel was found to bear excessive resemblances to Romain Gary's *La vie devant soi*, and Howard Buten's *Quand j'avais cinq ans, je m'ai tué* (Hitchcott 2007, 15). Although Beyala was condemned for plagiarism, the Académie Française controversially awarded her the Grand Prix du Roman for her novel *Les honneurs perdus* that same year. French literary critic Pierre Assouline reacted to the magazine *Les échos*: "Décidément, quelque chose ne va pas au royaume des écrivains. Plus Calixthe Beyala se defend des accusations de plagiat, plus on découvre avec effarement que ses livres sont truffés d'emprunts. À croire qu'il s'agit d'une méthode éprouvée. L'Académie Française l'a consacrée. À ses risques et périls" (Truly, something is not right in the kingdom of writers. The more Calixthe Beyala defends herself against accusations of plagiarism, the more we alarmingly find out that her books are filled with other people's writing. It is almost as if this has become a tried and true method. The Académie Française consecrated her, at its own risk) (Assouline 1997, par. 1). The Académie Française's ambiguous treatment of Beyala in 1996 reveals the control that the French literary institutions hold over *écrivains étrangers de langue française* (foreign authors who write in French): they have the ability to make or break them, consecrate and discredit them in the same year.

Before the "cas Beyala" (the "Beyala affair"), there had been investigations from established French literary authorities regarding the authenticity of African literature written in French in general, and Sub-Saharan literature in particular. Koffi Anyinefa explains in "Scandales. Littérature francophone africaine et identité ":

> Au commencement était donc le scandale, et depuis, chaque génération a connu le sien. Après la génération des pionniers (Bakari Diallo), il y a eu, pour la génération des écrivains de la Négritude, le scandale « Camara Laye »: l'auteur de *L'Enfant noir* (1953) s'est vu contester la paternité de son *Regard du roi* (1954) et reprocher une imitation excessive de Frantz Kafka; en 1968 éclate le scandale « Ouologuem » autour d'accusations de plagiat pour la génération post-négritudienne . . . Plus récemment enfin, en 1996, Calixthe Beyala de la génération des « afro-parisiens » a été accusée à son tour de plagiat.
>
> (At the beginning, therefore, was scandal. And since then, each generation has had one. After the generation of the pioneers (Bakari Diallo), there was, for the generation of the Negritude writers, the "Camara Laye" scandal: the *Enfant Noir* (1953) author had his authorship on his *Regard du roi* (1954) contested and was accused of excessively imitating Frantz Kafka; in 1968, the "Ouologuem" scandal appeared around accusations of plagiarism for the post-Negritude generation. . . More recently, finally, in 1996, Calixthe Beyala of the "afro-parisian" generation was accused of plagiarism.) (Anyinefa 2008, 458)

This trend of accusations seems to stem from an ethical prejudice that has French literary critics simultaneously demand an "authentic" African novel, but a novel which nevertheless narratively and/ or stylistically reflects a certain European influence. In this sense, the critic will not be able to recognize a text's authenticity unless it bears connotations to the French tradition either in its storyline (which should reflect the [post]colonial power structure) or style (it should be written in impeccable French). In return, in their zeal to find traces of French literary influence, the critics' over-examination of a given text could potentially lead to false accusations of plagiarism.

At the time of her trial, Beyala's works were published by the very popular and commercial Albin Michel. In failing to defend Beyala's interests, the publisher demonstrated complacency with an antiquated system that glorifies *littérature française* above all else. Albin Michel ultimately revealed its financial interests when, after the trial, Beyala's oeuvres were marketed according to colonial gender and ethnic stereotypes. These publishing practices (primarily paratextual, but also epitextual and editorial) essentially trade a fabricated exotic image of black female writers for the price of a paperback. This chapter examines the different ways in which the publishing industry associated the literature of French-African women writers with colonial and exotic paratexts at the turn of the century, thus surreptitiously forming an alternative category:

that of "Black" literature.¹ The subconscious association of the literature itself with the author's skin color and with a discourse of control and obedience appeared during the colonial period and continued throughout the twentieth century.² However, it is during the "Black-Blanc-Beur" years that the resurgence of the colonial truly imprinted itself onto these authors' book covers, and eventually onto their public identity. In producing essentialist African imagery that reminded the reader of the colonial and, in Beyala's case, of her submissive position to the French literary authorities, metropolitan publishers such as Albin Michel advertised the image of a Westernized compliant black woman, an *évoluée* whose success was largely attributed to her adherence to French values.

Evidently, the fabricated "Black" identity and "Black" literary label are still very present in the early twenty-first century, as exemplified by the continuing existence of Gallimard's *Continents Noirs* collection, and by cases like that of Marie NDiaye. After she won the Prix Goncourt in 2009 for her novel *Trois femmes puissantes*, NDiaye's identity was debated in literary circles as well as in the media: Was NDiaye to be considered French or francophone? Was she herself French? These questions arose from the preconceived and commonly acquired notion in France that one is not entirely French if one's skin color is anything but white. Because NDiaye was born of a Senegalese father and a French mother, she could not—for some—possibly be French. Dominic Thomas in *Africa and France: Postcolonial Cultures, Migration, and Racism* commented:

> Though the word was not publicly used, NDiaye was . . . treated as a latter-day *évoluée*. While deferring unconditional membership to that privileged club that was Frenchness, the French colonial authorities coined the category of *évolués* in order to designate certain colonized subjects which, through exposure to colonial educational and assimilationist mechanisms, had internalized French cultural and social norms. (Thomas 2013, 139)

The resurgence of the colonial in the NDiaye affair materialized on the front cover of *Trois femmes puissantes*'s Folio edition (2011) which was produced a year and a half after Gallimard's original Blanche hardcover edition (2009). The photograph of a black woman (not NDiaye) on the front cover of *Trois femmes puissantes*'s paperback visually recategorized NDiaye's work as "francophone" and "African" literature for the reader, thus contributing to the perpetuation of a "Black" literature category which exists separately from white literature written in French.³ The "cas NDiaye" of 2009 needs to be read in large part through the lens of the "cas Beyala" of 1996, and the fabrication of a "Black" literary identity during the "Black-Blanc-Beur" years. Indeed, this fabricated "Black" identity stealthily glorified the resurgence of colonial stereotypes and the authors' submission to the ideals of the French Republic, while officially promoting an artificial "Black" identity of successful integration (in the image of male soccer champion Lilian Thuram).

This chapter addresses the differential publishing strategies that were used by Beyala's main publisher, Albin Michel, as a result of the 1996 trial. After the "cas Beyala," the "cas Bessora" is examined through the paratextual choices of two of her publishers, Gallimard and Le Serpent à Plumes. Alongside the paratextual analysis of Beyala and Bessora's work, this chapter offers a literary analysis of Beyala's *Lettre d'une Afro-française à ses compatriotes* (2000) and Bessora's *53 cm* (1999). Despite the labels that were affixed to their identities by the media and the literary institutions, these authors were able to publish autofictional narratives and manifestoes which problematized the utopian thinking of that era in terms of immigration and integration in France. While Beyala's *Lettre* debated the contested hybrid identity of French black women, Bessora's *53 cm* used satire to criticize the French institutions as well as France's amnesia regarding its colonial past. Finally, Fatou Diome in *La préférence nationale et autres nouvelles* (2001) and *Le ventre de l'Atlantique* (2003) directly addressed the "Black-Blanc-Beur" utopia and exposed the reality of immigration and multiculturalism in France.

DEFINING BLACKNESS IN FRANCE: AFRICANS, AFROPOLITANS, AND *"LES BLACKS"*

The1996 Beyala trial spurred on a question in the metropolitan public discourse that was intimately tied to France's past relationship with Africa, and to Africa itself: can an African woman, despite her French nationality, write something genuine and of value, other than tales portraying Africa as exotic and desirable? This reasoning—which was never pronounced quite openly but rather subtly suggested by literary critics and the general media coverage—brought into focus the (self-) identifying process of Africans living in France: Africans who are, as is Beyala's case, writing in French, living in France, and have yet to be defined according to a set of geographical, racial, nationalistic, and societal traits that would reconcile their Sub-Saharan origin with their French education and residence.

This question was not asked of the male "Black" players on the "Black-Blanc-Beur" victorious French soccer team, "les Bleus," in 1998. The few black players on the team were actually all born in France or in French territories, except for Marcel Desailly who was born in Ghana but acquired the French nationality after being adopted by a French family and moving to the Metropole. Why weren't these "Black" players only known as French, or as

"Bleus" (the nickname of the French soccer team, in reference to the color of their jerseys)? Why was there a significant need to define these players of darker skin in relation to the rest of the team, "Blanc" and "Beur" players? In the documentary *Les Bleus: Une autre histoire de France (1996-2016)* cowritten by Pascal Blanchard and Sonia Dauger, author and activist Rokhaya Diallo compares the "Black-Blanc-Beur" slogan with the "Bleu-Blanc-Rouge" colors of the French flag and states: "Et finalement, le seul mot qui n'avait pas été modifié, c'était le mot "blanc." Comme s'il y avait une forme de normalité dans la blanchité que n'avaient pas les Noirs et les Arabes" (So the only word that wasn't altered [in the "Black-Blanc-Beur" slogan] was "White." As if whiteness was the norm, and being Black or Arab was not) (Blanchard and Dauger 2006, 20:00).

Before "Black" became a common occurrence in the French vernacular after the 1998 win, the term that would have been used to refer to people of Sub-Saharan or Caribbean descent in France would have commonly been "noir." But "noir" carried its own controversies, from being too reminiscent of France's colonial past (the Code Noir [Black Code] defined slavery in the French Caribbean), to its stark opposition to "blanc," subconsciously considered as the skin color of the typical French man and woman, the so-called *Français(e) de souche*. In contrast, saying "Black" was a way to avoid the term "noir" and encourage the amnesia around France's colonial past, while connoting an imagined urban, integrated, and modern (postcolonial) identity.

In *La condition noire: essai sur une minorité française*, French historian Pap Ndiaye begins:

Voilà que depuis quelques temps des observateurs semblent découvrir l'existence de populations noires dans notre pays . . . Cette remarque peut paraître incongrue, tant il est vrai qu'avoir la peau noire, en France hexagonale, n'est pas, à priori, la meilleure manière de passer inaperçu. Il conviendra de rendre compte de ce paradoxe: les Noirs de France sont individuellement visibles, mais ils sont invisibles en tant que groupe social et qu'objet d'étude pour les universitaires.

(It seems that, recently, observers are discovering the existence of black people in our country . . . This remark can seem odd, since it is true that having black skin in metropolitan France is not, at first sight, the best way to go unnoticed. We need to establish this paradox: Black people in France are individually visible, but they are invisible as a social group and as a research topic for academics.) (Ndiaye 2008, 17)

In his study, Pap Ndiaye seeks to analyze the status of black people living in metropolitan France since it has been understudied, mainly because of a law that makes it impossible to officially quantify any data regarding the black population—or any other ethnic minority—in France, but also because French academics' lack of interest in the matter (18).

Pap Ndiaye emphasizes that identifying as *noir* is not an ideal solution as it does not account for the various genetic or geographical patrimonies of individuals living in France but,[4] as he later notes, the notion of "race" becomes essential when working in the realm of social sciences, especially in the French context: "en tant qu'objet, la 'race' n'a aucun sens; en tant que notion pour rendre compte d'expériences sociales, elle est utile" (as an object, "race" does not mean anything; as a notion to interpret social experiences, it is useful) and "réfuter absolument la notion de 'race' au nom de l'antiracisme . . . est une position morale qui rend difficile la réflexion sur les caractéristiques sociales des discriminations précisément fondées sur elle" (to absolutely discredit the notion of "race" because of antiracism . . . is a moral position that makes it difficult to reflect on the social characteristics of discriminations that are precisely based on race) (33, 35). Thus, talking about a "black race" in France is for Ndiaye a viable option in order to allow for the study of the racist inequalities which black people endure in France. In his study, Ndiaye focuses on the black race's social hardships within metropolitan France, mostly from a "perspective minoritaire."[5] Unfortunately, while studies like *La condition noire* are helpful in creating a first contact between the social sciences and France's colonial past, they can also be accused of conveying the idea that black people in France only belong to a minority group (in itself an exclusionary connotation), and of not accounting for the seemingly successful "Noirs de France" (Ndiaye 2008, 17).

In recent years, Africans who are living in France and are strongly attached to the culture and history of Africa have begun to designate themselves, along with other Africans living in Western metropolises, as "Afropolitans," a term also used by academics such as Bernard De Meyer when speaking of Bessora, as seen later in this chapter. The term was first coined by Taiye Selasi, an author born in London and raised in Massachusetts who stated "I'm not sure where I'm from! I was born in London. My father's from Ghana but lives in Saudi Arabia. My mother's Nigerian but lives in Ghana. I grew up in Boston" (Selasi 2013, par. 2). Cameroonian philosopher Achille Mbembe further explained Afropolitanism in terms of self-consciousness and global awareness:

> Awareness of the interweaving of the here and there, the presence of the elsewhere in the here and vice versa, the relativisation of primary roots and memberships and the way of embracing, with full knowledge of the facts, strangeness, foreignness and remoteness, the ability to recognize one's face in that of a foreigner and make the most of remoteness in closeness, to domesticate the unfamiliar, to work with what seem to be opposites—it is this cultural,

historical and aesthetic sensitivity that underlies the term "Afropolitanism." (Mbembe 2005, 28)

Simon Gikandi, in his foreword to *Negotiating Afropolitanism: Essays on Borders and Spaces in Contemporary African Literature and Folklore* explains along the lines of Mbembe's definition: "To be Afropolitan is to be connected to knowable African communities, nations, and traditions; but it is also to live a life divided across cultures, languages, and states. It is to embrace and celebrate a state of cultural hybridity—to be of Africa and of other worlds at the same time" (Gikandi 2011, 9).

While a number of uprooted Africans who consider themselves global citizens have welcomed both Selasi's and Mbembe's definitions of Afropolitanism, several others have critiqued the academism and classism of the term. In "Is Afropolitanism Africa's New Single Story?" Brian Bwesigye decries the self-designated Afropolitan generation, stating: "It is now a trend that any story out of Africa that deals with deprivation, misrule and suffering is met with loud outcries of *poverty-porn* from a group of Africans Taiye Selasi defined as Afropolitans" (Bwesigye 2013, par. 1). Similarly, in response to Selasi's original text "Bye-Bye Babar" in which she declares "They (read: we) are Afropolitans—the newest generation of African emigrants, coming soon or collected already at a law firm/chem lab/jazz lounge near you. You'll know us by our funny blend of London fashion, New York jargon, African ethics, and academic successes" (Selasi 2005, par. 3), Marta Tvein in "The Afropolitan Must Go" asks: "But what about the non-affluent African diaspora?" (Tvein 2013, par. 6). These divergent views on Afropolitanism reflect the debate that has influenced the audience's reception of authors like Beyala, depending on the story they choose to tell in their novels. For example, with narratives of sexual abuse in Africa (such as *Tu t'appelleras Tanga*), the authenticity of Beyala's writing was never questioned as she was complying to the stereotype of the African writer writing about African poverty. However, as her *Petit prince de Belleville* was not yet another story about Africa but rather a call for attention regarding the living conditions of African immigrants in Paris, and because it was instantly met with literary success, it bore for the Académie Française the potential for a lack of authenticity.

Another term that has surfaced in recent years is "Afropean." Nicki Hitchcott and Dominic Thomas explain in "Francophone Afropeans": "Afropeans do not identify themselves in terms of either/or in relation to the African country of their ancestry and the European nation of their birth, but rather in relation to the transnational, diasporic space that is black Europe" (Hitchcott and Thomas 2014, 4). In the collection of essays *Francophone Afropean Literatures*, authors and academics come together to try and pinpoint what the term "Afropean" would signify in terms of national, but also racial and cultural identity. In the introduction, Hitchcott and Thomas point out the need that has existed since the Negritude movement to label the identity of uprooted Africans in Paris. From Bennetta Jules-Rosette's "Afro-Parisianism" to Cazenave's "Afrique-sur-Seine," Hitchcott and Thomas explain that these terms "have been indicative of the multiple attempts made to define the identities of people who are sometimes described in French as 'minorités visibles' [visible minorities]" (6). The absence of an official or permanent label that would identify Africans living in France has given free rein to not only critics attempting time and again to put a name on a constantly evolving population, but also to publishing houses which are left with the absolute power to define these authors and their works for the larger metropolitan reading audience.

It is not the possible self-defining process of Africans living in France that is at stake in what concerns us here, in the publication realm. As Pap Ndiaye explains in *La condition noire*: "les Noirs qui s'affirment comme tels ne disent jamais qu'ils ne sont que noirs, ni même qu'ils le sont tout le temps, mais ils incluent la carte noire dans leur portefeuille identitaire" (Black people who identify themselves as such never say that they are black only, or that they are black all the time, but they include the black card in their identity wallet) (Ndiaye 2008, 45). It is, however, the efforts *others* make to define Africans living outside of Africa that is of utmost importance to the questions that this book seeks to answer. The way publishing houses *define* their authors of Sub-Saharan descent is a direct reflection of the common status quo of the general metropolitan French unconscious regarding blackness, a pattern characterized by the unspoken yet ever-present "Black" label which gained national prominence during the "Black-Blanc-Beur" era.

Pap Ndiaye in *La condition noire* justly expressed the separation between black and white in the French subconscious when he wrote: "la différence entre les Français noirs et les autres Français dont les parents sont venus d'ailleurs est que l'identité française se trouve constamment suspectée dans le cas des premiers" (the difference between black French people and other French people whose parents came from elsewhere is that the French identity of the former is always treated with suspicion) (42). In this sense, when the paratext suggests an inalterable bond between the author, her text, and France's colonial past in Africa—thus creating a "Black" literature categoryz—it is simultaneously refusing the author's self-identifying process as possibly "French." For the sake of this book, and as explained in the introduction, I will term here and throughout as "Black publishing" the practice of publishing an author's piece along the lines of colonial stereotypes that directly descend from the French colonization of Africa. I do not wish to call it "Afropolitan publishing" or "Afropean publishing" out of respect for these terms which are self-designatory for parts of the African population living in

France who wish to find a label that portrays their global and transnational identity.

After the French soccer team's win of 1998, just as Zizou had become the ideal "Beur," the few Black players on the team had also come to incarnate an ideal, not of the *intégré* like Zidane, but of the *évolué*. Despite the fact that all "Black" players on the team except for Desailly had been born in France, in French overseas departments and territories (Thuram was born in Guadeloupe, Christian Karembeu in New Caledonia), or in former colonies (Patrick Vieira was born in Dakar, Senegal and obtained the French citizenship through his grandfather who had served in the French colonial army), the same stereotypes about African men which had served to justify the triangular trade were still very active in the 1998 French imaginary. Despite the persistent stereotypes that continued (and still continue) to plague the lives of black soccer players in France and abroad, the term "Black" served to somewhat modernize that relationship between France and the descendants of its formerly colonized countries. "Black" in and after 1998 inferred a notion of submission to the French nation, and implied an expected response of gratefulness from athletes, as well as the general black population in France—including women writers like Calixthe Beyala who had already been punished for disobeying the "rules of the game," and whose reputation had been publicly redeemed in a fabricated form or repentance.

CHALLENGING THE PARATEXTUAL EXOTIC: FROM "*ÉVOLUÉES*" TO "*FEMME NOIRES, FRANÇAISES*"

Calixthe Beyala

In a 1993 interview, to the question "Vous appartenez à un groupe ou un mouvement littéraire?" (Do you belong to a group or a literary movement?), Calixthe Beyala answered, "Disons aujourd'hui qu'on me considère un peu comme le chef de file d'un nouveau mouvement africain . . . C'est intéressant que ce soit une femme, pour une fois" (Let's just say that today, I am considered the leader of a new African movement . . . it's interesting that, for once, the leader is a woman) (Cevaer 1993, 162). Beyala's success on the 1990s metropolitan literary market and self-branding as the leader of a new African movement was matched in the paratext of her early publications with the image of a visibly Other yet Westernized author, an image that significantly evolved after the 1996 scandal.[6] As previously discussed in chapter 1, the most flagrant example of Beyala's works being marked as exotic and submissive after she was condemned for plagiarism was seen in the front cover of *Femme nue, femme noire*, which bore the image of a naked black woman partially hiding her body behind a large bouquet of flowers. This novel was also adorned with a red band that read "Un roman érotique africain" (an erotic African novel) effectively marking Beyala's work as exotic erotica. Albin Michel's marketing for her 1999 novel *Amours sauvages* had already paved the way for this new form of paratextual exoticism with the portrayal on the front cover of a black woman partially hiding her face behind her own hand. A promotional flyer created by Albin Michel for *Amours sauvages* advertised the novel in the following terms, which were attributed to the French newspaper *Le Figaro*: "Une œuvre originale et savoureuse: du caïman au piment et à la crème fraiche (Le Figaro)" (An original and tasty work: like caiman dressed with chili pepper and sour cream [Le Figaro]) ("Une oeuvre originale" 1999, par. 1).

In 2000, Beyala published with Mango Éditions *Lettre d'une Afro-française à ses compatriotes*, a non-fiction "lettre ouverte" (open letter) written in reaction to a recent poll in which 70 percent of French residents had declared themselves to be "a little, very, or absolutely racist" (Beyala 2000, back cover). This text echoes another "lettre" written by Beyala in 1995, *Lettre d'une Africaine à ses soeurs occidentales*, published with Spengler Éditions. It is crucial to note that these two nonfiction productions were not published by Albin Michel, Beyala's exclusive editor since 1992. Mango Éditions, which became an affiliate of a larger company, Fleurus Éditions, in 2003, is a small publishing house that today produces cooking manuals, children literature, and self-help books. Calixthe Beyala is not listed as one of their authors on their website. Similarly, Spengler Éditions is headed by Frank Spengler, the creator of the Éditions Blanche which specializes in erotic literature. Among the many collections comprised in the Éditions Blanche catalog, such as "romans érotiques" or "BD érotiques et mangas," the "essais et documents" collection houses a variety of texts such as Alain Soral's *Comprendre l'Empire* (Soral is known to be a Front National militant and affiliate of French humorist Dieudonné's anti-Semitic political movement), or lighter texts such as *Dictionnaire des fantasmes et perversions* (Blanche, "Essais et documents" 2019). Needless to say, both Spengler Éditions and Mango Éditions do not have the caliber of publishing houses to which Beyala had become accustomed in previous years.

As this book is concerned with the "Black-Blanc-Beur" years, we will not dwell on *Lettre d'une Africaine à ses soeurs occidentales* which was published in 1995, but rather focus on *Lettre d'une Afro-française à ses compatriotes*, as it was published *after* both the onset of the "Black-Blanc-Beur" cultural phenomenon, and Beyala's own trial and condemnation for plagiarism in 1996. Beyala's public image after the trial, beyond the paratextual manipulations operated by Albin Michel, was nothing short of that of a pariah. In *Pragmatic Plagiarism: Authorship, Profit, and Power*, Marilyn Randall points out Beyala's attractiveness to both the French media and institutions at the onset of her publishing career, when she was considered "the perfect writer to cleanse the French literary institution of its notorious misogyny and racism. Beautiful, young (her first novel was published at age twenty-five), talented, and an outspoken if self-appointed defender and promoter of African women's rights . . ." (Randall 2001, 183). After describing in detail French critic Pierre Assouline's relentless attempts at character assassination upon his discovery of Beyala's alleged repeat plagiarism in *Les honneurs perdus*, Randall exposes the author's strategy of "directly accus[ing] her accusers, appealing to the guilty conscience not only of the institution but of the nation" (186). In accusing the French literary institutions of racism and tokenism in 1996, Beyala started a "brand" for herself that followed her in her subsequent publications. As a matter of fact, she established herself as one that metropolitan literary institutions such as the Académie Française needs (a token successful black woman) as well as reviles: an outspoken, successful black French woman.

When Beyala declared "I am a black woman" at her trial, she evidently pointed to the hypocrisy of the old-fashioned (and all-white at the time, Assia Djébar having only been invited to join in 2005) Académie Française and, by extension, the metropolitan literary industry (187).[7] Four years later, *Lettre d'une Afro-française à ses compatriotes* is therefore a long, direct accusation of these very institutions that have made it nearly impossible for immigrants and their descendants to be considered by the French authorities and public as full-fledged citizens. Beyala states her thesis in the opening pages of her *Lettre*, one that relies heavily on the French Constitution: "Depuis vingt ans, les mécanismes de régulation semblent s'être rouillés: le principe républicain d'égalité devant la loi ne trouve plus d'application dans la réalité. Cette rupture entre texte et réalité est si profonde que notre pays multiracial et multiculturel perd ses spécificités et devient monocolore dans le monde du travail" ("In the last twenty years, the regulating mechanisms appear to have become rusty: the republican principal of equality in front of the law is no longer applied in reality. This rupture between text and reality is so deep that our multiracial and multicultural country is losing its specificities and becoming monochromatic in the realm of labor") (Beyala 2000, 13). The "rupture between text and reality" highlighted by Beyala directly refers to the French literary institutions' dual appreciation of its black French authors in the context of the "Black-Blanc-Beur" utopia: multiculturalism is laudable when it serves to build the façade of an egalitarian society, but it is decried as soon as it starts accentuating the faults of the French republican ideal.

While it seems at first that, in using the terms "multiracial" and "multicultural," Beyala would then outline the various ways in which all immigrants suffer from racism in France (she uses, for example, blanket terms such as "l'agressé"—"the harassed"—and "le minoritaire"—"the minority individual"—in the beginning pages of her *Lettre* [20]), her text actually focuses on minorities of African descent in France. Half-way through her pamphlet, Beyala exposes her definition of racism, which according to her is: "une idéologie qui envisage la hiérarchisation des groupes ethniques sous forme pyramidale. Au sommet, il y a l'Indo-européen et, tout au fond du précipice, survit l'Africain" (an ideology which foresees the hierarchization of ethnic groups in pyramid form. At the top stands the Indo-European and, at the very bottom of the abyss, the African survives) (36). She continues: "Les minorités noires ont une présence qui les accroche systématiquement à l'histoire des peuples d'Afrique, à ses souffrances, à ses misères, à ses esclavages et à ses dictatures" (Black minorities have a presence that systemically binds them to the history of Africa's peoples, to its sufferings, its miseries, its enslavements and its dictatorships) (37). Beyala's focus on racial hierarchies as they affect Africans in France highlights the autobiographical aspect of her *Lettre*, one written in response to her trial and to the Académie Française's relentless accusations.

In *Calixthe Beyala: Performances of Migration*, Nicki Hitchcott highlights that, in the *"Afro-française"* of Beyala's title, "the ethnic descriptor 'Afro' function[s] as a sub-category or 'type' to Frenchness," and that "although . . . the term appears to privilege French over African, the hyphen also points to an identity that might be located somewhere in between" (Hitchcott 2007, 89–90). However, when it comes to defining herself in the polarized structure outlined above, Beyala writes in her *Lettre* that she is a "femme noire, Française" (black woman, French) (Beyala 2000, 45), and not an "Afro-française" as the title of her letter had implied. She therefore positions herself in terms of her gender and race, without using the geographical and national locators of "Afro" and "French." In this sense, *Lettre d'une Afro-française à ses compatriotes* can be read as the longer version of what Beyala meant when she assessed in her 1996 defense against Assouline's accusations of repeated plagiarism, "I am a black woman." Beyala's critique of the French institutions is at the core of her *Lettre*, when she states: "Ceux qui en souffrent sont les Français d'origine étrangère qui, exclus systématiquement de la vie politique, économique, médiatique de notre pays, rejettent à leur tour ces principes dans lesquels ils ne se reconnaissent plus" (Those who suffer the most are the French of foreign origin who, as they are systematically excluded from the political, economic and media life of our country, reject in turn those principles with which they no longer identify) (13). Beyala clearly denounces the dangers of utopian thinking as she refers to the continuing rejection of "non-Blanc" French residents from the center, which in turns leads to discontent, social malaise and rebellion, as seen in the 2005 *banlieue* riots.

As she addresses the ambivalent structure of the institutions in their rapport with people of African descent in France, Beyala imagines a "Noir du seizième arrondissement parisien, vêtu de son costume trois-pièces, cravaté et attaché-case en main" (Black man from Paris' sixteenth arrondissement, dressed in his three-piece-suit, with a tie and a briefcase in hand) as the opposite example of the habitual "African" stereotype (in that he is not likely to be arrested by the police because of his Westernized appearance) (21), she expands in the following terms:

> Cet exemple de Noir riche est en soi significatif d'un des éléments essentiels sur lesquels se reposent les émotions racistes: la misère. L'étranger perçu comme un usurpateur de pain en devient le producteur, donc un ami, et en tant que tel, il est respecté. Il peut être aimé, et il n'est pas difficile, en ayant quelque peu l'esprit satirique, de l'imaginer en personnage d'importance griotienne, en feu de joie, autour duquel se recroqueville toute la haute bourgeoisie française pour s'instruire et se réchauffer. Rions donc.
>
> (This example of a rich black man is, in itself, significant of one of the essential elements upon which racist emotions are based: misery. The foreigner who was perceived as a bread thief is now a bread maker, therefore a friend and, as such, he is respected. He can be loved, and it is not difficult, if we have a somewhat satirical mind, to picture him as a character of *griot* importance, as a bonfire, around which every member of France's high bourgeoisie gathers in order to learn and warm up. Let's laugh, then.) (22)

According to the Oxford Dictionary of Literary Terms, a "griot" is "a kind of bard or itinerant minstrel found in western African societies, who usually sings of local legends, histories, genealogies, or heroic deeds" (Oxford 2019). Beyala's use of the term *griot* in "importance griotienne" creates a direct link between her *Lettre* and her rebellion against the French literary institutions at her 1996 trial, as she effectively denounces the process of intellectual slavery by which Westernized African authors are manipulated into producing entertaining literature for the former colonial empire. Beyala herself is a *griotte* and, as seen previously, used to be considered in her early professional years as a "[b]eautiful, young . . . talented" *Noire* (Randall 2001, 183) around whom the literary institutions used to gather, in exotically inspired admiration. In 2000, Beyala effectively reclaims her own *griotte* status with her *Lettre* in which she warns other Africans against the manipulations of the French literary institutions.

Bessora also addresses the specific role of the *griot* and, in particular, *griotte* in the French literary sphere in her semiautobiographical novel *53 cm*, which was published around the same time as Beyala's *Lettre*.[8] In the voice of her narrator Zara, Bessora writes: "Ce soir . . . je tiens mon rôle de griotte: le soir, à la veillée, je conte mon épopée" (Tonight . . . I assume my role of *griotte*: at night, after hours, I narrate my epic) (Bessora 1999, 84). Here and throughout *53 cm*, the creative process of the novel is subverted by the institutions that weigh on the narrator's future as she attempts to become a permanent resident of France, turning the text itself into a political manifesto akin to that of Beyala's *Lettre d'une Afro-française à ses compatriotes*. Both of these authors' duty as *griottes* in the French literary realm is to chronicle the lives of those that do not fit into the mold of the ideal "Black" of the "Black-Blanc-Beur" slogan in the years following 1998. Yet their role as *griotte* is constantly challenged by the metropolitan literary institutions, their own publishers included. In Bessora's case, as in Nina Bouraoui's, countless scholars and literary critiques have attempted to pinpoint and define the author's identity, most often along the lines of their geographic and ethnic lineage, and most often through the unsuccessful and misguided association of that lineage with the text itself.

Bessora

Bernard De Meyer writes in the abstract of his article "La sage-femme, l'exilée et l'écrivain ou les bébés hybrides de Bessora":

> Among the new generation of African women authors writing in French, Bessora occupies a very particular place. Daughter of "afropolitanism," she assumes her position in the literary field of African novel writing . . . while she is opposed to any form of determination (in particular racial and sexual), she herself succumbs to certain characterizations at the level of her writing, as she follows the path of her predecessors, in particular Mariama Bâ and Ken Bugul. (De Meyer 2006, 16)

De Meyer in his article argues that Bessora, like many of her contemporaries, has been known to, at times, look for inspiration in her ancestral roots in Africa (17). He states in particular: "Résultat d'une assimilation multiple et exagérée, son œuvre est le théâtre du flux et du reflux entre une prise de distance par rapport aux réalités littéraires et une implication dans cette même histoire" (The result of a multiple and exaggerated assimilation, her work is a theater of ebb and flow, between her distancing herself from the reality of literature and her implicating herself in that same history) (18). Bessora has indeed become quite a singular figure on the francophone literary scene (and French publishing market) as her style has been compared to that of French novelist Raymond Queneau, while her narratives continue to revolve around the topics of racial, gender, and sexual difference.

In spite of—or perhaps, because of—her eclectic writing style and acerbic political tone, Bessora and her oeuvre have been repeatedly cataloged as anything but French (francophone, colonial, postcolonial, and "Black") in the paratext chosen by her various publishers. Sandrine Bessora van Nguema, known as Bessora, a Belgian author of Gabonese descent, has become a prominent figure in the realms of French and francophone literature since the publication in 1999 of her very first novel *53 cm* by Le Serpent à Plumes. In *53 cm* and later in *Les tâches d'encre* (2000), Bessora denounces the effects of colonial stereotypes as they continue to be applied to immigrants in France today. Bessora's tone in her commentary on colonialism and postcolonialism is unique and one that the French literary institutions have been trying to define for years. On the back cover of *53 cm*, one can read "Petite-fille de Raymond Queneau et Alfred Jarry, Bessora propose ici une satire mordante d'une société déboussolée, s'entortillant dans la gestion des flux migratoires. Farce réjouissante, *53 cm* est un roman délirant et ubuesque, qui swingue sur le racisme bureaucratique et l'intolérance ordinaire" (The granddaughter of Raymond Queneau and Alfred Jarry, Bessora delivers a biting satire of a disoriented society that twists itself in its managing of migratory fluxes. A cheerful farce, *53 cm* is a grotesque and exuberant novel that swings on bureaucratic racism and ordinary intolerance) (Bessora 1999, back cover). The Serpent à Plumes publisher here places Bessora and her writing in a *littérature française* context (with the names of Queneau and Jarry), one that does not hint at her genetic connection (or narrative one according to De Meyer) to the African continent. However, the front cover image which was chosen for *53 cm* (that of a naked black woman's back—see chapter 1) effectively labels Bessora's first novel as "Other" and, in the context of the "Black-Blanc-Beur" years, as "Black" women's literature.

Bessora's writing is considered by critics as one of a kind and difficult to define, as Susan Ireland explains in "Bessora's Literary Ludics": "The wide range of comic devices used in the texts—farce, irony, intertextual allusions, pastiche, parody, quiproquos, and every kind of wordplay imaginable—produces a generically hybrid form, a metafictional novel with an immigrant twist that reflects Bessora's own mixed origins and constitutes an innovative means of voicing her opposition to discourses of the past" (Ireland 2004, 7). Yet this "hybrid" writing is not exactly recognized for its novelty or originality in the back cover summary of *53 cm*. Instead, it can be argued that, while it at first appears flattering, the paratext on the back cover presents Bessora as an *"évoluée"* in associating her with Queneau and Jarry while adding a short biography that lists her credentials: "Bessora est née en Belgique en 1968 de père gabonais et de mère suisse. Elle a grandi en Afrique, en Europe et aux Etats-Unis. Elle vit actuellement à Paris où elle prépare un doctorat en anthropologie après avoir fait HEC en Suisse et travaillé comme consultante" (Bessora was born in Belgium in 1968 of a Gabonese father and a Swiss mother. She grew up in Africa, Europe, and in the United States. She now lives in Paris where she is preparing a doctorate in anthropology after having attended HEC in Switzerland and working as a consultant) (Bessora 1999, back cover).

In *Packaging Post/Coloniality*, Richard Watts explains that the act of listing the author's degrees on the back cover is done as to give the oeuvre a sort of legitimacy (Watts 2005, 146). In this context, in listing Bessora's credentials *after* comparing her writing to that of two prominent French, white, and male authors, the publisher seems to be justifying its earlier comparison by outlining the French institutions' awarding of diplomas to Bessora, in a way legitimizing her place in the French intellectual sphere. In doing so, the publisher paints Bessora herself as a *hybrid*: her genetic predicament is that of an African ("de père gabonais") mixed with a European ("de mère suisse"), but she has risen above her condition and is working on her doctorate after having completed HEC, an elite business school in Switzerland. She should therefore not be seen by the reader as solely French, but rather "mixed." In this sense, Bessora appears to be publicly positioned as superior to Beyala: while *métissage* was publicized as impossible in the marketing of Beyala's *Femme nue, femme noire* at a time when "Black" and "Beur" were decidedly separated from "Blanc" (although the author herself was advocating for *métissage*, see chapter 1), it is advertised as being possible with Bessora. The combination of her educational pedigree and literary lineage to Queneau and Jarry position her as a perfect "*évoluée*," to reprise Dominic Thomas' term (Thomas 2013, 139).

The front cover of *53 cm* as published in its first edition by Le Serpent à Plumes portrays the naked back of a woman, her skin shaded in black but her buttocks emphasized with lighting effects to appear more prominent. This image is a direct reference to the narrator's own buttocks (or lack thereof) and, as is suggested in the narrative itself, to Sarah Baartman's. In the early nineteenth century, South-African slave Sarah Baartman (born Sawtche, renamed Saartjie Baartman, later baptized Sarah) was sent to London by Dutch settlers to be exhibited for her peculiar physical traits: her enlarged buttocks and genitalia were supposed to be a definite trait of the Hottentot tribe. From 1810 to 1814, she was shown in England by her Dutch master Caezar and British settler Alexander Dunlop. In 1814, she was purchased by Réaux, a showman of wild animals, and transported to Paris where she quickly became a fashionable kind of entertainment for bourgeois and later lower-class spectators. In Versailles, naturalist Georges Cuvier examined her and determined her supposed status in the evolution chain based on her physical appearance. T. Denean Sharpley-Whiting in *Black Venus: Sexualized Savages, Primal Fears, and Primitive Narratives in French* explains: "Baartman will be placed within this hole in the European system of representation as a highly developed animal, and then closely scrutinized in order to determine her relationship to other animals and human beings. She will be used as a yardstick by which to judge the stages of Western evolution, by which to discern identity, difference, and progress" (Sharpley-Whiting 1999, 23). The "science" of the time was simply based on the gaze and what the Western mind could deduce from what was seen, and therefore proved adept at producing biased and ethnocentric conclusions.

After Baartman's death, Cuvier made a plaster mold of her body and placed her brain and genitalia in jars to be displayed at the Musée de l'Homme, in order to educate the crowds on the evolution of Western civilization and the inferior status of indigenous people. While her brain and genitalia were restituted to her native land in 2002, Baartman's body cast remains in the archives of the Musée de l'Homme. Baartman's case is significant of the obsessive interest of France for the Other that subsisted well beyond her time, ethnographer Michel Leiris' extensive research on Africa being evident proof.[9] In the late twentieth century, Baartman's supposedly abnormal physical traits were still exposed as commodities to the gaze of the Parisian spectator. Baartman's body was in fact displayed as an object of consumption both in her lifetime (in the salons where she was forced to prostitute herself) and beyond, at the Musée de l'Homme.

Sarah Baartman in fact appears on the front cover of Bessora's narrative in pictorial form, as well as on the very first page of her narrative. As the narrator in Bessora's *53 cm* is trying to settle in Paris and obtain a *carte de séjour* for her daughter and herself, her daily encounters in the capital are tainted with the blatant objectification of black women, an objectification she experiences first hand at the gymnasium. On the opening page of *53 cm*, she recounts a strange conversation with a male French-African trainer on her first day at the gym:

- -Je suis pénisopyge, me déclare-t-il. Es-tu stéatopyge?
- Plaît-il?
- Tu es de race stéatopyge si, et seulement si, le périmètre horizontal de ton postérieur dépasse 791 millimètres. La stéatopygie est un caractère racial révélé par Cuvier et Montandon, des naturalistes célèbres et réputés; il faut connaître ses classiques. Alors, as-tu les fesses assez grosses, oui ou non?

("I am penisopygic, he declares. Are you steatopygic?"
"Excuse me?"
"You are of the steatopygic race if, and only if, the horizontal perimeter of your behind measures beyond 791 millimeters. Steatopygia is a racial trait revealed by Cuvier and Montandon, two famous and acclaimed naturalists; you have to know your history. So, is your behind rather big, yes or no?")
(Bessora 1999, 9)

In her first novel, Bessora immediately delineates the intricate network of colonial discourses that directs daily interactions between individuals in 1998–1999 Paris. Not only is the narrator being objectified based on the size of her buttocks (like Sarah Baartman before her), she is being placed in a colonialist and anthropological discourse devised by Georges Cuvier more than a century before her arrival in France. This discourse is in turn used by a French-African man who is attempting to define her based on those colonialist markers that he has already adopted in his own definition of himself.

The combination of the front cover of *53 cm* (the naked buttocks) and of the "inside" (as opposed to the cover) narrative makes for a mordant critique of the way black women are viewed and considered in late twentieth-century metropolitan France, specifically Paris, the center from which colonial constructions regarding women such as Sarah Baartman continue to be propagated into the French subconscious. The choice of the front cover by Le Serpent à Plumes can therefore be considered a display of satire considering Bessora's narrative regarding immigration in France and the innumerable hurdles her main character has to cross in order to obtain her *carte de séjour*. However, the front cover, as it does portray and advertise a black woman's naked body (or, as Bessora herself stated, a "cul racoleur," a "touting ass"),[10] also has the effect of publicizing Bessora's adherence to the fabricated "Black" literature category. The paratextual imagery for *53 cm* therefore appears to be encoded for two different types of audience, each one being offered an image that either confirms their prejudice or invites them to read the in-text narrative. In this sense, the Serpent à Plumes' publishing techniques resemble what Indian theorist Gayatri Spivak has termed "strategic essentialism." Spivak coined the term in her essay "Subaltern Studies: Deconstructing Historiography," pinpointing the solidarity expressed in the subaltern group around their particular essence (essence of the Other, be it woman, worker, nonwhite) in order to infiltrate the élite consciousness, "a *strategic* use of positivist essentialism in a scrupulously visible political interest" (Spivak 1988, 214). Essentialism, be it strategic or not, is problematic as it implies a fragmentation of the groups which entices fixity on both ends of the ethnic spectrum. While Spivak herself has abandoned the term because of its misuse, its application remains visible in paratextual practices such as Le Serpent à Plumes' in the context of Bessora's *53 cm*: the novel's paratext effectively advertises historical satire while appealing to a sense of exotic essentialism.

After *53 cm*, Bessora published two additional novels with Le Serpent à Plumes: *Les tâches d'encre* (2000) and *Deux bébés et l'addition* (2002). *Les tâches d'encre*'s front cover pictured a drawing of blue grapes on a white background, while *Deux bébés et l'addition*'s cover displayed two baby doll heads (one blond, one redhead) looking at each other, again on a white background. Therefore, beside the politically charged *53 cm*—and its ambiguous, essentialist paratext—Le Serpent à Plumes has mostly treated the Belgian author as a labelless author, and not as part of a larger commercial predicament that would have her sell a polished postcolonial version of Africa. The mention of her personal and academic background remains however a key element of the paratext of the three novels published by Le Serpent à Plumes when trying to attract a French reader into the world of a visibly black author whose voice is legitimized by the listing of her French degrees and French literary prizes.

Two of Bessora's novels were published in the *Continents Noirs* collection owned by Gallimard: *Cueillez-moi jolis Messieurs . . .* in 2007, and *Et si Dieu me demande, dites-lui que je dors* in 2008. It is essential to once again examine the denomination "continents noirs" ("black continents") as it was given to a specific literary collection by a major and very commercial publishing house. At first, such a name will have the (metropolitan French) reader ponder what other black continents there could be beyond Africa, suggesting the extent of the diaspora, but not quite so evidently to the average reader. Secondly, the designation "continents noirs" bears in itself a false sense of ethnicity regarding the literature and the authors that are part of this collection, as not all authors of these "continents noirs" are "noirs," an easy if not common association propagated by the commercialization of the "Black" paratext, as explained in this chapter.

What other continents (besides Africa) comprise that collection? On Gallimard's website, one can read the following description under the "*Collection* Continents Noirs" headline: "Avec près de quatre-vingt-dix titres et une quarantaine d'écrivains, la collection Continents Noirs vous propose de découvrir à travers son catalogue une littérature africaine, afro-européenne, diasporique, et ses auteurs" (With close to ninety titles and about forty authors, the Black Continents collection suggests that you discover through its catalog an African, Afro-European, and diasporic literature, along with its authors) (Gallimard, "Continents noirs" 2019). Most novels that appear under the headline and description are written by authors whose ancestry or nationality binds them to Africa, and whose narratives are set in what Gallimard presents to be the "noires" regions of the francophone world: Mali, Congo, but also the Reunion Island, New Caledonia, Louisiana . . . For example, Marie-Thérèse Humbert, an author born in Mauritius but a resident of Paris for most of her adult life, is classified under *Continents Noirs* along with her novel *Les désancrés,* whose action takes place in Louisiana. The effect of this cataloging is a harmonization of the former French colonial empire under one label that classifies these countries or regions' literatures, along with their authors, as *noirs*. Julia Waters in her article entitled "From *Continents Noirs* to *Collection Blanche*: From Other to Same? The case of Ananda Devi" (2008) pointedly argues:

> The very title chosen for Gallimard's collection—*Continents Noirs*—is problematic. Not only does this title, as the collection's overarching *raison d'être*, establish an essentialist link between geography and skin colour, but it is also redolent of a Conradian view of the African continent as a fascinating, awe-inspiring and ultimately inexplicable 'Heart of Darkness'—the very opposite of civilized, white Europe. Such implicit contrasts are, arguably, carried on in the semiotics of the cover design: minimal black and brown lettering and graphics on a stark, white background. (Waters 2008, 59)

In this sense, Gallimard's assumption that their reader would be attracted to a mystic or magic *Continents Noirs* label reveals just as much about its marketing strategies as it does about its lack of knowledge regarding the African diaspora in the postcolonial French-speaking world.

The paratext of these two novels follows the same lines previously unveiled in the case of Beyala, acting as a geographical locator of authorship and authenticity meant to reassure the reader as to the author's ability to write in French (Watts). On the back cover of *Cueillez-moi jolis Messieurs . . .*, one can therefore read in bold: "Née à Bruxelles d'un père gabonais et d'une mère suisse, Bessora vit à Paris. Elle a reçu le prix Fénéon 2001. *Cueillez-moi jolis Messieurs. . .*, où la tendresse le dispute au sarcasme, est son cinquième roman" (Born in Brussels for a Gabonese father and a Swiss mother, Bessora lives in Paris. She was awarded the Fénéon prize in 2001. *Cueillez-moi jolis Messieurs. . .*, where tenderness argues with sarcasm, is her fifth novel) (Bessora 2007, back cover). Here the author's qualifications to write a *Continents Noirs* novel are outlined quickly and efficiently: her father is from Gabon (she is black/African), her mother is Swiss (she is white as well), she lives in Paris (she speaks/writes/reads in French), she was awarded a prestigious prize (her literature is worth reading), and this is her fifth novel (she has a career in writing, and has been consistently published, therefore approved by the literary institutions). The description on the back of *Et si Dieu me demande, dites-lui que je dors* is more succinct: "Anthropologue de formation, Bessora est l'auteur de nombreux romans, dont *Cueillez-moi jolis Messieurs. . ., Petroleum, 53 cm*" (With a background in anthropology, Bessora is the author of numerous novels, including *Cueillez-moi jolis Messieurs . . ., Petroleum, 53 cm*) (Bessora 2008, back cover). The message displayed by these short paratextual descriptions of the author is efficient: a graduated anthropologist will surely know what she is talking about and again, she has written multiple novels.

"Black," "Afro-French," and "Évoluées" 99

In a recent interview, Bessora clarified her motivations to contract with different publishing houses (Le Serpent à Plumes, Gallimard, Belfond for *Cyr@no* in 2011), explaining: "Quand je cède mes droits, j'essaye de choisir une personne avant de choisir une maison. Pour mes derniers romans, j'ai choisi Pierre Bisiou . . . [ce qui] impliquait de publier aux éditions La Martinière, sous la marque du Serpent à Plumes. Mais je choisis d'abord des personnes, avant de signer avec des maisons (qui sont parfois de grands groupes, relativement désincarnés)" (When I release my copyrights, I try to first choose a person before choosing a publishing house. For my latest novels, I chose Pierre Bisiou . . . [which] meant choosing to publish with La Martinière, under the brand of Serpent à Plumes. But I first choose people before I sign with publishers (which are sometimes large companies, [thus] relatively disembodied) (Bessora 2019).[11] Regarding the different labels that have been attached to her works and authorial persona through the years, Bessora revealed that publishers and journalists alike have always wanted to classify her according to one particular label as opposed to a label or description that would reflect her mixed ethnic, cultural and geographical background. She stated:

> Je fais actuellement la promotion d'*Alpha* au Canada et en Croatie, sous l'étiquette "France." On m'accole parfois l'étiquette "Belgique," ou l'étiquette "Suisse." On a du mal à concevoir, en effet, qu'il soit possible d'être tout cela en même temps: le métissage, qui est vieux comme le monde, ou presque, est encore vu comme un avenir. . .heureusement éloigné du présent.
>
> (I am currently promoting *Alpha* in Canada and Croatia, under the "France" label. I am sometimes labeled as "Belgium" or "Switzerland." People have a hard time imagining that, actually, it is possible to be all of these at the same time: ethnic mixing, which has always existed, almost, is seen as a thing of the future . . . thankfully far from the present.) (Bessora 2019)

The question of identity, especially the identity of postcolonial Africans living in Paris, has always been at the center of Bessora's work. The main protagonist in *53 cm* resides in Paris but needs to obtain a *carte de séjour* in order to become a legal resident of France. The task proves to be extremely difficult as the various agents of the French bureaucracy she encounters give her inconsistent information regarding her case, and the sense that she does not exactly matter in the eyes of the government. The protagonist eventually encounters an official named Hermenondine Dumas who is supposed to help her receive governmental financial aid, known as the "allocations." Through this official character, Bessora invites History (*Histoire*), both factual and literary, in her immigrant protagonist's personal story (*histoire*) as she makes up Hermenondine Dumas to be the descendant of famed French author Alexandre Dumas' enslaved grandmother (Bessora 1999, 27). During their first meeting, Hermenondine Dumas proceeds to ask *53 cm*'s main protagonist questions regarding her identity: "Vous vous nommez Zara S . . . Sem . . . Andock; vous êtes née le 25 décembre 1968 à Bruxelles, d'une mère suisse romande et d'un père fang gabonais? Mais qu'est-ce que vous faites en France?" (Your name is Zara S . . . Sem . . . Andock; you were born on December 25, 1968 in Brussels, of a French-speaking Swiss mother and a fang Gabonese father? Why are you in France?) (28). Here the similarities between the main protagonist's personal information and the author's are striking, yet appear as no coincidence as *53 cm* begins to unfold as a manifesto exposing the flaws of the French immigration system, a system extremely tainted and influenced by France's colonial past and ensuing prejudices against Africans: in a word, *53 cm* is directly questioning the utopian "Black-Blanc-Beur" discourse of multiculturalism that was prevalent in 1999 France.

From that point on, the narrator begins to address the fictitious social worker Hermenondine Dumas as "mademoiselle Alexandre Dumas" (29), thus exposing the male literary identity that resists the test of time in the name itself and eclipses the personal, familial, and genetic patrimony of an individual. In the pages following the encounter with the social worker, it becomes hard to discern if it is the main protagonist speaking or Bessora herself, as she recounts her confrontations with prejudiced Parisians upon her arrival in the French capital:

Comment? Que font ces douceurs helvète et wallonne parmi cette parure nègre? Et vous autres? Que font ces haricots blancs et amérindiens comme du manioc dans votre cassoulet rose et gaulois? Syncrétisme originaire, Alexandre. Si. Pour être blanc, le plus blanc des Gaulois n'en est pas moins bâtard, pur ou impur.

(How? How is this Belgian and Swiss sweetness a part of this negro exterior? What about yourself? How are these Native-American beans, white as manioc, part of your pink and Gallic cassoulet? Native synchretism, Alexandre. Yes. Even though he is white, the whitest of the Gauls is still a bastard, pure or impure.) (30–31)

Here the narrator criticizes the silence that subsists around the multiculturalism of France born of colonial conquests in Africa, the Caribbean, and America that created mixed races and therefore debunks the image of the "pure" *Français de souche*. Despite the racialized and gendered paratext that accompanied *53 cm* and her contracting with Gallimard a few years later in their *Continents Noirs* collection, Bessora maintains—in-text—a global identity that unfolds in stark contrast with the national status quo. Bessora's unique use of textual resistance to the paratextual identification process that is forced upon her persona is similar to Fatou Diome's: in her texts published during the same time period as Bessora's, Diome also used the (semi) autobiographical genre in order to explicitly oppose the official version of multicultural bliss publicized by the "Black-Blanc-Beur" slogan.

DENOUNCING THE "BLACK-BLANC-BEUR" UTOPIA'S NEOCOLONIALISM

Like Beyala and Bessora, Fatou Diome is an author who is just as well known for her literature as she is for her honest tone and brazen political discourse, as seen most notably in television interviews. A video of Diome was, for example, omnipresent on social media during the 2017 French presidential election, in which the author was asked if she was afraid of presidential candidate and likely race finalist Marine Le Pen (daughter of former National Front leader Jean-Marie Le Pen) and answered "Je n'ai pas peur, c'est elle qui a peur de moi" (I'm not afraid, she [Le Pen] is afraid of me) (Diome 2017, 12:51). In 2017, the French author born in Senegal published an essay entitled *Marianne porte plainte!*, summed up on her publisher's website in these words: "Face aux attaques racistes, sexistes, islamophones, antisémistes, Marianne mérite mieux qu'une lâche resignation. Ne laissons pas les loups dévorer les agneaux au nom de l'identité nationale. Marianne porte plainte!" (As we are now faced with racist, sexist, islamophobic, and anti-Semitic attacks, Marianne deserves better than cowardly resignation. We cannot let the wolves devour the sheep in the name of national identity. Marianne is suing!) (Flammarion, "Marianne" 2018). Diome's militant and antiracist rhetoric was at the time directed toward far-right party National Front leader Marine Le Pen. However, it was not the first time that Diome's political prose was directed at the utopic French national identity and its oblivion of "Other" ethnicities.

La préférence nationale et autres nouvelles

Diome's very first published work was a collection of short stories gathered under the title of one of those stories, "La préférence nationale," and published by Présence Africaine. In the short story "Le visage de l'emploi," Diome recounts her arrival in Strasbourg's cold winter, which allowed her at first to hide her physical differences under scarves, hats, and coats, like the local Strasbourgeois. She writes: "L'égalité n'avait jamais aussi bien porté son nom, personne n'échappait à l'emballage: manteaux, gants, écharpes et bottes créent l'espace d'un hiver une race artificielle, celle des emmitouflés. Les gens n'étaient plus que boules de laine et couleurs industrielles. Les races étaient masquées" (Equality had never been named so appropriately, no one could escape its packaging: coats, gloves, scarves and boots create for a moment an artificial race, that of the swaddled. People had become balls of yarn and industrial colors. Races were concealed) (Diome 2001, 62). This public invisibility is however short-lived when summer begins, and people begin to shed their layers of winter clothing which, until then, kept their peculiarities hidden: "On ne traîna plus de manteaux, d'écharpes, de gants et de bottes, mais la totalité de ses origines, sa peau. Certains portèrent la leur comme un trophée, d'autres comme une croix" (They stopped carrying around their coats, scarves, gloves and boots, but showed the entirety of their origins, their skin. Some carried theirs around like a trophy, others like a cross) (63).

Unable to hide her Senegalese identity anymore, Diome describes her identification process in the public space in the same manner as Bessora in *53 cm*, referencing the natural sciences in the description of her inalterable genetic traits:

> Le visage, c'est un aéroport, une entrée, et son décor ne dévoile jamais assez le labyrinthe qu'il cache. Le visage, réceptacle de gènes et de culture, une carte d'immatriculation raciale et ethnique. Voilà donc pourquoi on me regardait tant: l'Afrique toute entière, avec ses attributs vrais ou imaginaires, s'était engouffrée en moi, et mon visage n'était plus le mien mais son hublot sur l'Europe.
>
> (One's face is an airport, an entryway, and its appearance never reveals enough about the labyrinth that is hidden behind it. One's face [is] the repository of genes and cultures, a racial and ethnic registration card. This is why I was observed so much: Africa in its entirety, with its attributes, real or imaginary, had taken me over, and my face was no longer mine but its window onto Europe.) (63-64)

Published in 2001, a short three years after France's World Cup win and the beginning of the "Black-Blanc-Beur" utopia, Diome's collection of short stories and very first published work revealed that, despite the media and institutional push for a multicultural and postcolonial France, not much had changed since the 1950s and Martinican philosopher Frantz Fanon's first impressions upon his arrival in Paris. In fact, the above-cited passage from "Le visage de l'emploi" (a pun on the French expression "la tête de l'emploi"—fit for the job—and "le visage," the true face of the employment process), is eerily similar to Fanon's in *Black Skin, White Masks* published in 1952:

Et puis il nous fut donné d'affronter le regard blanc. Une lourdeur inaccoutumée nous oppressa. Le véritable monde nous disputait notre part . . . J'étais tout à la fois responsable de mon corps, responsable de ma race, de mes ancêtres. Je promenai sur moi un regard objectif, découvris ma noirceur, mes caractères ethniques, -- et me défoncèrent le tympan l'anthropophagie, l'arriération mentale, le fétichisme, les tares raciales, les négriers, et surtout, et surtout: « Y a bon banania ».

(And then the occasion arose when I had to meet the white man's eyes. An unfamiliar weight burdened me. The real world challenged my claims . . . I was responsible at the same time for my body, for my race, for my ancestors. I subjected myself to an objective examination, I discovered my blackness, my ethnic characteristics; and I was battered down by tom-toms, cannibalism, intellectual deficiency, fetishism, racial defects, slave-ships, and above all else, above all: "Sho' good eatin.") (Fanon 1952/2008, 90–91/83–85)

This sentiment of internalized otherness of Diome's narrator is confirmed upon her meeting her future employer, a white woman who needs a housekeeper. The woman speaks to the narrator in a simplified, mocking, and colonial form of French that mirrors the "Sho' good eatin'" comment made by Fanon in 1952: "Toi y en a bien comprendre madame?" (You understand Misses?) (Diome 2001, 64). When the woman reports to her husband that "Elle ne semble pas savoir depuis quand elle est en France, mais elle a l'air de comprendre l'essentiel de ce que je lui dis" (She doesn't seem to know how long she has been in France, but she seems to understand most of what I tell her) (64), he answers "Mais qu'est-ce que tu veux qu'on fasse avec ça?" (Well, what do you want us to do with that?) (64). The narrator then reflects on her status in this household, in France, and in the larger postcolonial European realm, again in a way similar to Fanon's in the 1950s:

Je repensai donc à la question de Monsieur: "- Mais qu'est-ce que tu veux qu'on fasse avec ça?" C'était donc ça. C'est pour cela qu'on me regardait comme ça. Je n'étais pas moi avec mon prénom, ni madame, ni mademoiselle, mais *ça*. J'étais donc *ça* et même pas *l'autre*. Monsieur éprouvait à mon égard le sentiment que m'inspiraient ces mouches qui s'accouplaient dans sa vaisselle.

(I thought once more of Monsieur's question: "- Well, what do you want us to do with that?" That was it. That's why they were looking at me like that. I wasn't myself, with my name, or misses or miss, but *that*. I was *that*, not even *the other*. Monsieur thought of me the way I thought of those flies mating in his dirty dishes.) (Diome 2001, 66)

The paratext chosen by Présence Africaine for *La préférence nationale* seems to reflect the different narratives that make up Diome's collection of short stories. The front cover features a photograph of a broom and a rag in reference to the above-mentioned short story's lead character. The back cover first features what begins like a biography of Fatou Diome but dangerously assimilates the author with the "Le visage de l'emploi"'s narrator:

> De son île natale au sol français, de ses premiers émois à ses déceptions, c'est à un voyage géographique, social et mental que nous convie Fatou Diome. À travers ses nouvelles, dans une description sans fard et avec un humour féroce, usant d'une langue incisive et colorée, l'auteur raconte les aléas d'une femme de ménage en Alsace, un quotidien souvent fait d'humiliations pour survivre ... et payer ses études supérieures. Sombre tableau d'une difficile intégration que vient tempérer la nostalgie et la douceur des images de son enfance au Sénégal.

> (From her native island to the French land, from her first emotions to her disappointments, Fatou Diome invites us into a geographical, social, and mental journey. Through her short stories, with raw descriptions and a ferocious sense of humour, using an incisive and rich language, the author tells the tribulations of a cleaning woman in Alsace, and of her daily life often filled with humiliations that she she needs to survive... and to pay for her graduate studies. [This book paints] a dark image of a difficult integration process that is only countered with the nostalgic and fond images of her childhood in Senegal.) (Diome 2001, back cover)

On Présence Africaine's website, the opening blurb of the book's back cover has been altered in order to avoid any association in the reader's mind between the author and the narrator of "Le visage de l'emploi." The online description for *La préférence nationale* thus reads:

> De son île natale au sol français, de ses premiers émois à ses récentes déceptions, c'est à un voyage géographique social et mental, que nous convie la narratrice de ce recueil. Usant d'une langue incisive et colorée, la jeune romancière et poétesse sénégalaise y dépeint tant la brutalité des sociétés traditionnelles que la calme violence de nos sociétés d'exclusion.

> (From her native island to the French land, from her first emotions to her recent disappointments, this collection's narrator invites us into a geographical, social and mental journey. Using an incisive and rich language, the young Senegalese novelist and poet describes as much the brutality of traditional societies as the quiet violence of our excluding societies.) (Présence Africaine, "La préférence" 2019)

More recently then, Diome has become a "young Senegalese poet," who portrays "as much the brutality of traditional societies as the quiet violence of our excluding societies," while the narrator of the collection expresses her "recent" disappointments, even though Diome's book was first published in 2001.

The 2001 paperback edition also features on its back cover a short blurb about the author, akin to the ones those were placed on the backs of Bessora's novels published by Le Serpent à Plumes and by Gallimard: "Fatou Diome est née en 1968 à Niodor, une île du Sénégal. Elle vit actuellement en France où elle prépare un doctorat de lettres modernes à l'Université de Strasbourg. *La Préférence Nationale* est son premier livre" (Fatou Diome was born in 1968 in Niodor, an island of Senegal. She currently lives in France where she is working toward a doctorate in contemporary literature at the Université de Strasbourg. *La Préférence Nationale* is her first book) (Diome 2001, back cover). Like Bessora in 1999, Diome in 2001 is "legitimized" in her decision to write and publish in metropolitan France by her publishing house's establishing of her residence ("She currently lives in France") and of her intellectual development and adherence to the rules of writing ("she is preparing her doctorate in contemporary literature"). We can therefore assess that the tacit "Black literature" label, which propagated on the metropolitan literary scene during the "Black-Blanc-Beur" years with examples such as Beyala's *Femme nue, femme noire*, Bessora's *53 cm*, and Diome's *La préférence nationale*, not only exemplified literary colonial practices (Watts) but also established a pattern of identitarian control which these female authors of Sub-Saharan origin questioned and negotiated both within and outside of their narratives.

Le ventre de l'Atlantique

Fatou Diome's very first novel, *Le ventre de l'Atlantique*, published in 2003 with Anne Carrière Éditions, speaks directly to the "Black-Blanc-Beur" utopia and its immediate aftermath in former French colonies such as Senegal, where young men are ready to sacrifice everything in order to become the next "Black" ideal, in the vein of star "Bleu" player Lilian Thuram. All along the novel, Diome analyzes the different destinies of a group of men and women on the Isle of Niodior, off of the coast of Senegal, where the author herself was born. One of these characters is the late Moussa, a young man who aspired to become a star football player following the *Bleus'* victory in the World Cup final in July 1998. The unwavering love and desire for France as an idealized nation is presented all along the text through the narrator's eyes, Salie, a young Senegalese woman who resembles Diome in her realistic approach to what France (and Europe as a whole) truly has to offer young Africans. Salie explains that the story of Moussa is still told by the schoolteacher Ndétare in Niodior to try and prevent young aspiring men from following in the young soccer player's footsteps. The allure of France is presented with colonial undertones, ideals and impossible dreams of success emphasized by the "Black-Blanc-Beur" victory and ensuing slogan. In displacing the narrative from France to Senegal, Diome exposes the scope of the "Black-Blanc-Beur" utopia and its colonial identity politics.

With the story of Moussa, Diome addresses France's responsibility in recruiting young talented soccer players in former African colonies, as the country and its soccer recruiters rode the wave of the "Black-Blanc-Beur" ideal. She first expresses how Moussa was approached in Niodior by a recruiter, aptly named Jean-Charles Sauveur (Savior), who promised the young man instant success in France:

> Le recruteur n'eut aucune peine à convaincre le jeune poulain. Il lui avait suffi d'abattre ses cartes: un billet d'avion payé par le club, un logement garanti dans un centre de formation où on l'entraînerait avec les juniors, avant de le propulser vers la gloire au sein du grand club, et, surtout, la promesse d'un salaire mirobolant.
>
> (The scout had no trouble convincing the young lad. He had only to lay his cards on the table: a plane ticket paid for by the club, guaranteed accommodation in the training center where he'd be coached with the juniors before heading for fame playing for the great club —with, above all, the promise of a fabulous salary.) (Diome 2003/2008, 96/64)

While the book was written in 2003, these coercing methods and empty promises continue to be practiced, as was demonstrated in the 2012 film *Comme un lion* by Samuel Collardey. In the following pages, Sauveur is presented under the traits of a slave driver, consciously and openly evaluating the physical potential of Moussa for the success of the team, as opposed to his persona, psyche, or well-being. Moussa, in return, is described as blindly submitting to Sauveur's demands in an effort to please him, a reminder of the colonized-colonizer relationship: "Sous l'œil paternel de Jean-Charles Sauveur, Moussa se sentait investi d'une mission sacrée. Il ne devait pas faillir, Sauveur attendait impatiemment qu'il confirme ses talents pour rentabiliser son investissement" (Under Jean-Charles Sauveur's paternal eye, Moussa felt he was invested with a sacred mission. He must not falter; Sauveur was impatient for his talent to be confirmed so as to obtain the return on his outlay) (97/ 64).

As Moussa's hopes of becoming a member of Sauveur's team begin to fade, the young man becomes increasingly aware of his true status in Sauveur's plot (97/ 64-5). Diome writes that Moussa, in his pride of his home country, would have surpassed the 1998 players—in the following lines, Lilian Thuram specifically—in celebrating his goals with a typically Senegalese dance, the "mbalax":

Il s'était même inventé une pose victorieuse avant les glorieux acteurs du Mondial 1998. Non, Moussa ne se serait pas contenté d'un regard vague et d'un doigt posé sur la bouche pour inviter les spectateurs à admirer le merveilleux buteur épaté par son œuvre. Ce numéro de pantomime aurait été peu expressif à son goût. Enfant de la terre et du rythme, il exécuterait un mbalax endiablé avant de se jeter sur la pelouse, peut-être même qu'il ferait trois sauts périlleux pour prolonger les applaudissements.

(He'd even invented his victory salute well before the glorious 1998 World Cup team. No, Moussa wouldn't have been satisfied with a vacant look and a finger pressed to his mouth, inviting the adoring fans to admire the striker's amazing prowess. That pantomime wasn't nearly expressive enough for his taste. A child of rhythm and the earth, he'd execute a frenzied *mbalax* before throwing himself on the turf, maybe even three somersaults to prolong the applause.) (101/ 67)

In comparing Moussa's home pride to Thuram who after scoring the winning goal in the semifinal against Croatia in 1998 kneeled down on the field posing with a finger pressed against his mouth, Diome openly disses Thuram's compliance with a culturally neutral goal celebration as opposed to letting one's happiness burst freely in what the author perceives to be a more authentic way—displaying one's cultural difference with the performance of a visibly African dance.

In order to understand the cultural influence of the French soccer team on formerly colonized nations, we need to first explore the reasons why the game of soccer has always been a field for identity politics. In *Soccer Empire*, Laurent Dubois explains: "Today there is no sport more popular and powerful in its global reach, or more tightly linked to international politics, than football. Indeed football may well be the most universal language that currently exists, its empire more extensive than that of any political or religious ideology" (Dubois 2010, 4). On the 1998 French national team, Dubois particularly points out: "What makes the sport particularly powerful, though, is its unpredictability, the space for maneuver and improvisation it allows fans and players, many of whom, notably Zidane and Thuram, are many things at once, occupying shifting positions, taking on multiple affiliations, in the fields of football and politics" (7). Dubois' position in his aptly titled *Soccer Empire* is precisely to demonstrate that the French national soccer team has always been a reflection of its past history, in particular its colonial history as represented in the composition of the 1998 winning team.[12] In fact, Dubois confirms the cultural influence of soccer onto the colonized and formerly colonized as seen in Diome's *Le ventre de l'Atlantique* when he assesses: "While many colonial administrators saw football as a vehicle for inculcating the colonized with the values of European civilization, in many colonies, particularly in the Caribbean and Algeria, it rapidly became a powerful vehicle for individual and community expression, as well as for demands for equality and justice" (11). Dubois continues: "The story of the empire of French football condenses and illuminates the complexities and ironies of French colonialism. But it is also the story of how athletes used the equality and freedom of the playing, and winning, on the football field to confront the inequalities and injustices of the system in which they lived" (11).

Diome expresses this long-standing and unbreakable relationship between France and Senegal through the trope of soccer and its competition in the third opening chapter of her novel. She writes:

> La passion de mon frère pour le football est née assez tôt. Enfant, notre mère lui avait offert une petite balle en caoutchouc qu'elle avait achetée en ville. Il apprit à marcher et à taper du pied en même temps. Lorsqu'il tombait, il rampait jusqu'au ballon, se remettait debout et tapait dessus avant de retomber. Notre mère l'encourageait en l'applaudissant: - Bravo, mon fils, tu es un champion!
>
> (My brother's passion for football started early. When he was a child, our mother gave him a rubber ball she'd bought in town. He learned to walk and kick it at the same time. When he fell over, he'd crawl towards the ball, stand up and kick it, before falling over again. Our mother would encourage him with praise: 'Bravo, my son. You're a champion!') (Diome 2003/2008, 47/28)

Diome then outlines the context in which her character Madické grew up, a cultural context forever torn between the gendered traditions which were imposed on young girls and the dreams of success for men in France through sports as encouraged by the media. Diome reveals in this same chapter that for a long time, the French soccer idol most boys and young men sought to imitate in Niodior remained Michel Platini (48/ 29). Platini, a "Blanc" player of Italian ancestry, was a key player of the French soccer team between 1975 and 1987, leading France to two World Cup semifinals in 1982 and 1986, and to the winning of the European Championship in 1984. However, when a secondary character to the story nicknamed "l'homme de Barbès" (The Man from Barbès) brings back from France what is to be the island's very first television set (49/ 29), the young men's attention quickly drifts from the local soccer game and its Platini ersatz to actual games playing on television, which brings them instantly from the 1980s into the early 2000s, in the midst of the "Black-Blanc-Beur" utopia (53/ 32).

The instant broadcasting of European soccer games quickly becomes the main attraction in Niodior with the most attention being paid to the French soccer team, despite a number of competitions involving other European teams. Diome confirms the importance of France as the former colonizing power in Senegal in its continuing colonization of young minds:

> Pourtant, la télévision montrait aussi d'autres grands clubs occidentaux. Mais rien à faire. Après la colonisation historiquement reconnue, règne maintenant une sorte de colonisation mentale: les jeunes joueurs vénéraient et vénèrent encore la France. À leurs yeux, tout ce qui est enviable vient de France . . . Alors, sur l'île, même si on ne sait pas distinguer, sur une carte, la France du Pérou, on sait en revanche qu'elle rime franchement avec chance.
>
> (The television showed other big European clubs, too, but there was nothing doing. After the historically recognized colonization, a kind of mental colonization now prevails: the young players worshipped and still worship France. In their eyes, everything desirable comes from France. . . . Thus, on the island, even if we can't tell France from Peru on a map, we're always aware it rhymes with chance.) (53/ 32)

On one of her trips back home, the narrator, Salie, explains to a group of young hopeful men: "En Europe, mes frères, vous êtes d'abord noirs, accessoirement citoyens, définitivement étrangers, et ça, ce n'est pas écrit dans la Constitution, mais certains le lisent sur votre peau " (In Europe, my brothers, you're black first, citizens incidentally, outsiders permanently, and that's certainly not written in the constitution, but some can read it on your skin) (176/ 124). The narrator's brother, Madické, does not however long to be one of the famed former or new black players, nor does he long to become a player on the French team, which is a surprise both to the narrator and the reader. Madické's idol is an Italian player named Paolo Maldini, which allows Diome to express the universalist aspect of the colonizing process of these young men's minds.

As mentioned above through Dubois' *Soccer Empire* and Diome's remembrance of Michel Platini's impact on the younger populations of Senegal, French soccer players of Italian origins have long made the roster of the national team and become representative of France's history of immigration. On a larger scale, Italy is home to the A.C. Milan, a highly renowned and successful team. In this sense, Madické's admiration for Maldini is not as misplaced as it can first appear since it is indeed rooted in the European-African colonial relationship, as well as in larger expressions of Eurocentrism and European exceptionalism. Madické's attachment to Maldini's success instead of French player Thuram's is expressed in the very first pages of Diome's novel, as her narrator Salie, in Paris, is watching the same game opposing Italy and Holland in the 2000 European cup as Madické, who is watching on The Man from Barbès' small television in Niodior (15/ 4). Madické's colonial-like identification to Maldini is later expressed by Salie in her repeated implorations perhaps to God, perhaps to the French institutions or even the reader, to make sure that Maldini remains a hero, a glimmer of hope for Madické:

> Alors, dites à Maldini que ses cartons jaunes ou rouges sont trop lourds et m'écrasent le cœur. . . . Dites-lui surtout que je l'ai vu, à Niodior, courir sur le sable chaud derrière une bulle de rêve. Car un jour, sur un terrain vague, mon frère est devenu Maldini. Alors, dites à Maldini son corps de lutteur, ses yeux noirs, ses cheveux crépus, son beau sourire et ses dents blanches. Ce Maldini-là, c'est mon petit frère englouti par son rêve.
>
> (So tell Maldini his yellow or red cards are too much to bear, they're crushing my heart. . . . Tell him above all that I saw him, in Niodior, chasing the bubble of a dream over the warm sand. Because one day, on waste ground, my brother turned into Maldini. So tell Maldini about his wrestler's body, his dark eyes, his frizzy hair, his gorgeous smile and white teeth. That Maldini is my little brother, swallowed up in his dream.) (18/ 6)

When *Le ventre de l'Atlantique* was released in 2003 by Anne Carrière Éditions, the novel was adorned by a white and blue front cover on which one could read the name of the author, the title of the work, the word "roman" (novel), and the name of the editor with its logo (Diome 2003, front cover). By all means, and as this book has sought to demonstrate, such a neutral use of the paratext allows the author to work from within the narrative and also—especially in Diome's case—the epitext, in order to teach her reader about the reality of the "Black-Blanc-Beur" utopia. When the text was reedited by *Le Livre de poche* in 2005 in a smaller, cheaper format, the front cover was adorned with a photograph of a sailboat at sunset, with a shadowed figure steering the boat. *Le Livre de Poche* is a collection that belongs to Hachette, one of the main French publishers, and, since the beginning of the twenty-first century, one of the main five publishers in the United States, along with Simon and Schuster, Penguin Random House, HarperCollins, and MacMillan Publishers (all are known as the "Big Five"). With Hachette being no novice on the literary market, it comes as no surprise that the cheaper format of Diome's novel portrayed on its front cover a rather romanticized image of migration.

When the British publishing house Serpent's Tail published *The Belly of the Atlantic*, Diome's first novel in translation in 2008, several paratextual shortcuts to the story were prominently and strategically placed on the book's front cover as well. The photograph placed at the top of the front cover featured a bare-chested black man rowing in a traditional pirogue on the water, while the larger bottom half of the cover featured a close-up photograph of a black child's bare legs, one of his foot on a soccer ball with, in the background, what is portrayed to be a typical African village. Besides these photographic pseudo-geographical, cultural and narrative shortcuts, three words are printed below the author's name, along with the name of the woman who uttered them: "'Charming, vivid and poetic' Michela Wrong" (Diome 2008, front cover). Wrong is a British journalist who has previously lived in Africa and published a number of non-fiction books on various topics in relation to the continent. Since Serpent's Tail is based in Great Britain, the intention behind the act of including Wrong's input on the front cover of Diome's work in translation appears to be quite essentializing as it casts a white British reporter as the voice of authority validating Diome's published novel in terms that do not touch at all on the political dimension of the novel, as has been outlined in this chapter.

However, the back cover features a longer quote by Wrong, one that alludes to the political dimension of Diome's work: "This charming, vivid and poetic book captures the poignancy of immigrant life and all the unresolved pain of Africa's relationship with its former colonial powers" (Diome 2008, back cover). The front cover's isolation of the first three words of an otherwise compelling political commentary on France and Africa's postcolonial relations is indicative of the British publisher's essentialist marketing practices. In trying to minimize Diome's actual discourse on Europe's responsibility in the continuing psychological colonization of young African men, Serpent's Tail reveals that publishing houses beyond France's metropolitan market equally partake in the commodification of African identities, and of the narratives of French authors of African descent.

CONCLUSION

The fabricated label of "Black" women's literature written in French at the turn of the millennium, one of colonial-like compliance to the literary institutions, was directly inscribed in the paratext of Calixthe Beyala, Bessora, and Fatou Diome's publications. While a handful of athletic "Black" men were glorified for their "integration" within French society, "Black" women writers were degraded on their book covers, and sometimes vilified in the media for their perceived arrogance. This stark resurgence of colonial stereotypes as seen in the textual and visual paratexts of Beyala's *Femme nue, femme noire*, Bessora's *53 cm*, and Diome's *La préférence nationale*, conflicted with the three authors' textual resistance and dissidence against the institutional portrayal of an ideal "Black-Blanc-Beur" French society. In their semiautobiographies, autofictions, and manifestos, the three authors developed accurate portrayals of ethnic minority women writers living in post-1998 France, and of the struggles they faced as black women striving for institutional recognition.

After her condemnation for plagiarism in 1996 and Albin Michel's reductive portrayals of herself and her texts, Calixthe Beyala chose to publish her manifesto with a minor publishing house, and outlined in it her identity as an African woman living in Paris, concurrently warning against the mirage of an easy integration process in France. Bessora's anthropological analysis of the French people and institutions in *53 cm* revealed the colonial hierarchies that subsisted in 1999 France in spite of the "Black-Blanc-Beur" euphoria. Through irony and satire, Bessora's approach to her own *métissage* and mixed literary identity directly contradicted the paratextual elements put in place by her publisher who wished to portray her as an educated *évoluée*. Finally, in *Le ventre de l'Atlantique*, Fatou Diome not only denounced but also warned young African men against the dangers of utopian thinking: in directly addressing the athletic success portrayed in the highly mediatized realm of soccer, Diome lamented the neocolonial propaganda that affects young black men in the development of their lives and identities.

NOTES

1. This chapter along with the larger theme of this book is purposefully focused on female authors whose ancestry ties them directly to Sub-Saharan Africa. While famed Caribbean authors such as Gisèle Pineau and Maryse Condé have been subjected to similar differential practices in the publication of their oeuvres—Condé's Folio edition of *Moi, Tituba sorcière* . . . donning on its front cover Marie-Guillemine Benoist's *Portrait of a Negress*—the departmentalization of the French Caribbean islands of Guadeloupe and Martinique in 1946 pose in this book's context a different predicament for these authors who are considered to be of French nationality through their birthright.

2. In *Packaging Post/Coloniality*, Richard Watts explains: "In the earliest works of colonial subjects using their newly acquired literacy in French and, more to the point, recent mastery of French cultural forms (namely, the novel), the paratext often functions as a marker of colonial ownership. In the preface of a colonial administrator, the dedication by an author to a colonial governor, and the reduction of indigenous culture to a visual cliché in the book cover's illustration, the authority over the text and the cultures it represents passes from its expected possessor, the author, to the predominant voice in the paratext, that of the colonizer." (Watts 2005, 5).

3. See Mouflard, Claire. "Évoluée or Intégrée: Black and Beur Publishing Practices in Contemporary Metropolitan French Women Writing."

4. "Parler des Noirs ne serait-il pas un abus de langage, dans la mesure où les différences culturelles et de classe entre personnes noires ou réputées telles sont si

notables qu'il faudrait renoncer à parler des Noirs en général?" ("Wouldn't talking about Blacks be an abuse of language, since cultural and class differences among black people or people known as black are so noticeable that we would have to forgo talking about Blacks in general?) (Ndiaye 2008, 39).

5. "Ce livre se situe globalement dans la « perspective minoritaire », même s'il emprunte parfois à la « perspective identitaire », susceptible de proposer des éclairages anthropologiques précieux sur les « postcolonisés », d'analyser finement les représentations discursives, en particulier l'eurocentrisme, de mobiliser des disciplines variées (sciences sociales, philosophie, psychanalyse, histoire de l'art, etc. . . . .)" ("This book is globally situated in a 'minority perspective,' even though it borrows at times from the 'identitarian perspective,' which has the potential to provide precious anthropological outlooks on the 'postcolonized,' to finely analyze discursive representations, especially eurocentrism, to mobilize various disciplines (social sciences, philosophy, psychoanalysis, art history, etc. . . .") (21).

6. See Mouflard, Claire. "Évoluée or Intégrée: Black and Beur Publishing Practices in Contemporary Metropolitan French Women Writing."

7. "If 'I am a black woman' can be used to counter accusations of plagiarism, it is also an unanswerable challenge to the Académie to deny that these same conditions may have motivated their choice." (Randall 2001, 187).

8. See Mouflard, Claire. "The Digital Griotte : Bessora's Para/Textual Discourses on Identity Politics and Neocolonialism in Contemporary France."

9. Michel Leiris started a collection of ethnographic works in 1931 that ended in 1967 with the publication of *Afrique Noire*. These works are partly composed of accounts of his own trip between Dakar and Djibouti. His research was meant to help complete the collections at the Musée de l'Homme, at the time Musée d'Ethnographie, at the Trocadéro.

10. See Bessora's interview in chapter 1.

11. The La Martinière company acquired the Serpent à Plumes publishing house in 2017.

12. "Three legendary players led the team through its best periods: Raymond Kopa, the son of Polish immigrants, in the 1950s; Michel Platini, grandson of an Italian immigrant, in the 1980s; and Zinedine Zidane, the son of Algerian colonial migrants, in the 1990s and in 2006. These three men embody the history of immigration into France, recalling the vast migration of Polish workers to the mines of northern France before World War II, the arrival of Italian workers throughout the twentieth century, and the large-scale migration of North Africans that began with individual male laborers in the 1920s and then accelerated, and increasingly involved entire families, from the 1950s to the 1970s" (Dubois 2010, 8).

Chapter 4

Franco-Vietnamese Literature
The Unspoken Making of Anna Moï and Linda Lê

In the introduction to her 2011 study entitled *Le roman vietnamien francophone: Orientalisme, occidentalisme et hybridité*, Ching Selao explains:

> Au Québec comme en France, les Vietnamiens bénéficient d'un préjugé favorable, celui qui les définit comme une communauté immigrante tranquille et silencieuse, qui ne se plaint pas, ou si peu en comparaison d'autres communautés aux demandes parfois « déraisonnables ». Tout se passe comme si on se serait attendu au même silence en littérature.

> (In Quebec as in France, Vietnamese people benefit from a favorable prejudice, that which defines them as a quiet and silent immigrant community, one that does not complain, or so little when compared to other communities who sometimes have "unreasonable" demands. Everything then happens as if the same silence in literature should be expected.) (Selao 2011, 11)

These stereotypes mentioned here by Selao were certainly a factor in the French metropolitan editors' decision-making process regarding the editing and marketing of authors like Anna Moï and Linda Lê during the "Black-Blanc-Beur" years (1998–2005). In France—and, according to Selao, in Quebec as well—citizens of Asian descent are not often represented in the media. As Selao suggests, they are not considered to be as "demanding" of the State's attention, as are—supposedly and stereotypically—other immigrant populations namely, as we have seen in the case of 1990s metropolitan France, populations emigrating from the African continent. In fact, in reviewing the political context and identitarian rhetoric of the 1990s in France in this book's opening chapter, we were reminded of President Chirac's infamous 1991 interview in which he criticized "le bruit et l'odeur" (the noise and the smell) of immigrants in France, specifically of "[les] musulmans et les Noirs" (Muslims and Blacks). Selao's statement therefore rings true as this book has so far demonstrated the State and the media's near-obsession with portraying idealized versions of "Black" and "Beur" immigrants in late 1990s-early 2000s France, without any mention or regard to immigrants of Southeastern Asian origin, namely from the former Indochina colonies.

In addition, Selao underlines another crucial point regarding populations of Asian descent in France, specifically in relation with their impact on world politics, and in the French and francophone literature realm. Selao writes:

> C'est oublier qu'avant d'être des *boat people* et des exilés « sans voix », les Vietnamiens ont été des colonisés et que ce peuple dit silencieux a, dans les années 1950, représenté le cri de liberté et de libération pour de nombreux auteurs francophones . . . Non seulement la littérature vietnamienne francophone existe et a connu sa période prolifique dans les années 1950, mais les premiers textes ont paru au Vietnam et en France dès le début des années 1910.
>
> (This means forgetting that, before they were *boat people* and a "voiceless" exiled population, the Vietnamese were colonized, and that this supposedly silent people represented in the 1950s the cry of freedom and liberation for numerous francophone authors . . . Not only does francophone Vietnamese literature exist and it was at its height in the 1950s, its first texts were published in Vietnam and in France at the beginning of the 1910s.) (11–12)

In these circumstances, considering that Vietnamese authors in France and their descendants have been part of the literary landscape for nearly a hundred years, how can we explain that their work has been, at best, downplayed to that of a minor presence and influence? Considering the metropolitan publishing market's efforts to create and publicize subjective literary categories that reflected the State's portrayals of immigrants during the "Black-Blanc-Beur" years, can we pinpoint the editing and marketing practices that simultaneously kept authors of Vietnamese origin in the French literary sphere's periphery, all the while quietly installing them as a staple of near-*littérature française* (thus reproducing the stereotypes of "a quiet and silent immigrant community" outlined by Selao)?

In order to answer these questions and before we delve into the specific cases of Anna Moï and Linda Lê's authorial careers in the early 2000s, it is essential to further explore the stereotypes outlined by Selao in her study—stereotypes which are in no way seldom but rather ethnically and coloniallyfounded. In *Le roman vietnamien francophone*, Selao returns to the creation of the notions of Orientalism and Occidentalism as she attempts to debunk their existence and certain authors' reliance on, compliance with, or distance from these concepts that were fabricated during the colonial era. Needless to say, this chapter's goal is not to reproduce Selao's study nor is it to apply her research methods to Anna Moï and Linda Lê's oeuvres and authorial identities. In fact, this chapter rather seeks to pinpoint parallels between what Selao perceives as stereotypically colonial constructions of immigrants of Southeastern Asian descent as "tranquille et silencieux," and the paratextual construction of a "tranquille et silencieuse" *near*-French literary category in the works of Anna Moï and Linda Lê in early 2000s France.

Ultimately, this chapter demonstrates that this silent yet near-French literary presence in "Black-Blanc-Beur" France served to offset the heavily stereotyped "Black" and "Beur" literatures of the time. In so doing, the common efforts of the Gallimard, L'Aube and Christian Bourgois publishing houses succeeded in anchoring Franco-Vietnamese literatures within—and not outside—the French literature landscape, while never quite construing them exactly as *littérature française*. This chapter finally unveils the varying degrees of paratextual manipulations in the case of both Anna Moï and Linda Lê's oeuvres and authorial identities. While Gallimard repeated its othering ethnic and gender branding of Moï's literature (marketing techniques also visible in Moï's publications with l'Aube), Christian Bourgois proved to be the only publisher to attach the most neutral forms of paratext to Linda Lê's oeuvre, in line with the author's utter dislike for literary labels.

FRANCO-VIETNAMESE LITERATURE ON THE METROPOLITAN MARKET

For Edward Saïd, what has been known for centuries in Western sociocultural circles as "the Orient" is a fabricated space filled with stereotypical notions meant to emphasize the grandeur and intellectualism of the West. This construct functions as a theater stage or a spectacle, designed to reassure the West of its own idea of uniqueness and superiority. Saïd writes:

> Our initial description of Orientalism as a learned field now acquires a new concreteness. A field is often an enclosed space. The idea of representation is a theatrical one: the Orient is the stage on which the whole East is confined. On this stage will appear figures whose role it is to represent the larger whole from which they emanate. The Orient then seems to be, not an unlimited extension beyond the familiar European world, but rather a closed field, a theatrical stage affixed to Europe. (Saïd 1994, 63)

What was true at the time of Saïd's study originally published in 1979 remains valid when considering our study of the metropolitan publishing market in the early 2000s. As the "Black-Blanc-Beur" France of the early twenty-first century was redefining itself according to a utopic idea of cohesion that did not account for the existence of Franco-Asian populations in its construction of an ideal society, publishing houses tended to reproduce the construct of a far-off colonial "Orient" in their marketing of texts written in French by Franco-Vietnamese authors. This strategy effectively offset the strong focus on "Black" and "Beur" identities which were portrayed in the paratextual elements of several "non-Blanc" literary productions with the comforting and equally fabricated idea that the "Orient" remained a subdued space, a remnant of the colonized world's allegiance to France.

These stereotypical and colonial concepts are visible in Gallimard's production of *Riz Noir* by Anna Moï in 2004, and in its reproduction as a Folio in 2006. Timing here is key for Gallimard: in 2006, the publishing giant was producing Moï's memoir on writing entitled *Espéranto, Desesperanto: la francophonie sans les Français* (*Espéranto, Desesperanto: Francophonie Without the French*) in their Blanche (French literature) collection. Their reproduction of *Riz Noir*, which is set in postcolonial Vietnam, as a stereotypical Folio that same year, was in fact used to confirm Moï's place in the "field" and "enclosed space"—to use Saïd's words—of Vietnam, a space quite distinct from *littérature française*. These negotiations in the production of Moï's oeuvres reveal the power dynamics at play between the literary production of a major publishing house and the ambient politics and public constructions of Others in France in 2006, a year after the *banlieue* riots and the end of the "Black-Blanc-Beur" utopia. The following sections will analyze Anna Moï's productions with Gallimard and l'Aube (a smaller publishing house based in Provence), before moving onto the case of Linda Lê. Lê's loyalty to Christian Bourgois coupled with her publisher's lack of paratextual markers of ethnic and gender identity seem to have shielded the author from literary and political labels throughout her writing career.

Jack Yeager's foundational work, *The Vietnamese Novel in French: A Literary Response to Colonialism* paved the way for further and more recent studies regarding the works of Vietnamese authors writing in French and publishing in metropolitan France. Selao indicates in her own study that Yeager's work, because of its timing, is incomplete and at times hypothetical on a certain number of points (Selao 2011, 28). In fact, Yaeger recognized in his introduction: "Recently there has been increasing attention paid to other foreign literatures in French. But Vietnamese Francophone literature still remains virtually unknown. . . . Most people are completely unaware that such a literature exists" (Yaeger 1987, 1–2). This impeding factor in Yaeger's study—yet its motivator—was true in 1987 and continued to be true in 1998 and beyond. In the 2000s, few metropolitan French readers were aware of Linda Lê's extensive body of work published with the Éditions Christian Bourgois.

As the present book sets out to examine the role of metropolitan French publishing houses in the distribution of texts written by French-Vietnamese women during a very specific time-period (1998–2005), it is essential to note that Vietnamese literature written in French did not become a popular research field until recently. Two recent works have gained academic attention, mainly among North-American researchers in the field of *francophonie*: Nathalie Nguyen's *Vietnamese Voices: Gender and Cultural Identity in the Vietnamese Francophone Novel* (2003), and Karl Ashoka Britto's *Disorientation: France, Vietnam, and the Ambivalence of Interculturality* (2004). Selao underlines that, in France, studies in Vietnamese literature are so sparse that they remain in the "stade de la présentation du corpus" ("corpus presentation stage") (Selao 2011, 31). More recently, Catherine H. Nguyen established in "Vietnam by Removes: Storytelling and Postmemory in Minh Tran Huy": "Responding to the French colonization of Indochina, Vietnamese literature in French, Vietnamese francophone literature, and Vietnamese French literature participate in and produce a postcolonial literature that interrogates French and American (neo)imperialism in their lingering effects on the Vietnamese diaspora" (Nguyen 2018, 96). Nguyen adds: "The very multiplicity of this literary terminology speaks to the diverse cultural production arising from the displacement of large populations of Vietnamese people to France after the military conflicts of the First Indochina War/ Anti-French Resistance War and the Second Indochina Was/ Vietnam War/ American War" (96).

In turn, Selao points out that the very few French scholarly publications on the topic of Vietnamese literature are inspired by an already-existing interest for colonial Vietnam under French rule, Indochina (Selao 2011, 32). Citing further studies that vaguely and quickly brush onto the topic of Vietnamese literature in French, encapsulating "it" as minor when compared to larger postcolonial literary movements such as the Negritude (35), Selao quite aptly concludes: "Ce genre de généralisations nourrit la perception qu'il n'existe pas de littérature vietnamienne francophone, même si cette production n'est pas négligeable" ("This type of generalizations feeds into the perception that francophone Vietnamese literature does not exist, even though its production is not insignificant") (36). Yaeger in 1987 already noted that francophone Vietnam was often absorbed into a larger sense of *francophonie* which did not exactly relate its specificity, assessing, for example, that "[t]he Francophone literature of Viet Nam thus shares common characteristics with other Francophone literatures. Yet like other such literatures, it is historically and culturally unique within the classification" (Yaeger 1987, 5). In his seminal study, Yaeger examined twenty-five novels written by thirteen authors between 1920 and 1969, the majority of which were published in Paris with the exception of five published in Vietnam (6). Yaeger established that these works had combined the mode of first and third-person narratives found in French eighteenth- and nineteenth-century literature with typical Vietnamese literary constructions such as the "[f]olktales and Vietnamese *truyen* or verse romances" (7). Yager concluded that these literary hybrids were "neither fully Vietnamese nor fully French" (7), before adding: "This is a literature of contradiction and irresolution, one challenging French colonial authority; it is thus implicitly political. At the same time, it questions both Vietnamese and French culture and literature, ultimately denying both. It is therefore an anomaly, a distinctive cultural phenomenon: a literary response to colonialism" (8). These literary "anomalies" preceded the literary hybrids written by Franco-Vietnamese women like Kim Lefèvre, Anna Moï, and Linda Lê: these women's oeuvres, like those of their predecessors, expressed "a literary response to colonialism," as well as identity politics and attitudes toward Otherness in postcolonial France.

How were these "literary hybrids" negotiated by publishing houses with differential marketing practices such as Gallimard and L'Aube at the time of the "Black-Blanc-Beur" utopia? What interests lay in their publishing Franco-Vietnamese literature written by women when the country's attention was focused on the overwhelmingly mediatized influx of fabricated Black and Beur identities? At the turn of the millennium, ten years after Yaeger's study, were these works still "challenging French colonial authority," or were they actually challenging the French national identity politics that excluded their identity, history, and literary voices? The following sections examine the works of Anna Moï and Linda Lê published during the years of the "Black-Blanc-Beur" utopia as literary negotiations of both sociopolitical and literary identities.

CONFRONTING HISTORY: ANNA MOÏ, L'AUBE, AND GALLIMARD

Anna Moï's literary works—her novels and essays—have for the most part been published by Les Éditions de l'Aube and Gallimard (*Violon* was published by Flammarion in 2006, and *L'année du cochon de feu* by the Éditions du Rocher in 2008). The next section contrasts and compares the oeuvres published by l'Aube and Gallimard between 1998 and 2006 in each of the publishers' choice of paratext for Moï herself, and for each of her texts. An examination of both paratextual and narrative elements in *Riz noir* (Gallimard 2004) and *Espéranto, désésperanto: la francophonie sans les Français* (Gallimard 2006), studied in contrast with *L'écho des rizières* and *Parfum de pagode* (originally published by l'Aube in 2001 and 2004) reveals that the texts which Moï published with Gallimard are evidently more political. Through them, the author seeks to inscribe and establish the irremediable link between *Histoire* (history) and her own *histoire* (personal story) in the larger postcolonial context, and in particular in the lives of the postcolonial Vietnamese diaspora. The examination of the paratextual choices for these four texts that were published at the time of the "Black-Blanc-Beur" utopia and its blatant erasure of postcolonial Vietnamese identities exposes exclusionary practices from the *littérature française* corpus by both Gallimard and l'Aube. While l'Aube has reproduced some of the "othering" marketing practices previously exposed in the study of Gallimard's paratextual content, the motives of the smaller publishing house have been justified by their desire to create visibility around a Franco-Vietnamese literary corpus until then disregarded by the metropolitan literary market (Hennebert 2019).

Whatever the motivations of these two publishers may have been at the time of the "Black-Blanc-Beur" utopia—either reinforcing the author's Otherness as opposed to a sacrosanct French white identity in the case of Gallimard, or promoting her Otherness yet similitude with French literature through the promotion of her hybrid Franco-Vietnamese identity at l'Aube—it is safe to say that Moï's career was quietly defined during these key years of the early twenty-first century. Moï is known today to be a discreet yet renowned author whose texts published with l'Aube are integral to a growing corpus of select few publications on the topics of historical memory and reconciliation for the postcolonial Franco-Vietnamese diaspora. On the other hand, her texts published with Gallimard have gained acclaim in larger circles whose participants were most likely eager to define and classify a form of *littérature asiatique en français*, as evidenced in Moï's inclusion in the *littérature-monde* debate of 2007 as the only signatory of Southeastern Asian descent, a strategic inclusion which will be further discussed in this book's conclusion.

Riz noir

Anna Moï's first publication with Gallimard, *Riz noir*, was included in the publisher's Blanche, *littérature française*, collection in 2004, but was not adorned with the habitual Blanche collection cream-colored, plain front cover.[1] Instead, it bore a faded black and white photograph of two young women wearing white dresses and looking directly at the camera. Unlike the visibly and stereotypically fabricated "Black" or "Beur" texts produced by Gallimard in order to "fit"—yet further complicate—the post-1998

"Black-Blanc-Beur" era, this photograph clearly confines *Riz noir* along with its author Anna Moï in an unresolved French colonial past, that of the former Indochina. However, the narrative of *Riz noir* begins long after the Geneva Accords of 1954 and focuses on the internal violence that spread through Vietnam after the colonial era. While *Riz noir* was first published with what one would recognize as a typically marked Asian and female cover, its reedition in 2006 in the Folio collection was marked as what one would recognize as typically Vietnamese, yet this time foregoing an obvious marker of gender. The front cover in the re-edition also does not appear to bear the marks of a familial story (as portrayed by the faded photo of two women who could possibly be related on the first edition's front cover), and instead pictures the backs of two fishermen (or women) who appear to be relaxing on a pontoon—an image that is in stark contrast with *Riz noir*'s narrative of political torture perpetrated on two young sisters in the Poulo Condor prison in 1968.

In the original 2004 edition, the only information about the author is located at the bottom of the back cover, and is very succinct: "Anna Moï est née et reside une partie de l'année au Vietnam. *Riz noir* est son premier roman" (Anna Moï was born and resides for part of the year in Vietnam. *Riz noir* is her first novel) (Gallimard 2004, back cover). In its 2006 Folio version, the novel opens with a longer presentation of the author by Gallimard, which was inserted on a page inside of the book itself, before the beginning of the actual narrative:

> Anna Moï est née au Vietnam et partage sa vie entre Paris et Saigon, sa ville natale. Écrivain, journaliste, mais aussi styliste de mode, elle écrit exclusivement en français des histoires inspirées de son pays natal. *Riz noir* est son premier roman.
>
> (Anna Moï was born in Vietnam and splits her time between Paris and her hometown of Saigon. A writer, journalist, but also a fashion designer, she writes stories inspired by her native country, exclusively in French. *Riz noir* is her first novel.) (Gallimard 2006)

This introduction of Moï to the French metropolitan reader in 2006 seems fairly strategic on the part of Gallimard since it presents and formats the author according to certain standards to which we have become accustomed since our examination of fabricated "Beur" and "Black" literature and authorial identities during the years of the "Black-Blanc-Beur" utopia. With this particular introduction of the author, Gallimard reproduces the pattern of identification of "other yet written in French" literature, akin to the fabricated "évoluée" and "intégrée" subcategories used to market authors for North-African and Sub-Saharan origin after 1998. In this summary of her personal

Figure 4.1 Front Cover of *Riz noir* by Anna Moï, Published by Gallimard (Folio, 2006).

life and professional accomplishments, Anna Moï is first marked as "other" in that her birthplace is the very first information to be given about her identity, "born in Vietnam," a piece of information which is reinforced with the words "her hometown of Saigon." Next, Moï's authority (and authorization) to write and to be published in metropolitan France is authenticated with the words "author" and "journalist," the mention of her third occupation as "fashion designer" appearing to be a marker of gender and originality, all the while notifying the reader that writing may not be her primary interest, passion, or line of work, therefore potentially minimizing the quality and importance of the text to follow. In addition, to mention that "she writes stories inspired by her native country, exclusively in French" is, in a way, to assess and confirm Moï's dedication to the French language and, by extension, to the history of French colonialism in Vietnam, while purporting a certain sense of nostalgia for colonial Vietnam that the author may seek to impress upon her writing.

Finally, to assess that Moï writes "stories" ("histoires") is to lessen the importance of her entire body of work in general, and of *Riz noir* in particular. The narrative of *Riz noir* is truly a work of History (*Histoire*) and of historical research regarding the aftermath of colonialism in Vietnam following the signing of the Geneva Accords in 1954. The connotation of the word "stories"/"histoires" (personal stories versus History in French) is one of imagination and fiction as opposed to one anchored in reality and historical facts; as such, the term "histoires" positions Moï's work in a repetitive realm of nostalgic colonial Orientalism, outside of the West's consideration for chronological time and reality—in a word, outside of History. Yet, in its narrative, *Riz Noir* reveals itself to be a site of resistance where History, racial and gender constructs, as well as identity and language, are deconstructed and rebuilt in order to counter the Western narrative of uniqueness that is embodied—in a sense—in Gallimard's marketing decisions for such an oeuvre. As *Riz noir*'s narrative takes place in the 1960s and 1970s, it is not a reflection by the author on the "Black-Blanc-Beur" era like the other works studied in this book. In addition, because it is neither autobiographical nor autofictional, its analysis for the purpose of this chapter will remain paratextual. As a matter of fact, *Riz Noir*'s paratext demonstrates some of Gallimard's strongest authorial identity markers in the case of Franco-Vietnamese women's literature.

Gallimard's final note that "*Riz noir* is [Moï]'s first novel" is slightly incorrect and quite revealing of the publishing house's self-assigned role as a guardian of *littérature française*, one that publicly decides and publicizes who can and cannot enter the sacrosanct realm of French literature. *Riz noir* is not Moï's first published work by any means, as she had already published *L'écho des rizières* in 2001 with the Éditions de l'Aube—even though there is no mention of this work in Gallimard's publication of *Riz noir*. She had also published *Parfum de pagode* in 2003, although that work would not be classified as a novel, but rather as a collection of short stories. Nevertheless, in assessing that "*Riz noir* is her first novel" while discarding her previous published works with l'Aube, Gallimard presents itself as Moï's first publisher and simultaneously connotes for the reader a sense of guardianship and literary patronage over the author and her work (and, eventually, any of her future works).

There are notable differences between the back covers of the original 2004 edition by Gallimard and its 2006 Folio reproduction. In the 2004 edition, the writing of the back cover summary is clearly attributed to the author herself, Anna Moï, who signed "A.M." at the end of the short text. The beginning of the text itself frames the novel chronologically, and is similar in both editions: "En 1968, la guerre du Vietnam bascule. La violence parvient à son paroxysme lors de l'offensive du Têt: Saigon est à feu et à sang" (In 1968, the Vietnam War takes a turn. Violence reaches its peak during the Tet Offensive: Saigon is set ablaze) (Gallimard 2004, back cover). Reading these first few lines, a potential reader who is used to Gallimard's publishing practices and aware of the publisher's authority in the field might be comforted that Moï's novel is indeed being published by Gallimard, France's publishing giant, this fact alone giving it a seal of approval in terms of historical and factual authenticity.

This sentiment is further conveyed by the author herself as she establishes the partial veracity of the narrative, noting: "Ce roman m'a été en partie inspiré par l'histoire authentique de Tan, que j'ai connue au lycée, et de Tao, deux soeurs de quinze et seize ans arrêtées, torturées puis internées dans le bagne de Poulo Condor, au large de Saigon, à la fin des années 1960" (I was partly inspired to write this novel because of the authentic story of Tan, whom I met in high school, and of Tao: two sisters, fifteen- and sixteen years old, who were arrested, tortured, and imprisoned in the labor camp of Poulo Condor, off the coast of Saigon, in the late 1960s) (Gallimard 2004, back cover). This section is reproduced in the Folio but is written in the third person, as there is no mention of Moï having authored this back cover summary (emphasis on changes are mine): "Ce roman a été en partie inspiré par l'histoire authentique de *deux soeurs adolescentes* internées dans le bagne de Poulo Condor, au large de Saigon" (This novel was partially inspired by the authentic story of *two teenage sisters* imprisoned in the penal colony of Poulo Condor, off the coast of Saigon) (Gallimard 2006, back cover).

In 2006, the author's involvement in the narrative, from her writing of the back cover summary to her actual familiarity with some of the characters in the novel, has all but vanished. We need to remember other Folio editions which were studied in the previous chapters of this book: in all the cases examined, the publishing of Folio editions by Gallimard has followed a pattern of simplifying, de-authorizing, and marketing the text to the largest audience possible while comforting them in neocolonial stereotypes that may or may not have already been ingrained in their minds as a result of media-enforced nationalist discourses. In removing Moï's authorship and authority over the narrative—one that is not usually present in a back cover summary, but which was clearly inscribed in the 2004 edition—Gallimard sought to market *Riz noir* to a much larger audience than its first 2004 hardcover edition.

This publishing strategy was evidently confirmed in the production of a stereotypically Vietnamese front cover (traditionally dressed men who appear to be fishermen), which was in addition void of authenticating identity traits as it did not show the faces of the people pictured in the photograph, as opposed to the original 2004 edition which bore the photo of the two women. Although there is no mention in the 2004 edition of the origin of the front cover photograph or of the identity of the two young women pictured, it would be rather safe to assume, having read the back cover summary written by Anna Moï, that the two women would have been sisters, or perhaps students at a high school in Saigon in the 1960s. They could even have been Tan and Tao, the two sisters who were kidnapped, tortured, and imprisoned in Poulo Condor. But we must tread lightly in analyzing the oeuvre's visual paratext according to its written paratextual elements, as we could be falling into all too common essentialist conclusions drawn directly from the publisher's strategic marketing practices. At least, the composition of the original 2004 front cover offers some similitudes with the back cover summary written by the author and what we as readers know to be the essence of the narrative of *Riz noir*. The 2006 Folio cover, in contrast, seems to have been composed to attract a larger reading public into a generally accessible narrative about Vietnam.

Other elements of the 2006 back cover summary were altered in order to remove the female gender marker from the paratext of *Riz noir*. Where Anna Moï in the 2004 edition summary wrote "À travers la mémoire des jeunes prisonnières" (Through the memory of the young female prisoners), Gallimard in 2006 transformed her words into "À travers la mémoire des *personnages*" (Through the memory of the characters), effectively removing markers of gender ("prisonni*ères*" being the female form of "prisonniers"—"prisoners"—as opposed to "personnages," a gender-neutral noun in French). Possibly the most notable change between the 2004 and the 2006 versions are located at the end of the summary. In 2004, Moï wrote: "Le livre est dédié *à Tan et Tao*, ainsi qu'à *toutes les femmes vietnamiennes*, filles de dragon selon la tradition, filles d'eau et de feu, fragiles et invincibles" (The book is dedicated *to Tan and Tao*, as well as to *all Vietnamese women,* daughters of the dragon according to tradition, daughters of water and fire, fragile and invincible). In 2006, this portion of the back cover summary reads: "*Riz noir* est aussi *un livre sur la perte de l'innocence*, et *un hymne aux femmes vietnamiennes*, filles de dragon selon la tradition, filles d'eau et de feu, fragiles et invincibles" (my emphases) (*Riz noir* is also *a book on the loss of innocence,* and *a hymn to Vietnamese women*, daughters of the dragon according to tradition, daughters of water and fire, fragile and invincible).

Evidently, the possible identity of the sisters Tan and Tao, which had already been removed from the front cover photograph in 2006 and from the back cover summary is once again removed in favor of a blanket statement regarding the characters' "loss of innocence" (an understatement considering the violent acts of torture the two sisters endured in Poulo Condor). In addition, the novel is no longer "dedicated" to Tan and Tao and to Vietnamese women, but it has instead become "a hymn to Vietnamese women": what would first appear as a simple semantic change actually reflects yet another dispossession of authority from the author, who it seems has no longer worked to "dedicate" her novel to Vietnamese women, but whose text now exists outside of her control in having become "a hymn," a different literary object in and of itself dispossessed of authorial intention.

On its website, Gallimard classifies *Riz noir* as both "*littérature française*" (French literature) and "*littérature étrangère*" (foreign literature), finishing its description with "*pays: Vietnam*" (Country: Vietnam) (Gallimard, "Riz noir" 2018). In contrast, Moï's essay *Espéranto, désespéranto: la francophonie sans les Français*, published only two years after *Riz noir*, is classified as "*philologie, linguistique*" (philology, linguistics), and "*XXIe siècle*" (twenty-first century); yet, *Espéranto, désespéranto*'s description once again ends with "Country: Vietnam" (Gallimard, "Espéranto" 2018). These various labels and descriptions leave Anna Moï and her texts in an undefined space between France ("*littérature française*") and Vietnam, between the present and the past, at a time when visible efforts were being made by major publishing houses such as Gallimard to define the Other in France as an "evolved Black" or "integrated Beur"—in essence leaving no discursive space to define Franco-Vietnamese people in France. In keeping Moï and her oeuvre partially in "Vietnam," Gallimard participated in the "Black-Blanc-Beur" utopia, one in which there was no room for authors of Southeastern Asian descent to be identified. Yet, as previously mentioned, Moï's narratives reveal themselves as sites of resistance to this very practice led by institutions in France that define Others according to colonial and neocolonial criteria.

L'écho des rizières, Parfum de pagode

In contrast with Gallimard's secluding publishing practices (keeping the author and her text in literary "Vietnam" while conceding them a share of "*littérature française*" by default, seemingly because the text is written in French and published in metropolitan France), the Éditions de l'Aube during the "Black-Blanc-Beur" years built Anna Moï and her oeuvre in the contemporary and realistic cultural hybridity of the Vietnamese expatriates in France. These works published with l'Aube at the turn of the millennium, *L'écho des rizières* and *Parfum de pagode*, carry just as much historical weight and controversy as *Riz noir* but have been defined according to criteria which contain Moï and her oeuvre in a different space than that of a nostalgic colonial era like Gallimard's publication of *Riz noir*.

On its website, l'Aube describes Moï in the following terms: "Écrivain et styliste, Anna Moï est née à Saïgon et partage sa vie entre France et Vietnam" (Author and stylist, Anna Moï was born in Saigon, and shares her life between France and Vietnam) (l'Aube 2018). This lifestyle choice—also emphasized by Gallimard—is reflected in *L'écho des rizières*, her first novel published in 2001 with l'Aube. In it, Moï describes a life split between a 1990s postcolonial Vietnam which continues to lack Western luxuries, and France, which she barely describes.[2] The book, in and of itself, is very marked in terms of gender and ethnicity. The front cover bears a photograph of Moï herself, taken by her husband Léon-Paul Schwab, as indicated in the inside cover (and confirmed by Marion Hennebert in her 2019 interview). This inside cover also indicates that *L'écho des rizières* is simultaneously classified in the "collection *Regard croisés*" directed by Marion Hennebert (a collection which currently comprises the works of Maïssa Bey, and several other authors who would be classified as "francophone" by other publishing houses), and in the "Le Viêt-nam" section of l'Aube's catalog (alongside Kim Lefèvre's *Métisse blanche*, among others). This "Le Viêt-nam" collection is no longer accessible from l'Aube's online catalog—in fact, both Jean Viard and Marion Hennebert have confirmed that this collection no longer exists (2019). How can we understand this classification by l'Aube in 2001 when we have already established that the exclusion of Vietnamese writers from the *littérature française* realm—as exemplified by Gallimard's two editions of *Riz noir*—was an ideologically segregating practice? Does the first signifier of "Regards croisés" (which remains today) supersede what perhaps l'Aube considered a "necessary" or "positive" segregation of these authors in order to give them a voice in an exclusive "Black-Blanc-Beur" France, which did not recognize the history or the descendants of the French colonization of Vietnam?

Ching Selao in *Le roman vietnamien francophone* effectively criticizes l'Aube's marketing practices for both Anna Moï and Kim Lefèvre. She writes: "En littérature, on remarque que les Éditions de l'Aube, qui publient les récits de Kim Lefèvre, les recueils de nouvelles d'Anna Moï . . . utilisent très souvent des images de femmes asiatiques sensuelles ou de paysages exotiques pour la couverture de leur livre" (In the literature realm, it is noticeable that the Éditions de l'Aube, which publish Kim Lefèvre's works, Anna Moï's collections of short stories . . . very often use images of sensual Asian women or exotic landscapes on their books' front covers) (Selao 2011, 54). She concludes: "Ces exemples montrent néanmoins à quel point l'exotisme et l'évocation de l'érotisme favorisent la vente des livres—même critiques et sérieux—et que l'Orient demeure somme toute féminin" (These examples demonstrate, nevertheless, the extent to which exoticism and the evocation of eroticism favor the sale of books —even critical and serious works—and that the Orient overall remains feminine) (54). In fact, Jean Viard, co-founder of the Éditions de l'Aube, confessed, as previously noted in chapter 1 that "il faut reconnaître que la ligne vietnamienne a toujours été surchargée en photos féminines" (it is important to acknowledge that the Vietnamese field has always been overloaded with feminine photographs) (Viard 2019).

Evidently, l'Aube applied the same neocolonial marketing practices as their colleagues at Gallimard, one of the largest publishing houses in the francophone world (including metropolitan France) which, as we have established in this book, has profited from marketing non-Blanc authors as "Other" since the late twentieth century. However, while these essentialist marketing practices clearly followed a pattern which was quite widespread during the "Black-Blanc-Beur" years, l'Aube also attempted to garner visibility for its Asian literature catalog: this goal was achieved when Chinese novelist Gao Xingjian received the Nobel Prize in 2000 after translations of his works were first published by l'Aube in 1995 (*La montagne de l'âme*), 1997 (*Une canne-à-pêche pour mon grand-père*) and 2000 (*Le livre d'un homme seul*). In fact, Viard explains that "il y avait une vraie curiosité pour la littérature asiatique, chinoise et vietnamienne" (there was a true interest for Asian literature, Chinese and Vietnamese) during the "Black-Blanc-Beur" years, and that l'Aube's differential cataloging practices were partially responsible for this success as they reflected and eventually met the late 1990s–early 2000s reading audience's desire for the Orient (Viard 2019).

When asked why l'Aube's geographicallymarked collections such as "Le Viêt-nam" had been discontinued, Viard explained that it all comes down to strategy and to meeting the literary market's demands: "Aujourd'hui, honnêtement, les Français lisent surtout des Français, voire des Américains, beaucoup moins les auteurs asiatiques. Et du coup, nous, on a un peu diminué notre production littéraire . . . c'est une stratégie commerciale" (Today, honestly, French people mostly read French authors, even American authors, much less Asian authors. As a result, we've diminished our literary production a little . . . it's a commercial strategy) (Viard 2019). According to Viard, the French reading audience's interests have shifted to the point that geographical and identitarian markers now matter less than the book's general appeal. However, to this day, the strategic sexualization of Asian female authors continues, as recently seen in the publication of French-Laotian author Loo Hui Phang's *L'imprudence* by Actes Sud: its front cover bears the black and white photograph of a young Asian woman lying in bed under a sheet which she is holding over her chest, while the back cover's summary describes a "premier roman sensuel et audacieux" (first novel, sensual and audacious) in which the main character "sent, elle saisit, elle invite, elle donne, elle jouit" (feels, she takes hold, she invites, she gives, she orgasms) (Actes Sud 2019, back cover).

Reeditions of both *L'écho des rizières* and *Parfum de pagode* appear in the "L'Aube poche" collection, also directed by Marion Hennebert. Both novels in their original and "pocket" formats reveal a specific pattern in marketing Moï's work to the early twenty-first century metropolitan French reader. Unlike *L'écho des rizières*, *Parfum de pagode* does not overtly address the colonial or postcolonial relationship between France and Vietnam. It is a collection of semi-autobiographical short stories written by Moï while she lived in Vietnam where she returned as an adult with her family. Because *Parfum de pagode* does not speak directly to the "Black-Blanc-Beur" utopia in terms of addressing multiculturalism in the Metropole, we will not dwell on its narrative impact but rather on its paratextual elements.

In its first re-edition in the Poche collection in 2004, *Parfum de pagode* was given the same front cover as the original hardback. However, in its 2007 reedition—still in the Poche collection—a new design was added to the front cover: that of a lone fisherman at sunset, in what appears to be a more current or modern photograph. When asked about the front cover illustrations chosen for *Parfum de pagode* and *L'écho des rizières* during a 2019 phone interview with the author, Marion Hennebert explained that these photos were chosen in agreement with Anna Moï, that they were free of copyrights, and that they pictured Ha Long Bay in Vietnam (Hennebert 2019). The first re-edition of *Parfum de pagode* includes on its back cover short excerpts of reviews from the newspaper *La Voix du Nord* ("Un recueil de nouvelles très humaines écrites avec poésie, humour, spiritualité, et tendresse," "A collection of very human short stories, written with poetry, humor, spirituality and tenderness"), the *Bulletin de l'association franco-vietnamienne* ("*Parfum de pagode* nous fait respirer toutes les fragrances du Viêt-nam d'aujourd'hui," "*Parfum de pagode* allows us to smell all of contemporary Vietnam's fragrances"), and French journalist Danièle Mazingarbe from the magazine *Le Figaro Madame* ("Une écriture d'une simplicité totale avec un air de ne pas y toucher enchanteur. . .," "Her writing style is fraught with total simplicity and her apparent detachment [from the subject matter] is enchanting . . .") (l'Aube 2004, back cover). These chosen reviews seem to frame Moï's text within rather gendered (feminine) qualities such as "spirituality and tenderness" while highlighting its "simplicity" and "enchanting" qualities. One could wonder if the goal of these paratextual choices (particularly the remarks on the text's simplicity by minor reviewers) was to "simplify" the text for the readers in order to reassure them in their choice of a work that is part of the "Le Viêt-Nam" catalog: where

Franco-Vietnamese Literature

Figure 4.2 Front Cover of *Parfum de pagode* by Anna Moï, Published by Éditions de l'Aube (2004).

potential contemporary metropolitan French readers might find themselves at a loss in terms of historical, geographical, or sociocultural markers, the back cover paratext of *Parfum de pagode*'s 2004 Poche edition certainly put their minds at ease all the while gendering (feminizing) Moï's work.

Espéranto, désespéranto: La francophonie sans les Français

Although Moï's treaty on the status of *francophonie* was adorned with a cream-colored cover reminiscent of Gallimard's "Blanche" collection, *Espéranto, désespéranto* was included in the publisher's *Connaissance*

Figure 4.3 Front Cover of *Parfum de pagode* by Anna Moï, Published by Éditions de l'Aube (L'Aube Poche, 2007).

(knowledge) series. The front cover does not bear any photograph or information other than the title, the author's name, and the publisher's name: Gallimard. This text, because of its publication date, falls outside of the time period considered for this book, 1998–2005. However, we should consider Moï's *Espéranto, désespéranto* as a self-reflective work which also signals the transition from the "Black-Blanc-Beur" era and its restrictive literary labels to the 2007 "littérature-monde" era (and its debate on "world literature" in French). *Espéranto, désespéranto* was published a year after Linda Lê's autobiographical memoir and self-reflection on her writing practice and literary labels, *Le complexe de Caliban*: both texts were thus written at a time when the ideal of a multicultural France was about to end or had just ended, which implies that there were ramifications from the *banlieue* riots, and that these ramifications reflected onto the literary realm of *littérature française* or *littérature "presque" française* ("almost" French).

When *Espéranto, désespéranto* was published in 2006, the utopia of an integrated and cohesive multicultural France was no longer discussed or present in the public's mind. In fact, the preoccupation of numerous authors, academics, and politicians at that point was then-President Chirac's "law on colonialism," which was enacted in 2005 as one of four "lois mémorielles" (memory laws). The law titled "Loi portant reconnaissance de la Nation et contribution nationale en faveur des Français rapatriés" (Law regarding the recognition of the Nation and national contribution in favor of the repatriated French) aimed at financially compensating and publicly recognizing the Harki families who had fought alongside the French army during the Algerian War of Independence. Article 4 of this law in particular stated: "Les programmes scolaires reconnaissent en particulier le rôle positif de la présence française outre-mer, notamment en Afrique du Nord, et accordent à l'histoire et aux sacrifices des combattants de l'armée française issus de ces territoires la place éminente à laquelle ils ont droit" (School programs recognize in particular the positive role of the French presence overseas, notably in North Africa, and afford history and the sacrifices of the French army's soldiers from these territories their rightfully eminent place) (2005, par. 3). As this specific article mandated history teachers in French public schools to emphasize the positive outcomes of colonization in the French colonies, several history teachers and professors, authors and philosophers (among others, Patrick Chamoiseau and Edouard Glissant) and historians (with Benjamin Stora at the helm of the movement) expressed their discontent and their desire to see the law abrogated (Van Eeckhout 2005).

In the midst of this debate, Glissant and Chamoiseau (who would later write against Nicolas Sarkozy's opening of a Ministry of Immigration, Integration, National Identity and Co-Development in 2007) wrote a letter to then-Minister of the Interior Sarkozy before a scheduled state visit to Martinique: in it, the two authors reminded Sarkozy that postcolonial France was indeed multiethnic, and that France's rich patrimony was built on the horrors of colonialism and slavery. Glissant and Chamoiseau thus started their letter to Sarkozy in such terms:

> Martinique is an old ground of slavery, of colonization, and of neo-colonialism. But this interminable sorrow is a treasured master: it has instructed us in exchange and sharing. Dehumanizing situations have such worth that they preserve, in the heart of the dominated, palpitations where a demand for dignity always grows. Our land is one of the most eager. (Glissant 2005, par. 1)

Later, Aimé Césaire declared that he would not meet with Sarkozy in the midst of the debate on the 2005 law, stating: "Parce que, auteur du discours sur le colonialisme, je reste fidèle à ma doctrine et anticolonialiste résolu. Et ne saurais paraître me rallier à l'esprit et à la lettre de la loi du 23 février 2005 . . . [et du] rôle positif de la présence française en outre-mer" (Because, as the author of the Discourse on Colonialism, I remain true to my doctrine and a determined anticolonialist. And I would not like to appear as if I was supporting the spirit or wording of the law of February 23rd 2005 . . . and of the positive role of the French presence overseas) ("Aimé Césaire refuse" 2005, par. 2). Sarkozy eventually cancelled his state visit to Martinique. In 2006, under pressure from the public opinion and accusations of historical revisionism, Chirac repealed article 4 of the law.

As the law in particular spoke to the recognition of the role of the Harkis in the Algerian War, and as article 4 underlined the positive effects of French colonization "notably in North Africa," it appeared that the divisive and restrictive discourse of the "Black-Blanc-Beur" utopia continued to differentiate between the various French-speaking postcolonial identities, highlighting one group of the formerly colonized of North Africa *above* other formerly colonized countries, such as Vietnam. While this was clearly not the type of governmental or public recognition that Algeria and even Martinique (in the words of Glissant, Chamoiseau, and Césaire) desired or expected, it appeared that, once more, Vietnam was not considered as part of the equation that constituted postcolonial France in the eyes of the government, nor was there room for a voice to officially speak in the name of the descendants of the formerly colonized Indochina. The absence of a voice which, like Glissant's or Césaire's, would have had such a powerful impact as to effectively shake the confidence of the French government and even the French president's proved significant of the latent disregard emanating from the French metropolitan discourse regarding the Franco-Vietnamese postcolonial population and their aspirations.

Although Anna Moï seemingly constrains her discourse on postcolonial multiculturalism within the realm of Gallimard's restrictive publishing practices in 2006, she effectively articulates in *Espéranto, désespéranto*, through her analysis of language and writing (*l'écriture*), the position of the Franco-Vietnamese within this crucial time of redefinition of the French postcolonial identity. *Espéranto, désespéranto* evidently is, through its reflections and conclusions on language, literature, and identity, an opportunity for the author to reflect on the space she occupies as a female author who writes in the French language and publishes in metropolitan France about her bicultural life. Before further slogans and definitions were to appear on the public stage (notably, the evanescent and idealized *"littérature-monde"* label as advocated by Glissant, Chamoiseau, and others in 2007), Moï's *Espéranto, désespéranto* is an attempt at delineating her own authorial identity within the metropolitan French publishing realm. Throughout this rather short essay (66 pages), Moï recognizes her multilingual upbringing and desire for a universal language, as well as her own redefinition as *moï* (the "sauvage," now "minorité ethnique," "ethnic minority" in Vietnamese) as she expresses her hope for an unrestricted, unlabeled vision of literature and language (Moï 2006, 21–22, 43).

In *Espéranto, désespéranto*, Anna Moï argues that she does not seek to reproduce the languages which she already knows (Vietnamese, French, English, and German) in her writing, but that she would rather create a language that can express everything she experiences in all these languages. Thus, she states in the first section of *Espéranto, désespéranto* entitled "Manifeste" (Manifesto): "les langues ne sont qu'un instrument de traduction d'une langue indicible concoctée par l'auteur, page après page" (languages are nothing but tools to translate an unspeakable language concocted by the author, page after page) and "[j]e ne me suis pas demandé un jour: 'De quelle nationalité sera mon époux?' ni 'Dans quelle langue vais-je écrire?' mais: 'comment enregistrer tous ces échos qui résonnent—rires, pleurs, balbutiements, rugissements?'" (I did not ask myself one day: 'What nationality will my spouse be?' or 'In which language will I write?' but: 'how can I record all these echoes that resonate—laughs, cries, babblings, roars?') (15–16). Moï then debates the use of a universal language, first discussing English and then Espéranto, a language invented by Ludwig Zamenhof in 1887 which inspired the title of her memoir (21-22). However, for Moï, neither of these languages is universal nor is any other widelyspoken language such as Russian or Chinese. According to her, "[c]ette langue universelle existe" ([t]his universal language exists) (22) as she addresses the emotions that are transmitted in any language through singing—a reflection which ties into her own experience of learning how to sing in Vietnam as outlined in her first novel *L'écho des rizières*. In disavowing the traditional construct of language (Vietnamese or French) and moving toward the *sound* of a universal language, Moï effectively deconstructs the very strict definitions of identity put in place during the "Black-Blanc-Beur" years, and especially around the time of the 2005 "lois mémorielles."

Espéranto, désespéranto constitutes one of the most public statements made by Moï at that time regarding racial and political labeling in France itself, and in metropolitan literature in particular—notions that she would address again in 2007 as the only signatory of Southeastern Asian descent of the "Pour une 'littérature-monde' en français" manifesto, and in 2017 as the winner of the Prix Littérature-Monde for her novel published in

Gallimard's Blanche collection, *Le venin du papillon* (see this book's conclusion). Indeed, as Moï muses in *Espéranto, désespéranto* about her identity as an author *d'expression française*, she asks a question that has appeared in this study to be quintessential of the selected women's autobiographical quests for their public and authorial identity: "Écrire dans sa langue maternelle, mais laquelle?" (To write in one's native tongue, but which one?) (29). As a native of Vietnam, Moï could have chosen to write in Chinese, Sino-Vietnamese or *quôc gnu* (32). However, she does not believe that her creative productions should be constrained by a single language or by the geographical and historical notions that such a language would simply represent. Rather, she argues:

> Je considère que dans l'exercice d'un art, le choix du matériau, quel qu'il soit—mots, instruments de musique, pigments, marbre—, est toujours légitime: il s'agit, *in fine*, de générer un langage original indifférent aux frontières; de délivrer l'artiste d'un corps physique hérité et de le laisser, en toute liberté, forger d'autres créatures, anges et démons.
>
> (I think that, in the exercise of an art, the choice of the material, whatever it may be—words, musical instruments, pigments, marble— is always legitimate: it is, *in fine*, about generating an original language that does not take borders into account; about liberating the artist from a physical body which he inherited, and to allow him to forge other creatures, angels and demons, in total freedom.) (32)

As the creative force of the artist surpasses its medium, Moï concludes, at a time of self-(re)definition on the metropolitan French literary scene in 2006:

> On écrit toujours dans une langue étrangère, fût-elle sa langue maternelle. Aucun pays n'offre un territoire idéal où l'écrivain tracerait sa géographie et il n'est pas étonnant que celui-ci éprouve le besoin, de temps à autre, d'aller s'enfermer dans les murs neutres d'une residence solitaire extraterritoriale.
>
> (We always write in a foreign language, even if that is our native language. No country provides an ideal territory where authors can trace their own geography and it is not surprising that they feel the need, from time to time, to go isolate themselves within the neutral walls of an extraterritorial solitary residence.) (33)

This deterritorialization of language and of identity that Moï has had to perform as a Vietnamese author who writes in French was completed when she reterritorialized her own identity in choosing her own name, in a sense *labeling* herself before she even began to write. She explains that:

En adoptant le pseudonyme d'Anna Moï, j'usurpai une nouvelle identité qui me rendit doublement libre, presque hérétique: *moï* signifie sauvage—bon sauvage ou mauvais sauvage selon les cas. Aujourd'hui, le mot est politiquement incorrect et il est remplacé par la locution "minorité ethnique" . . . Je revendique, de *moï*, la qualité ou la tare, les défauts de couleur de peau et d'appartenance. Je suis consanguine des sauvages et des étrangers sur tous les sols piétinés et n'échangerai ma condition contre aucune autre.

(In adopting the pseudonym Anna Moï, I appropriated a new identity that made me free in two ways, almost heretic: *moï* means savage—good savage or bad savage depending on the case. Today, this word is politically incorrect and it has been replaced with the phrase "ethnic minority" (. . .) I claim, in the name *moï*, the attribute or the flaw, the faults of one's skin color and belonging. I am related to the savages and foreigners on all trampled grounds, and I would never trade my condition for another.) (43)

Here Moï's assessment of her active and voluntary "consanguinage" with "savages and foreigners" serves to affirm her voice and identity as a postcolonial Franco-Vietnamese author within the confines of Gallimard's "Connaissance" series, itself packaged in similar paratextual elements to the unique and homogenous "Blanche," *littérature française* collection.

In 2006, Moï represented francophone Vietnam as part of the "Francofffonies!" Festival. According to Selao in *Le roman vietnamien francophone*, Moï's presence in the line-up of authors writing in the French language had the effect of essentializing francophone Vietnamese literature, fixing it in terms of gender and time for a metropolitan audience that was at that time unaccustomed to the very concept of francophone Vietnamese literature. Selao explains:

Auteure de deux recueils de nouvelles et de trois romans, Anna Moï a littéralement été le visage vietnamien de ce festival, puisque, parmi les photos de quelques artistes qui défilaient sur la page d'accueil de son site officiel, se trouvait la sienne. Mais le visage de cette écrivaine, qui n'a commencé à publier en France qu'au début des années 2000, a peut-être fait oublier que la littérature vietnamienne de langue française ne date pas d'hier, loin de là.

(As the author of two collections of short stories and three novels, Anna Moï literally was the Vietnamese face of this festival since her photo was among those of the few artists that would cycle through the official site's home page. However, the face of this author who only began to publish in France in the early 2000s may have eclipsed the fact that Vietnamese literature written in French is not at all that new.) (Selao 2011, 22)

The focus on Moï in 2006 was also problematic in that she is, according to Selao, a contradictory author who claims that she does not want to be labeled, yet often labels herself as "littérature francophone" (38).³ Selao then expands on Moï's disregard for literary labels (akin to Linda Lê's) and argues that it appears to be manufactured in that, contrary to Lê, Moï still resides partially in Vietnam, and in addition, writes narratives that are set in Vietnam (38).

I would respectfully disagree with Selao here since, as we have attempted to demonstrate in this book, the location of the narrative and the private life of the author should not be given any importance in classifying their work. These factors have only come into account when they have been used by the publishing industry in order to market the text and its author in a way that corresponds to sociocultural trends, which are themselves most often linked to governmental and media-driven identity politics. Therefore, Moï's desire to *not* be labeled as Vietnamese or francophone despite—per Selao—her visibly "Vietnamese" corpus should not be seen as disingenuous but rather as a way to distance herself from the colonial labels which have resurfaced in the past twenty years. However, I would agree with Selao in admitting that Moï's self-labeling, or lack thereof, has often coincided with discourses (literary, political, and academic) denouncing the resurgence of colonial labels in the realm of literature written in French. These identity politics which bled into the metropolitan literature realm developed further after 2006, when Nicolas Sarkozy was elected president, in a way forcing the literary realm and its agents (authors and publishers) to enter a discourse that would result in new forms of labeling, albeit aligned with postcolonial aspirations.

CHRISTIAN BOURGOIS AND LINDA LÊ: FORMATTING IN-DIFFERENCE

Far from Anna Moï's discourse on classification and from the various labels attached to her work and her persona by l'Aube and Gallimard, Linda Lê appears as radically opposed to any sort of essentialist—or nonessentialist for the matter—labeling of her works. Her autobiographical memoir *Le complexe de Caliban* pointedly enumerates all the authors, canonical and noncanonical, French and non-French, who have inspired her to write and helped her find her voice, define her style: that of an *écrivaine* who refuses any form of labeling. Ching Selao in *Le roman vietnamien francophone: orientalisme, occidentalisme et hybridité* points out that Lê has long refused the label of "écrivaine vietnamienne francophone" and that renowned authors such as Nancy Huston in *Professeurs de désespoir* have considered her as an equal alongside awarded European French-speaking authors (Selao 2011, 18). Lê is not an author who has worked in the styles of Orientalism or Occidentalism as she has herself admitted that she does not know Vietnam very well. Rather, her style is one that exists in a morbid space of fantasy, as Selao puts it: "Son oeuvre n'est pas tant enracinée dans la tradition littéraire vietnamienne que dans l'obsession d'un pays, d'un père, tous deux devenus, par la distance géographique et temporelle, des fantasmes, des fantômes qui hantent son écriture" (Her oeuvre is not as rooted in the Vietnamese literary tradition as it is in the obsession of a country and a father who have both become, through geographic and chronological distance, fantasies and phantoms that haunt her writing) (18–19).

In *Professeurs de désespoir*, Nancy Huston outlines two periods in Lê's writing career, marked by her return to Vietnam in 1996. Before, Lê (who has lived in France since her mother moved her away from Vietnam in 1979 at age sixteen along with her two sisters) would only use male narrative voices in her novels and short stories. Huston establishes: "Dans les premiers récits, l'action est presque toujours décrite du point de vue d'un protagoniste masculin, soit à la première, soit à la troisième personne: c'est qu'il est plus facile pour un homme que pour une femme d'assumer la haine de la chair mère" (In her first narratives, the action is almost always described from the point of a view of a male protagonist, either in the first or the third person: it is actually much easier for a man than it is for a woman to accept the hatred of the mother's flesh) (Huston 2004, 326). Huston describes Lê's early texts (and Lê herself) as "néantistes" (annihilators) (324). In particular, she comments:

L'univers de ses livres est celui du déracinement, de l'errance, de la déchéance, de la laideur, de la mendicité, des mauvaises odeurs, des non-rencontres, des meurtres et des suicides. Son style, en revanche (surtout si on le compare à celui de Houellebecq, dont les thèmes sont proches), est élevé, ciselé, presque cioranien dans sa concision (du reste, elle fait souvent allusion à Cioran sans le nommer).

(The universe of her books is that of uprooting, wandering, decline, ugliness, begging, foul smells, missed connections, murders and suicides. Her style however [and especially if we compare it to Houellebecq's, whose themes are similar] is grand, chiseled, almost Cioran-like in its concision [besides, she often alludes to Cioran without naming him].) (325)

In Huston's words, Lê is an enigma, an anomaly on the French literary market, as she notes "elle [Lê] fuit la publicité" (she [Lê] avoids publicity) (325). Yet, her undeniable talent as underlined above by Huston has placed Lê in a revered position in the French literature realm, as she openly draws from a variety of literary traditions in order to express her malaise as an uprooted young Vietnamese woman who is writing in French in metropolitan France.

After her return to Vietnam in 1996, Huston notes a break in Lê's "néantisme" characterized by the production of a trilogy (the beginning of her professional alliance with Christian Bourgois) and by the chosen gender of Lê's narrators, "à chaque fois une femme, maintenant" (every time a woman, now) (329): "En 1996, après dix-sept ans d'exil, après la mort de son père à elle, Lê retourne au Viêtnam. Cet événement donnera lieu à une trilogie romanesque (*Les trois parques*, *Voix* et *Lettre morte*) où on la voit en train de lutter pour se dégager de la position nihiliste/masochiste" (In 1996, after seventeen years in exile, after her own father's death, Lê goes back to Vietnam. This event will lead to a fictional trilogy [*Les trois parques*, *Voix* and *Lettre morte*] in which we can see her fighting to escape the nihilistic/masochistic position) (329). While the trilogy is anchored in the questions of family and filiation (especially in light of the disappearance of Lê's father figure), Huston notes on Lê's collection of short stories *Autres jeux avec le feu* published in 2002 that the dilemma of exile ("tous les dilemmes de l'exil") had resurfaced for the author: "l'autre soi qu'on avait laissé dans le pays natal, et qui reprend vie; la culpabilité d'avoir abandonné sa maison, son pays, sa langue d'origine; la hantise de perdre sa deuxième langue, celle de l'écriture . . ." (the other self that we had left in the native land, and who comes back to life; the guilt of having abandoned one's home, one's country, one's native tongue; the fear of losing one's second language, that of writing. . .) (330). Lê's return to Vietnam parallels Moï's own return and, like Moï's, this return took place during the years of the "Black-Blanc-Beur" utopia, a time of redefinition of national identity in metropolitan France, and a time of self-reflection for the exiled author, neglected and excluded from this idealized version of a multicultural French identity.

As underlined by Huston, Lê's return to Vietnam engenders on one hand a shift in her literary production (the return of the theme of exile, the transition to a female narrator) and, on the other hand, ushers an era of self-reflection for the author both in terms of her own identity as Franco-Vietnamese woman, and in terms of her literary identity as a postcolonial writer of the French language. Yet, Lê's oeuvre—her trilogy in particular—was never marketed or classified by Christian Bourgois as anything other than French literature, despite the latent themes of exile and self-(re)definition which she developed in her narratives. In fact, the specific cataloging and design of Lê's publications during the "Black-Blanc-Beur" years, starting with *Les trois parques* (1997) and ending with *Le complexe de Caliban* (2005), have fashioned the Franco-Vietnamese woman as a writer of French literature away from the limelight and identity politics of "Beur" and "Black" publishing. Her discrete yet solid presence on the French publishing market have made her one of the most prolific contemporary authors, as Huston had already noted in 2004 that "il n'y a presque pas eu d'année sans livre" (there has nearly not been one year without a book) (324). Lê's self-reflective process regarding her position as a Franco-Vietnamese author on the "Black-Blanc-Beur" metropolitan literary market is very clearly addressed in *Le complexe de Caliban*, a memoir on the author's writing process which is examined later in this chapter. First, it is essential to address Christian Bourgois' neutral marketing practices which contributed to Lê's cataloging as *littérature française* despite her own dislike of literary labels.

The Éditions Christian Bourgois (located in Paris proper) offer an extensive catalog with some rather traditional categories (*Littérature étrangère, Littérature française,* and *Essais*), and other more specific categories (*Théâtre, Théâtre de l'Odéon, Compacts,* and *Titres*). Christian Bourgois also offers a selection of collections including a "*Bibliothèque asiatique.*" However, unlike Gallimard, Christian Bourgois has always classified Linda Lê's works under "*Littérature française,*" never under "*Bibliothèque asiatique.*" The "*Bibliothèque asiatique*" page on the publisher's website only lists six works which are all "*traduits du chinois*" (translated from Chinese), but one historical work by French journalist Francis Deron (Christian Bourgois "Bibliothèque asiatique" 2019). The overt inclusion of Lê's work into their French Literature collection from the beginning of their collaboration in 1993 with *Calomnies* (Lê's first published work), has served to anchor Lê and her works within a larger sense of French literature, one that is not Other, Oriental, or postcolonial in any way, and one which has allowed the author herself to escape the labels that she abhors.

Christian Bourgois's presentation of the author on their website is thus focused on Lê's voluntary detachment from all labels: "Née en 1963 au Viêtnam, Linda Lê avoue volontiers qu'elle n'a plus une connaissance intime de sa langue natale. Le français, appris dès l'enfance, à Saigon, est devenu, sinon sa patrie, du moins un espace mouvant qui lui permet tout ensemble de se désabriter et de trouver une ancre flottante" (Born in 1963 in Vietnam, Linda Lê willingly confesses that she no longer possesses an intimate knowledge of her native tongue. French, which she started learning as a child in Saigon, has become, if not her country, at least a moving space that allows her to altogether unshelter herself and to find a floating anchor) (Christian Bourgois, "Linda Lê" 2019). While the description goes on to recount the various publications of the author, including the literary prizes which she has won and those for which she was nominated, the right-hand side of the webpage includes a headshot and a quote by Lê: "La littérature n'est pas faite pour les acquittés, elle n'est pas faite pour les élus. Elle est dans le camp des victimes et des sacrifiés, dans le camp des condamnés qui essayent, comme moi, de trouver leur salut et qui se cassent les dents" (Literature is not for the acquitted, it is not for the elected. It sides with the victims and those that were sacrificed, it sides with those condemned that try, like I do, to find their salvation and hit a brick wall) (Christian Bourgois, "Linda Lê" 2019).

It is important to note that, while Christian Bourgois' inclusion of Linda Lê in their French literature collection coupled with their neutral paratextual practices regarding the marketing of the author's oeuvres, have helped Lê establish herself outside of the restrictive geographical and raciallybased labels that had become (overtly and surreptitiously) habitual during the years of the "Black-Blanc-Beur" utopia, two elements on this webpage presenting the author echo colonial and postcolonial practices previously analyzed in this book as first examined by Richard Watts. First, the inclusion of a list of literary prizes signals the legitimacy of the author in her writing in French and being published by a metropolitan publishing house, all the while legitimizing her aptitude to write *about* the topic to which she is thought to speak: Vietnam. This is reinforced by a headshot of Lê which, in a second reference to Watts' study, establishes for the reader a supposedly logical bind between the name of the author, her ethnicity, and the topic(s) addressed in her works.[4]

These practices, while reminiscent of the colonial and immediately post-colonial literary marketing of "Other" authors in metropolitan France (Watts) were however, as we have seen, not uncommon during the years of the "Black-Blanc-Beur" utopia. In fact, could Christian Bourgois have managed to establish on one hand the "French literature" quality of Lê's writing while, on the other, affirming her presence within "Black-Blanc-Beur" France as a Vietnamese woman, the descendant of the formerly colonized? It is in fact possible, especially when we consider Christian Bourgois' online mention of Lê's exile to France as a young adult, and her finding solace in literature (something Lê has mentioned herself on numerous occasions): "Arrivée en France en 1977, deux ans après la fin de la guerre du Viêt-Nam, elle a pris le chemin de la littérature" (As she arrived in France in 1977, two years after the end of the Vietnam War, she began writing) (Christian Bourgois, "Linda Lê" 2019). However, the question remains: how would this practice of presenting an-Other author, one who does not fit into the "Black-Blanc-Beur" utopia, be different from that of Gallimard's or l'Aube's which were examined earlier in this chapter? One answer to this question goes back to the material aspect of Lê's literature: her classification in *Littérature française*, and the neutral paratextual elements in the packaging of her books published by Christian Bourgois, notably in the *Titres* collection.

The books in the *Titres* collection (Christian Bourgois' own version of a "Pocket" or "Folio" format) are adorned with blue covers that do not indicate the gender or ethnicity of the author (despite her first and last name being printed in black block letters): in this sense, these blue covers may appeal to a larger audience since they do not advertise any particularity of the text (as opposed to, perhaps, a specialized audience that would be actively looking for books written by Franco-Vietnamese authors, about Vietnam). More importantly, these blue covers resemble those of Stocks's *La Bleue* collection in which a majority of Nina Bouraoui's novels have been published, under the "French literature" label—effectively fabricating her authorial persona as an integrated second-generation immigrant, one who represented the ideal of the "Beur" in the "Black-Blanc-Beur" utopia. In a 2012 article entitled "Les couleurs du succès" ("Colors of Success"), Didier Jacob remarked that every established and influential publishing house had one main collection whose publications were characterized by a solid color front cover. The premise of the article was encompassed in its opening questions: "Que serait Gallimard sans sa célèbre «collection blanche»? Et Grasset sans sa «jaune»? Du Seuil à Actes Sud ou à Christian Bourgois, comment se fabriquent les grandes couvertures?" (Where would Gallimard be without its famous "white collection"? And Grasset without its "yellow" [collection]? From Seuil to Actes Sud and Christian Bourgois, how are great front covers made?) (Jacob 2012, par. 1). Jacob's accentuating of these publishers' front covers as "grandes" (great) confirms the identity and literary politics that are represented in the choice of the front cover for an author's publication, in that it will or will not grant him or her access into a certain literary category (here, and most likely quite often, the "grande" French literature" category).

In fact, before Christian Bourgois moved onto to illustrated front covers and even the 2007 *Titres* collection with its blue covers, the late Parisian editor sought out the most neutral, most unremarkable front cover for his publication, as Didier Jacob recounts:

> Il se souvient avoir même demandé au directeur artistique de chez Havas de lui dessiner une couverture *«agressive d'illisibilité»*. Elles seront blanches donc, avec des caractères disposés à la main, et ce logo de la maison, aujourd'hui légendaire, qu'il appelle toujours *«le bidule»*. Seulement les libraires rouspètent: la couverture ne se distingue pas assez de la «blanche».

> (He actually remembers asking the artistic director from Havas publishing to draw him an "aggressively unreadable" front cover. They will be white then, with letters that have been positioned by hand, and the [publishing] house's logo, which has today become legendary, which he still calls *"the thingy."* But bookstore owners grumbled: [Christian Bourgois'] front cover was not distinguishable enough from [Gallimard's] "white" [cover].) (par. 8)

In order to no longer compete with Gallimard's "Blanche" collection with its cream-colored front covers, Christian Bourgois progressively moved away from plain white covers to covers that included small illustrations which became larger with time and ultimately filled up the entire front cover of the publishing house's productions. Christian Bourgois' return to a solid color cover with the *Titres* collection in 2007 marked the publisher's return to an unmarked form of labeling for its authors, one which benefited Linda Lê even further than the illustrated yet gender and ethnicallyneutral covers that had adorned her first editions with the publisher.

With the *Titres* reprints of *Les trois parques* and *Lettre morte* in 2011, Lê and her publisher are not vying in any sense to establish a specific label that would align the author and her text to any form of identity politics in effect at the time of publication. Rather, these covers have the effect of further removing Lê from any formal or subtle labeling, something for which she continues to strive as expressed in *Le complexe de Caliban* as well as in later interviews. *Voix* on the other hand, published in a smaller format not with Christian Bourgois in the *Titres* collection but with Pocket, bears on its front cover a drawing resembling Edvard Munch's 1893 painting entitled "The Scream." Contrary to other Folio and Livre de Poche editions studied in this book's previous chapters on "Beur" and "Black" publishing between 1998 and 2005, Pocket's edition of *Voix* does not bear any paratextual elements of gender or ethnic identity about its author, Linda Lê. However, on the back cover, a short blurb about Lê is included following a summary of the novel, which reads: "D'origine vietnamienne, Linda Lê vit à Paris. C'est de sa propre expérience qu'elle se sert pour décrire la folie de son personnage" (Originally from Vietnam, Linda Lê lives in Paris. She uses her own experience to describe her character's madness) (Pocket 1999, back cover). *Voix* is cataloged in Pocket's "Nouvelles Voix" ("New Voices") collection which includes among others (and as indicated across from the inside title page) French writers Christine Angot and Marc Bonnet as well as Algerian author Yasmina Khadra (Pocket 1999, 4). In this sense, Lê has not been classified by Pocket according to her gender or ethnic heritage but rather in terms of "novelty" literature at the time of her novel's second publication by Pocket in 1999. Pocket thus followed the example of Christian Bourgois in choosing to not mark Lê and her oeuvre as different from another oeuvre of French literature.

Lê has only published two of her twenty-two novels, memoirs, and collections of short stories, with a publisher other than Christian Bourgois: *Marina Tsvetaeva: comment ça va la vie?* with Éditions Jean-Michel Place in 2002, and *À l'enfant que je n'aurai pas* in 2011 with Éditions NiL. With the Éditions Jean-Michel Place (f. 1974), now known as Nouvelles Éditions Place since a 2009 merger, Linda Lê's *Marina Tsvetaeva* was categorized in their "Collection Poésie" ("Poetry"), in which, according to their website:

"chaque titre est une monographie singulière consacrée à un poète contemporain ou du XXème siècle—singulière parce qu'écrite à travers le regard d'un autre poète. Loin des analyses académiques, chaque auteur éclaire une poésie à la lumière de son encre" (each title is a singular monograph dedicated to a contemporary or twentieth-century poet—singular because it is written through the lens of another poet. Far from academic analysis, each author sheds light on a form of poetry using the light of his or her own ink) (Place 2019). Here Lê is cataloged as a "poet" analyzing the work of another poet (Marina Tsvetaeva, a renowned Russian poet, who was exiled in Berlin, Prague, and Paris). The reason why this work was not published by Christian Bourgois appears to be due to the nature of the work itself: a poetic analysis of a single figure of foreign literature, a form of literary practice which is common at the Nouvelles Éditions Place where it pertains to a specific collection, would not have easily found its place in Christian Bourgois' catalog which is more inclined to publish fiction and memoirs.

CALIBAN AND CANNIBAL: TRANSNATIONAL RECONCILIATIONS

In *Le complexe de Caliban*, an autobiographical memoir in which she enumerates and explores the works of various international authors who have inspired her, Lê appears to be less attached to other francophone writers of the recently decolonized Africa, Maghreb, and French Caribbean, and more attuned to the woes of exiled Russian and Eastern European writers (in fact, as noted earlier, Lê dedicated an entire work to Russian author Marina Tsvetaeva published by Jean-Michel Place in 2002). In *Le complexe de Caliban*, Lê speaks of Andreyev (exiled in Finland during the Bolshevik Revolution), Dostoyevsky (exiled in Siberia) and Cioran (exiled in France during the World War II). Lê also identifies with Herman Melville and Shakespeare—both of the Anglo-Saxon tradition—but curiously, not with Martiniquan and Negritude founder Aimé Césaire who adapted Shakespeare's *Tempest* in 1969 amid civil unrest in France and in the former colonies, as her title *Le complexe de Caliban* may have denoted. It could then be inferred, from Lê's lack of African, North-African, and Caribbean references, that the focus on fabricated "Black" and "Beur" identities during the "Black-Blanc-Beur" period encouraged her to position herself among famed Western (white and male) authors as opposed to authors who, like her, had origins or ancestry in countries formerly colonized by the French. However, it is more likely that Lê may have seen in the lack of representation of Franco-Vietnamese authors in France at the time of the "Black-Blanc-Beur" utopia an opportunity to de-essentialize what was known (and continues to be known in a majority of circles) as "francophone" literature, in de-emphasizing the ethnic characteristics of nonwhiteness and shining a light on the common denominator between all nonwhite authors writing in "white" languages: the need and right to express oneself regardless of the identity politics that are tied to the language being used.

In fact, Lê found more kinship at the time with authors who, like her, had suffered from exile as opposed to authors who had suffered or were still suffering from being ostracized in metropolitan France because of the color of their skin. Lê considers exile as not only physical, but also linguistic. Early on in *Le complexe de Caliban*, she explains that it is the commonality of exile that influenced her reading of other authors who had been exiled. She writes:

> Ma résolution de devenir écrivain s'affermit en lisant les grands auteurs—Flaubert, Dostoïevski, Shakespeare—l'un après l'autre. Mais je commençais à ressentir profondément ma différence . . . Il y avait en moi une fêlure que j'essayais de comprendre en me tournant vers les écrivains qui ont trahi leur langue natale: Conrad le Polonais qui écrivait en anglais, Cioran le Roumain et Beckett l'Irlandais écrivant en français.
>
> (My resolution to become a writer was affirmed as I read great authors—Flaubert, Dostoïevski, Shakespeare—one after the other. But I started to sense deeply that I was different . . . There was in me a fissure that I tried to understand by turning to writers who betrayed their native tongue: Conrad the Pole who wrote in English, Cioran the Romanian and Beckett the Irish who wrote in French.) (Lê 2005, 41)

Lê did not seem to find commonality with her fellow postcolonial authors of the francophone realm, those who were raised, like her, both in their native language and in French and who chose to write in French. Rather, she became fascinated by those she calls the "grands auteurs" (great authors) of which very few—if any—had roots in the formerly colonized French realm.

In her chapter entitled "Je me souviens" ("I remember"), Lê however mentions Algerian author Kateb Yacine, who "disait que la langue française est un butin de guerre" (used to say that the French language was spoils of war) (94). In this same chapter, she mentions German poet Heinrich Heine, Marcel Proust's male character Bergotte in *À la recherche du temps perdu*, Mariana Tsvetaeva, French writers Henri Calet and Violette Leduc, and William Blake (96-97). Yacine is one of very few iterations of a potential postcolonial francophone kinship on Lê's part, and appears to be drowned in a sea of "white" canonical and noncanonical references. Yet, Lê's "cannibalization" of white literature (as referred to in the very title of her autobiographical memoir, *Caliban's Complex*) falls into a tradition that is more aligned with that of

Aimé Césaire, Suzanne Césaire and Maryse Condé in the French Caribbean, than it is with that of Proust, Blake, or Shakespeare's.

The figure of Caliban and of the cannibal ("Caliban" being an imperfect anagram of the word "cannibal"), have resurfaced over the years in various postcolonial literary traditions (francophone, anglophone, hispanophone) as a trope of subversion of authority and adaptation. In rewriting stories which are originally part and parcel of the Western European white literary canon, nonwhite postcolonial authors express their desire and ability to create a new form of literature and to subvert the power structure of colonialism that had seeped deeply into all realms of life for the colonized, as far as the constructs of language, literature, self, and identity.

In the Caribbean literary tradition, both Maryse Condé and Suzanne Césaire addressed the trope of literary cannibalism. In her study of Condé's *Histoire de la femme cannibale* (Gallimard 2005), Dawn Fulton in *Signs of Dissent: Maryse Condé and Postcolonial Criticism* relates the title and storyline of Condé's 2005 novel to the Guadeloupian author's larger philosophy and legitimacy of literary cannibalism:

> Condé herself has written in recent essays about this . . . strategy of "literary cannibalism," identifying its emergence in Brazilian modernism via Oswaldo de Andrade's anthropophagist movement and tracing a literary history through such intellectual figures as Martinican critic Suzanne Césaire and Argentine-Chilean writer Ariel Dorfman . . . Firmly situated in a New World geography, Condé's framework foregrounds the violence and incorporation associated with cannibalism as a mode of creative freedom. (Fulton 2008, 124)

The *Manifesto Antropófago* published in Brazil in 1928 by Oswaldo de Andrade stands as an anchor point to literary cannibalism and adaptation studies around the world. De Andrade (as translated by Leslie Bary in 1991) thus exclaims: "We want the Carib Revolution. Greater than the French Revolution . . . Without us, Europe wouldn't even have its meager declaration of the rights of man" (De Andrade 1991, 39), and "Heritage. Contact with the Carib side of Brazil . . . Montaigne. Natural man. Rousseau. From the French Revolution to Romanticism, to the Bolshevik Revolution, to the Surrealist Revolution and Keyserling's technicized barbarian. We push onward" (39).

Suzanne Césaire also wrote about literary cannibalism and the mixing of colonialist culture with native culture in the literary revue *Tropiques* which she cofounded with her husband and was published between 1941 and 1945. Her main argument in her text entitled "Malaise d'une civilisation" expressed how the mimicry encouraged by the colonizer had given way, after the abolition of slavery, to a creative force that was no longer a product of simple imitation and reproduction, but rather a creolization of the original, and the production of a symbolic and nationalist artform. Suzanne Césaire wrote:

> Il ne s'agit point d'un retour en arrière, de la résurrection d'un passé africain que nous avons appris à connaître et à respecter. Il s'agit, au contraire, d'une mobilisation de toutes les forces vives mêlées sur cette terre où la race est le résultat du brassage le plus continu; il s'agit de prendre conscience du formidable amas d'énergies diverses que nous avons jusqu'ici enfermées en nous-mêmes. Nous devons maintenant les employer dans leur plénitude, sans déviation et sans falsification. Tant pis pour ceux qui nous croient des rêveurs.
>
> (It is not at all about a backwards return, a resurrection of an African past that we have learned to know and respect. On the contrary, it is about the mobilization of every living strength brought together upon this earth where race is the result of the most unremitting intermixing; it is about becoming conscious of the incredible store of varied energies until now locked up within us. We must now deploy them to the maximum without deviation, without falsification. Too bad for those who consider us mere dreamers.) (S. Césaire 1942, 48–9/33)

Suzanne Césaire is considered by many as the precursor of *créolité* later claimed and developed by Patrick Chamoiseau and Edouard Glissant. Indeed, while her husband Aimé strongly advocated for a return to common African roots in the spirit of the Negritude philosophy, Suzanne was writing about the reality and creative impulse of a "brassage continu" (unremitting intermixing), already separating herself from a homogenous definition of identity, one that would be strictly opposed to the white colonial world. In this sense, we can say that Suzanne Césaire was a precursor to Linda Lê's refusal of literary labels, and to her drawing on multiple literary traditions to find her own voice and identity—reviving in the meantime the figure of the literary cannibal.

Lê's work in *Le complexe de Caliban* is therefore aligned with the practices of rewriting and adaptation that have been integral parts of what continues to be termed "francophone literature," which Glissant, Chamoiseau, and others sought to rename "littérature-monde en français" in their 2007 manifesto. However, it is essential to consider Lê's perpetual and public detachment from literary labels in order to understand her lack of affiliation with the rest of the postcolonial francophone literary group. In her 2018 study entitled "Linda Lê, On Writing and Not Writing," Leslie Barnes establishes from the beginning of her article: "Linda Lê has noted that writing shapes her identity more than any origins or affiliations, a knowledge which she claims allows her to occupy with ease the illegitimate spaces between homeland and adopted country, between belonging and unbelonging" (Barnes 2018, 21). For the purpose of this study, it is critical to reposition Lê's *complexe de Caliban*—which she herself presents as an autobiographical memoir on her coming to writing—in the context the "Black-Blanc-Beur" utopia, in terms of the creation of subversive literary classifications for non-Blanc authors at that time, and in terms of the author defining her practice of writing as distinct, yet inspired from various literary traditions including that of the formerly colonized.

The following commentary highlights the way in which Lê adopts the position of postcolonial revolt, as it was demonstrated in Aimé Césaire's adaptation of Caliban in *Une tempête* (1969), in claiming autonomy and anonymity from the colonial literary labels which resurfaced at the turn of the millennium alongside differential national identity politics.[5] In doing so, Lê exposes how she overcame her "Caliban's complex" while reflecting on her position as a postcolonial author publishing in the metropolitan France of the *banlieue* riots in 2005. Lê's desire to shed all literary labels while overcoming her Caliban traits ultimately brings her and her work closer to Aimé Césaire than she has perhaps been willing to admit. In this sense, Lê successfully transcends literary labels at a time when neocolonial labels were fabricated in line with the "Black-Blanc-Beur" utopia; in a way, Lê subtly honors the memory of one of the first leaders of the francophone postcolonial cause, Aimé Césaire.

When Césaire adapted Shakespeare's *Tempest* "pour un théâtre nègre" (for a black theater) (A. Césaire 1997/2000, 5/1), Charles de Gaulle, the actor of the 1946 law on departmentalization, was facing civil discontent in France and in the overseas departments of Guadeloupe and Martinique. In 1959, three Martiniquans had died at the hands of the French police after riots had erupted following the death of a black man who had been run over by a white driver in Fort-de-France. Later in 1967 in Guadeloupe, the French police fired at a large group of protesters demanding better wages and civil rights, killing about 100 Guadeloupeans. While Césaire as a politician did have a heavy hand in making Guadeloupe and Martinique overseas departments in 1946, he also recognized, in 1969, that the condition of the black man in the French Caribbean had not changed for the better. In her article titled "Maintaining the State of Emergence/y in Aimé Césaire's *Une tempête*," Lucy Rix argues that "at the time, the very act of rewriting the *Tempest* was seen as an audacious literary siege; for Césaire it provided a potent strategy by which to throw aside the rules of colonial culture, and to dramatize the destinies of the colonized" (Rix 2000, 236). The dependency theory between colonizer and colonized, as outlined in Octavio Mannoni's 1964 study entitled *Prospero and Caliban: the Psychology of Colonization*, was, according to Lucy Rix, rejected by Césaire—and yet, Césaire was "influenced by the idea that dependency established following colonization could be psychological and not exclusively economic" (248).

In his *Tempest*, Césaire demonstrated that this psychological colonization further expanded to the realms of language and literature. In Act I, scene 2, Prospero the colonizer chastises Caliban for using the Swahili word for freedom, "Uhuru," telling him: "Encore une remontée de ton langage barbare . . . tu pourrais au moins me bénir te t'avoir appris à parler. Un barbare! Une bête brute que j'ai éduquée, formée, que j'ai tirée de l'animalité qui l'engangue encore de toute part!" (Yet another return of your savage tongue . . . you might at least give me your blessing for having taught you to speak at all. A savage! A brute animal I educated, trained, dragged up from the bestiality that still festers all over him) (A. Césaire 1997/2000, 24–25/19), to which Caliban replies "Tu ne m'as rien appris du tout. Sauf, bien sûr à baragouiner ton langage pour comprendre tes orders . . . Quant à ta science, est-ce que tu me l'as jamais apprise, toi? Tu t'en es bien gardé! Ta science, tu la gardes égoïstement pour toi tout seul, enfermée dans les gros livres que voilà" (You haven't taught me anything at all! Except of course to jabber away in your language so as to understand your orders . . . As for your knowledge, did you ever impart any of that on me? You took care not to. You selfishly keep all your knowledge to yourself alone, sealed up in big books like those (25/ 19). Here Césaire's use of the present tense "keep" in 1969 seeks to accuse the unbalanced relationship between France and Martinique which he sees as directly affecting the Martiniquans' lives as well as their ability to express themselves in a language and literature other than strictly those of the colonizer.

In *Le complexe de Caliban*, Lê addresses similar notions of dependence, and self-declared (as opposed to granted) independence from the French language and culture. When she establishes that "[l]'écrivain exilé qui choisit d'écrire en français souffre du complexe de Caliban. Sa dévotion à la langue est mêlée d'hérésie" (the exiled writer who chooses to write in French suffers from Caliban's complex, his devotion to language mixed with heresy) (Lê 2005, 102), she addresses the same question as Césaire in 1969: can the formerly colonized surpass this Caliban complex and create a new literary space and tradition for him or herself? From the very first pages of her memoir, the discursively forsaken Vietnam of Lê's childhood mirrors the island of Césaire's *Tempest* along with the power dynamics that exist on the island originally owned by Caliban, then colonized by Prospero. Lê's way of quietly revolting against the poor living conditions and the political persecutions of postcolonial Vietnam was to read and thus obtain knowledge until then "sealed up in big books" like those of Prospero in Césaire's *Tempest*. Indeed she notes: "Celui qui savait lire était pour moi le maître du monde" (To me, the one who knew how to read was the master of the world) (8).

Throughout her various readings of canonical authors such as Flaubert, Dostoyevsky, and Shakespeare, as well as others who had experienced before her the hybrid spaces of anglophone and francophone literatures—she names

Conrad, Cioran, and Beckett—Lê finally finds a literary figure with which she can identify and which allows her to find her own voice: that of Bartleby the Scrivener, written by American author Herman Melville in 1853, whom she describes as "un orphelin et un opposant" (an orphan and a protester) (44). Lê expresses this liberating moment as follows:

> Il est difficile de mesurer le retentissement que provoque dans l'imaginaire d'une exilée incertaine de son identité l'apparition de Bartleby . . . À tout ce qu'on lui propose, il répond: "I would prefer not to. Je préférerais ne pas." Ce refus tranquille, cette résistance passive, cette formule simple et pourtant séditieuse, jaillit comme la manifestation même de la pureté . . . Sa solitude est l'annonce d'un monde qui dénie l'autorité et se libère de tout lien. Son détachement indiquait à l'adolescente déracinée que j'étais une attitude de défi serein.

> (It is difficult to measure the impact that the apparition of Bartleby, the young scribe, had on the mind of a young, uncertain exiled woman . . . To everything that is asked of him, Bartleby answers "I would prefer not to." This calm refusal, this passive resistance, this simple yet subversive formula, arose like the perfect manifestation of purity . . . His solitude is the announcement of a world that denies authority and frees itself from all bonds. His detachment indicated to the uprooted teenager that I was an attitude of serene defiance.) (45)

It is indeed Bartleby's quiet and passive opposition to the world order that best characterizes Linda Lê's ascending writing career in the late 90s and early 2000s. When Lê wrote *Le complexe de Caliban* in 2005, the "Black-Blanc-Beur" utopia had become fraught over the years with separatist political discourses on the *Français de souche* (the "truly French" according to some) and their Others (first and second-generation immigrants), and it was nearing a violent end marked by the *banlieue* riots of October and November 2005. *Le complexe de Caliban* was therefore published at a time when the resurgence of colonial practices forced Lê into a space of self-reflection. In her memoir, Lê reviews the various authors, French and others, who inspired her to write and encouraged her quiet anchoring into French literature as a form of resistance to literary labels and self-determination. As Lê's writing was never marketed by her publishing house Christian Bourgois as anything other than French, both in the visual paratext and in the cataloging of her works, she managedtopubliclyshedher"Other"—non-Blanc,non-*Françaisdesouche*—labels in favor of a quasi-incognito literary identity (her full name still appears on her book covers, marking her Vietnamese heritage).

In lacking a label that would present her as "Other" to her readership, Lê resembles Césaire's Caliban when he asks Prospero to stop labeling him as a slave, and to only be known as "X" the figure of absence (Césaire 28/ 21-22). As Lê echoes Césaire's Caliban in his refusal to be labeled according to his dependence to the colonizer, she asserts her liberation from the literary labels inspired by France's divisive identity politics which culminated in the *banlieue* riots of 2005. Like Bartleby the Scrivener, she "would prefer not to" succumb to the identity formation processes of the French literary institutions, as she declared in a 2008 interview recorded by Leslie Barnes: "I know that, in general, people consider me a French author, but I don't feel like a French author. Then again, I don't feel like a Vietnamese author either. It's true that I've doubted and that I've questioned my real identity, but I've also always been aware that the only real identity I can have is the one I create for myself through the books I write" (Barnes 2008, 53–54). The figure of Caliban therefore seems to resurface at times of revolt and defiance of the established postcolonial world order as a literary trope which reveals the francophone diaspora's yearning for self-determination, as exemplified by Césaire in 1969 and Lê in 2005. In adapting Césaire's postcolonial revolt, as incarnated by his iteration of Shakespeare's Caliban, to the quiet opposition of Melville's Bartleby, Lê builds on several literary and cultural contributions in order to form her own literature of dissent, autonomy, and creativity—in a sense establishing "an audacious literary siege" (Rix 2000, 236) in the manner of Césaire in 1969.

Lê's masterful distancing from common literary labels that would have marked her as "Other" (Vietnamese and/or francophone) is visible in the paratext chosen by Christian Bourgois for *Le complexe de Caliban*. On the front cover, the publisher added a photograph of six book spines representing canonical titles of French literature: Jules Barbey d'Aurevilly's *Les diaboliques* (1874), Gustave Flaubert's *Madame Bovary* (volume one and two, 1856), Stendhal's *La Chartreuse de Parme* (volume one and two, 1839), and Stendhal's *Le rouge et le noir* (1830). This front cover resembles Lê, her oeuvre, and her self-appointed lineage as expressed in *Le complexe de Caliban*. In anchoring Lê's text in canonical French nineteenth-century literature while advertising a title that connotes both Shakespeare's tempest from 1610 and Césaire's *Une tempête* from 1969, Christian Bourgois appeals to the French reader's ability to identify a validated work of French literature, as well as the reader's potential curiosity about its *métissage* with non-French (Shakespeare) and "non-Blanc" (Césaire and Lê) literature.

CONCLUSION

The stereotypical view of the Southeastern Asian population living in France as "a quiet and silent immigrant community" (Selao 2011, 11) transpired into the paratextual composition of the oeuvres written by Franco-Vietnamese women during the "Black-Blanc-Beur" years. Visual clues and back-cover summaries confined these authors and their works within an Orientalist space of colonial and gendered nostalgia, set to offset the brutality and perceived arrogance of "Black" and "Beur" authors. While the general tendency was to constrain these authors and their works into a specifically utopic space of colonial allegiance to France, select publishers genuinely strove to spark the metropolitan reading audience's interest for Franco-Vietnamese literature. That is the case of the Éditions de l'Aube who, despite their use of paratextual elements which often marked Anna Moï and her texts as decidedly feminine and Vietnamese, expressed a true interest in publishing and bringing attention to the Franco-Asian literary corpus. On the other hand, Christian Bourgois never published Linda Lê's works as anything other than *littérature française*, and never used paratextual elements which would indicate or reinforce her geographical origins or France's colonial past.

In the same manner as the authors studied in chapters 2 and 3 of this book, Anna Moï and Linda Lê used the autobiographical genre to examine their roles on the metropolitan literary market, as well as to explore their own identity formation processes as women writing in the colonizer's language. Moï, as will be exposed in this book's conclusion, continues to vacillate between labels, a hesitation in part due to her continuing relationship with Gallimard. Lê, on the other hand, has established her literary lineage, one of transnational contestation and deep love of writing, as her authorial identity on the metropolitan literary scene. The focus on "Black" and "Beur" identities at the turn of the century encouraged the Éditions de l'Aube and Éditions Christian Bourgois to create a space in which Moï and Lê's autobiographical identity formation processes were able to materialize. In turn, their oeuvres were promoted as near-*littérature française* despite the use of colonial paratextual markers by certain publishers. This "integration" process is especially visible in the case of Linda Lê who benefited from a transparent relationship with her publisher and, as such, remains one of very few ethnic minority women authors in France to hold some authority over the presentation of their oeuvres.

NOTES

1. Two of Moï's later works were also published in Gallimard's Blanche collection (*Rapaces* in 2005, and *Le Venin du papillon* in 2017), while her essay *Espéranto, désespéranto: la francophonie sans les Français* was published as part of Gallimard's Connaissance (*Knowledge*) series.

2. About 1990s Vietnam, she writes: "En quatre-vingt-dix, je suis revenue au Viêtnam pour la première fois, après une absence de presque vingt ans. L'électricité était coupée cinq jours sur sept, de six heures du matin à six heures du soir" ("In ninety,

I came back to Vietnam for the first time after having been gone from about twenty years. The power was out five out of seven days, from six in the morning until six in the evening") (14), and "L'été à Saigon, je suis désoeuvrée sans l'être vraiment. La majeure partie du temps est passé à attendre. Le réparateur de toit (car il pleut beaucoup). Le réparateur de la photocopieuse (elle tombe souvent en panne). Le réparateur du modem (grillé par la foudre)" ("In the summer in Saigon, I am inactive without really being inactive. The better part of the day is spent waiting. The roofer (because it rains a lot). The copier repairman (it is often out of service). The internet repairman (hit by lighting)") (41).

3. Selao argues that Moï's work and authorial self-perception are more similar to the previous generation of Franco-Vietnamese writers than to Linda Lê and her "refus d'écrire explicitement sur le Vietnam afin d'éviter tout type de catégorisation" ("refusal to write explicitly about Vietnam as to avoid any type of categorization"). While she is considered to be "la représentante de la littérature vietnamienne francophone contemporaine" ("the representative of contemporary Francophone Vietnamese literature"), Selao argues that Moï oddly refuses the "Vietnamese" label although some of her narratives are set in Vietnam and she spends part of each year in Vietnam where she writes her books (Selao 38).

4. Watts explains in *Packaging Post/Coloniality*: "The effect of the curriculum vitae . . . is to remove the work from the realm of creative fiction, endow it with anthropological authenticity, and thrust it unambiguously into the realm of testimony . . . [Paratexts] simply vouch for the reliability of the woman writer and of her appropriateness as witness to a particular event or, more often, sociological condition." (146).

5. Parts of the research for this section were presented at the Modern Language Association annual convention in Chicago, Illinois, in a paper entitled "Writing as Caliban: Aimé Césaire, Linda Lê, and Transnational Autobiographies" (January 4-7 2018).

Conclusion
Beyond "Black-Blanc-Beur": Negotiating Labels and "littérature-monde"

Although ethnic minority women were excluded from the main discourse of the "Black-Blanc-Beur" utopia, they were actually often used by the publishing and news media to broadcast a certain neocolonial image of "non-Blanc" women in France. Ethnic minority women consequently became instrumental in the perpetuation of France's multicultural ideal: while the athletic success of "non-Blanc" men was acclaimed as a mark of integration and allegiance to France, the sexualities and difficult lives of "Black" and "Beur" women accentuated by the media confined them in a premodern space adjacent to the men's. Against this negative press, *banlieue* women led by Fadela Amara and Samira Bellil had to march through France in order to disrupt the social order and force the media's attention on sexual violence in the projects. As was highlighted in chapter 2, the attention they gained turned out to be a double-edged sword, as it solidified for the general public the role of the French institutions in safeguarding these women from the violence of "non-Blanc" men. Although women may have seemed secondary to the "Black-Blanc-Beur" utopia, they were only given a more tortuous and heavily stigmatized path into the construction of a supposedly perfect version of 1998 France. As exposed in chapters 2 and 3, subcategories of female identities emerged in the media and publishing realm, such as the exotic Black woman, or the "*banlieue* victim" Beur woman. Meanwhile, as seen in chapter 4, women of Southeastern Asian descent and their oeuvres garnered much less public and media attention in the context of the "Black-Blanc-Beur" utopia. These authors were consequently afforded a somewhat less burdened path into a near-French literature category, despite some of their publishers' essentialist and colonialist publishing strategies.

The desire to label the literature written by second- and third-generation "non-Blanc" immigrants in metropolitan France did not vanish after the

"Black-Blanc-Beur" years: if anything, it increased as evidenced by the reactions of ethnic minority authors who wished to define themselves and their literatures in a context of increased governmental xenophobia. When Nicolas Sarkozy won the 2007 presidential election, the "Black-Blanc-Beur" slogan and utopian image of a multicultural France had indeed become utopic vestiges of the past. The various displays of Sarkozy's exclusionary identity politics, which had begun with the closing of the Sangatte refugee camp in 2002 and the 2004 headscarf ban (when Sarkozy was Minister of the Interior), continued with the president's inflammatory comments upon his visit to the projects in the midst of the 2005 riots.[1] In 2007, Sarkozy created the Ministère de l'Immigration, de l'Intégration, de l'Identité Nationale et du Développement Solidaire (Ministry of Immigration, Integration, National Identity and Co-Development), which prompted Patrick Chamoiseau and Édouard Glissant to publish a manifesto entitled "Les murs" in the newspaper *L'Humanité*.

In their expanded publication entitled *Quand les murs tombent: l'identité nationale hors-la-loi* (published one month after "Les murs"), Chamoiseau and Glissant advocated for a deterritorialized definition of identity as it pertains to language and literature, one which exists beyond the geographical and historical framework of France's former colonial empire. They wrote: "nous n'appartenons pas en exclusivité à des « patries », à des « nations », et pas du tout à des « territoires », mais désormais à des « lieux », des intempéries linguistiques . . . des terres natales que nous aurons décidées, des langues que nous aurons désirées, ces géographies tissées de matières et de visions que nous aurons forgées" (we do not exclusively belong to "countries," "nations", and not at all to "territories", but, from this point forward, to "places", to linguistic storms . . . to native lands which we will have chosen, to languages which we will have desired, to these geographies woven from materials and visions which we will have forged) (Glissant and Chamoiseau 2007, 16–17). The rhizomatic identity outlined here by Chamoiseau and Glissant cannot be controlled by institutional forces; rather, it is formed through a self-determination process which resembles that of the authors studied in this book who continue to build and represent their multifaced literary identities in their autobiographical and autofictional works.

After 2005, questions relating to the interplay between the government's discourse on postcolonial immigration and the Metropole's institutional publishing practices (from the awarding of literary prizes to the categorization and marketing of oeuvres) surfaced in a much more open and contentious manner than ever before. In fact, a few months before the publication of "Les murs" and *Quand les murs tombent*, a collective of authors including Michel Le Bris, Édouard Glissant, Maryse Condé, and Anna Moï, had penned another manifesto entitled "Pour une 'littérature-monde' en français" (also published in *Le Monde*). "Pour une 'littérature-monde' en français" was signed by a large number of "francophone" authors who no longer wished to be considered as such after several members of that artificial literary category had won, that year, the most prestigious metropolitan literary prizes. They argued notably:

> Combien d'écrivains de langue française, pris eux aussi entre deux ou plusieurs cultures, se sont interrogés alors sur cette étrange disparité qui les reléguait sur les marges, eux "francophones", variante exotique tout juste tolérée, tandis que les enfants de l'ex-empire britannique prenaient, en toute légitimité, possession des lettres anglaises?
>
> (How many authors who write in French, stuck in between two or more cultures, have wondered about this strange disparity which relegated them, the "Francophones," to the margins, as an exotic yet barely tolerated variation, while the children of the former British empire rightfully took possession of the British letters?) (Barbery et al. 2007, par. 7)

A number of scholars have rejected the term "*littérature-monde*" as yet another label which potentially excludes "non-Blanc" literature written in French, as it unwittingly reproduces a chiasm between the publishing center of the (French) Metropole and the rest of the (francophone) world. As Jean-Xavier Ridon asks in "*Littérature-monde*, or Redefining Exotic Literature?": "how is the reproduction of an exotic representative type to be avoided when the very concept of *littérature-monde* is linked, by Le Bris and others, to travel literature? For these authors, literary success is confirmed by the unqualified adoption by the French literary establishment" (Ridon 2010, 197). It is critical to note that none of the authors studied in this book have adopted the "*littérature-monde*" label, nor have they adhered to any particular official or unofficial label through their literary self-determination process.

Anna Moï was the only author of Southeastern Asian descent (and the only *female* author of Asian descent) to be included among the signatories of the "Pour une 'littérature-monde'" manifesto.[2] Moï's inclusion as the sole representative of Franco-Vietnamese literature indicates her position within the metropolitan literature realm, that of an accepted "*intégrée*" ethnic minority female author who belongs to the inner circle of French metropolitan publishing. As Laura Reeck notes in "The World and the Mirror in Two Twenty-First Century Manifestoes: 'Pour une "littérature-monde" en français' and 'Qui fait la France?'", most of the "Pour une 'littérature-monde' en français" signatories, including Anna Moï, were already associated with the metropolitan literary market (unlike those of "Qui fait la France?", another manifesto published in 2007 by a collective of authors led by Mohamed Reziane). Reeck further establishes that Glissant, Condé, and Moï (among others) had already entered the French canon by winning prestigious literary prizes (Reeck 2010, 265), and that "most of them [were] world travelers, migrant intellectuals and not uncommonly tenured members of foreign academic institutions" (267). In addition, Jean-Xavier Ridon notes that Alain Mabanckou, himself a signatory of the manifesto, had noted in his contribution to the *Pour une littérature-monde* volume published by Gallimard that "most so-called Francophone authors do not exist and are not recognized until they sign with a French, invariably Parisian, editor" (Ridon 2010, 196).

Anna Moï has previously published her own manifesto on literary labels entitled "Francophonie sans Français" in *Le Monde*. Moï's essay was published on November 24 2005, about a week after the recorded end of the *banlieue* riots. The author opens with this declaration: "À la veille de l'Année de la francophonie annoncée [pour 2006] par le président de la République, des émeutes font désordre dans ce beau paysage coloré des peuples francophones" (On the eve of the Year of francophonie announced [for 2006] by the President of the Republic, riots are causing unrest in this beautiful colored landscape of francophone peoples) (Moï 2005, par. 1). As her essay is directly inspired by the rioters' dissent, Moï aims to highlight the sociocultural and ethnic divide between centers and peripheries in metropolitan France, as well as between *littérature française* and other literatures written in French.

Like the future signatories of the 2007 manifesto, she invokes the former British colonial empire as a counterpoint to the exclusionary labeling of "francophone" literatures—yet, unlike her 2007 cosigners, Moï is openly vocal regarding the continuing racism of the English-speaking literary realm, stating "Allez! Ils sont bien un peu racistes — *"nobody's perfect"*. Par exemple, en 2004, ils recensèrent cent Britanniques remarquables. On constata qu'aucun de ces individus n'était d'origine ethnique" (Well! They are a little bit racist —*"nobody's perfect"*. For example, in 2004, they published a list of a hundred remarkable British people. It was noted that none of these individuals was of ethnic origin) (par. 2). Similarly to the upcoming 2007 manifesto, Moï's essay clearly addresses the racist tendencies which continue to rule the metropolitan literary realm, stating: "Nul ne pensa à recenser des personnalités françaises remarquables, et donc encore moins des personnalités remarquables d'origines ethniques diverses. D'ailleurs, les personnalités françaises noires sont absentes en France: la différenciation ethnique est anticonstitutionnelle" (No one thought to make a list of remarkable French public figures, let alone of remarkable public figures of diverse ethnic origins. In fact, public figures who are French and black are invisible in France: ethnic differentiation is anticonstitutional) (par.4).

Moï's further statements on French and francophone literatures are however perplexing as she discusses her own classification within the French publishing market. She declares: "Dans le même ordre d'idées, il n'y a plus de littérature française, mais une littérature francophone. Je note cependant que mes romans, écrits en français et publiés par Gallimard dans la collection « Blanche » , sont répertoriés dans le département de littérature vietnamienne à la Fnac" (Similarly, there is no more French literature, but Francophone literature. I noticed however that my novels that are written in French and published by Gallimard in the "Blanche" collection are classified in the Vietnamese literature department at the Fnac [bookstore]) (par. 5). Unfortunately, against Moï's claim, the "French literature" category still existed in 2005; in fact, the exclusionary practices of publishers and booksellers who still classified her works as Vietnamese—although they were published in Gallimard's French literature collection ("La Blanche")—continue to this day.

In 2017, after she received the Prix Littérature-Monde (created in 2013) for her novel *Le venin du papillon* published by Gallimard in the Blanche collection, Moï declared in an interview: "Je suis ravie d'être 'noyée' maintenant au milieu des autres auteurs, d'être lue pour mes textes et non en raison de mes origines géographiques ou de ma supposée identité vietnamienne" (I'm delighted to now be 'drowned' among other authors, to be read for my texts and not because of my geographical origins or because of my supposed Vietnamese identity) (Raspiengeas par.7). However, *Le venin du papillon* is classified by Gallimard as "littérature française" (French literature), "littérature étrangère" (Foreign literature) "du continent asiatique et Proche-Orient non-arabe—Francophones" (of the Asian continent and non-Arabic Middle-East—Francophones) and "Viêtnam" (Gallimard "Le venin" 2019). Therefore, although Moï sees her work and herself as now being "drowned" among other authors and labels, the author and her work actually continue to be subjected to essentialist marketing practices and identity formation processes, similar to those of the "Black-Blanc-Beur" years.

NOTES

1. Marie des Neiges Léonard in "The Effects of Political Rhetoric on the Rise of Legitimized Racism in France: the Case of the 2005 French Riots" explains: "As soon as the riots began on 27 October 2005, using the same kind of unrestrained words he had used in prior months, then-Minister of Interior Sarkozy commented on the events by denouncing the actions of the rioters, whom he labeled 'scum' and 'thugs' (the now-infamous French word '*racaille*')" (1093).

2. Dai Sijie is the only other Asian author (he was born in China and resides in France) who is among the signatories of the "Pour une 'littérature-monde' en français" manifesto.

Appendix
Further Reading

Bessora. *Cyr@no*. Paris: Belfond, 2011.
———. *Deux bébés et l'addition*. Paris: Le Serpent à Plumes, 2002.
———. *La dynastie des boîteux*. Paris: Le Serpent à Plumes, 2018.
———. *Le testament de Nicolas*. Paris: La Margouline, 2016.
———. *Les tâches d'encre*. Paris: Le Serpent à Plumes, 2000.
Beyala, Calixthe. *La plantation*. Paris: Albin Michel, 2005.
———. *Le petit prince de Belleville*. Paris: Albin Michel, 1992.
———. *Les arbres en parlent encore*. Paris: Albin Michel, 2002.
———. *Les honneurs perdus*. Paris: Albin Michel, 1996.
———. *Lettre d'une Africaine à ses soeurs occidentales*. Paris: Spangler Editions, 1995.
———. *L'homme qui m'offrait le ciel*. Paris: Albin Michel, 2007.
———. *Maman a un amant*. Paris: Albin Michel, 1993.
———. *Tu t'appelleras Tanga*. Paris: Stock, 1988.
Bouraoui, Nina. *Avant les hommes*. Paris: Stock, 2007.
———. *Beaux rivages*. Paris: JC Lattès, 2016.
———. *La vie heureuse*. Paris: Stock, 2002.
———. *Le jour du séisme*. Paris: Stock, 1999.
———. *Mes mauvaises pensées*. Paris: Stock, 2005.
———. *Poing mort*. Paris: Gallimard, 1992.
———. *Poupée Bella*. Paris: Stock, 2004.
———. *Sauvage*. Paris: Stock, 2011.
———. *Standard*. Paris: Flammarion, 2014.
———. *Tous les hommes désirent naturellement savoir*. Paris: JC Lattès, 2018.
Cazenave, Odile. *Afrique-sur-Seine, Une nouvelle génération de romanciers africains à Paris*. Paris: L'Harmattan, 2003.
Chu Lai. *Rue des soldats*. La Tour d'Aigues: Éditions de l'Aube, 2003.
Condé, Maryse. *Histoire de la femme cannibale*. Paris: Gallimard, 2005.
———. *Moi, Tituba sorcière*. Paris: Gallimard, 1988.

Devi, Ananda. *La vie de Joséphin le fou*. Paris: Gallimard, 2003.

———. *Le long désir*. Paris: Gallimard, 2003.

———. *Pagli*. Paris: Gallimard, 2001

———. *Soupirs*. Paris: Gallimard, 2002.

Dương, Thu H. *Histoire d'amour racontée avant l'aube*. Translated by Kim Lefèvre. La Tour d'Aigues: Éditions de l'Aube, 2003.

Guène Faïza. *Kiffe Kiffe demain*. Paris: Hachette, 2004.

———. *Kiffe Kiffe Tomorrow*. Translated by Sarah Adams. Orlando: Harcourt Books, 2006.

Humbert, Marie-Thérèse. *Les désancrés*. Paris: Gallimard, 2015.

Imache, Tassadit. *Une fille sans histoire*. Paris: Calmann-Lévy, 1989.

Jules-Rosette, Bennetta. *Black Paris: The African Writers' Landscape*. Urbana: University of Illinois Press, 1998.

Lê, Linda. *À l'enfant que je n'aurai pas*. Paris: Éditions NiL, 2011.

———. *Autres jeux avec le feu*. Paris: Christian Bourgois, 2002.

———. *Calomnies*. Paris: Christian Bourgois, 1993.

———. *Cronos*. Paris: Christian Bourgois, 2010.

———. *In memoriam*. Paris: Christian Bourgois, 2007.

———. *Lame de fond*. Paris: Christian Bourgois, 2012.

———. *Les aubes*. Paris: Christian Bourgois, 2001.

———. *Les dits d'un idiots*. Paris: Christian Bourgois, 1995.

———. *Les trois parques*. Paris: Christian Bourgois, 1997.

———. *Lettre morte*. Paris: Christian Bourgois, 1999.

———. *Marina Tsvetaeva: comment ça va la vie?* Paris: Éditions Jean-Michel Place, 2002.

———. *Voix*. Paris: Christian Bourgois, 1998.

Leiris, Michel. *L'Afrique fantôme*. Paris: Gallimard, 1931.

Levain, Myriam. "Nora Hamdi: 'On peut réussir hors de la culture des cités'." *Be*, 2011.

Memmi, Albert. *Portrait du colonisé*. Paris: Buchet/Chastel, 1957.

Moï, Anna. *L'année du cochon de feu*. Paris: Éditions du Rocher, 2008.

———. *Le venin du papillon*. Paris: Gallimard, 2017.

———. *Rapaces*. Paris: Gallimard, 2005.

———. *Violon*. Paris: Flammarion, 2006.

More, Thomas. *Utopia*. Oxford: Oxford University Press, 1999.

Mouflard, Claire. "Évoluée or Intégrée: Black and Beur Publishing Practices in Contemporary Metropolitan French Women Writing." *Romance Notes* 56, no. 2 (2016): 305–320.

———. *L'Autre en Mouvement: Representations of the Postcolonial Urban Other in Contemporary Metropolitan French Art, Literature and Cinema*. Seattle: University of Washington, 2014.

———. "The Digital Griotte: Bessora's Para/Textual Discourses on Identity Politics and Neocolonialism in Contemporary France." *Humanities* 8, no. 1 (2019): 1–15. https://doi.org/10.3390/h8010002.

NDiaye, Marie. *Trois femmes puissantes*. Paris: Gallimard, 2009.

Nguyen, Nathalie Huynh Chau. *Vietnamese Voices: Gender and Cultural Identity in the Vietnamese Francophone Novel.* DeKalb, IL: Southeast Asia Publications, Center for Southeast Asian Studies, Northern Illinois University, 2003.
Pierrat, Jérôme. *La mafia des cités: économie souterraine et crime organisé en banlieue.* Paris: Denoël, 2006.
Schiffrin, André. *The Business of Books: How International Conglomerates Took Over Publishing and Changed the Way We Read.* London: Verso, 2001.
Shakespeare, William and Mark McMurray. *The Tempest.* Canton, NY: Caliban Press, 2001.
Thuram, Lilian. *Manifeste pour l'égalité.* Paris: Autrement, 2012.
Xingjian, Gao. *La Montagne de l'âme.* La Tour d'Aigues: Éditions de l'Aube, 1995.
———. *Le livre d'un homme seul.* La Tour d'Aigues: Éditions de l'Aube, 2000.
———. *Une canne-à-pêche pour mon grand-père.* La Tour d'Aigues: Éditions de l'Aube, 1997.
Zappi, Sylvia. *La maison des vulnérables.* Paris: Seuil, 2016.
Zoubir, Latifa. *Je m'appelle Latifa: une "intégration à la française."* Paris: Denoël, 2009.

Bibliography

Achille, Étienne and Lydie Moudileno. *Mythologies postcoloniales: pour une décolonisation du quotidien.* Paris: Honoré Champion éditeur, 2018.
AFP. "Mondial-1998: vingt ans après, le mythe lointain du "black-blanc-beur." *Le Point*, June 5, 2018. https://www.lepoint.fr/sport/mondial-1998-les-20-ans-vingt-ans-apres-le-mythe-lointain-du-black-blanc-beur-05-06-2018-2224262_26.php.
"Aimé Césaire refuse de recevoir Nicolas Sarkozy." *Le Monde*, December 6, 2005. https://www.lemonde.fr/societe/article/2005/12/06/aime-cesaire-refuse-de-recevoir-nicolas-sarkozy_717977_3224.html.
"Albin Michel: Amours sauvages, Calixthe Beyala." Poster, 1999. 1719.5. Institut Mémoires de l'édition contemporaine.
Amara, Fadela and Sylvia Zappi. *Breaking the Silence: French Women's Voices from the Ghetto*. Translated by Helen Harden Chenut. Berkeley: University of California Press, 2006.
———. *Ni Putes Ni Soumises*. Paris: La Découverte, 2003.
Angelo, Adrienne. "Vision, Voice, and the Female Body: Nina Bouraoui's Sites/Sights of Resistance." In *Francophone Women: Between Visibility and Invisibility*, edited by Cybelle McFadden and Sandrine Teixidor, 77–98. New York: Peter Lang, 2010.
Anyinefa, Koffi. "Scandales: littérature francophone africaine et identité." *Cahiers d'études africaines* 48, no. 191 (2008): 457–486.
Arendt, Hannah. *Origins of Totalitarianism*. New York: Shocken Books, 1954.
Assouline, Pierre. "L'affaire Beyala rebondit: l'Académie Française a pris le risque de cautionner un auteur dont l'oeuvre est truffée de plagiats." *Les échos*, February 1997.
Au Diable Vauvert. n.d.a. "Plaqué or." Accessed April 4, 2019. https://audiable.com/boutique/cat_litterature-francaise/plaque-or/.
———. n.d.b. "Présentation." Accessed April 4, 2019. https://audiable.com/presentation/.

Augé, Marc. *Match retour: anthropologie de la revanche et autres textes*. Paris: Payot & Rivages, 2019.
Barbery, Muriel, Tahar Ben Jelloun, Alain Borer, Roland Brival, Maryse Condé, Didier Daeninckx, Ananda Devi, et al. "Pour une 'littérature-monde' en français." *Le Monde*, March 15, 2007. https://www.lemonde.fr/livres/article/2007/03/15/des-ecrivains-plaident-pour-un-roman-en-francais-ouvert-sur-le-monde_883572_3260.html.
———. "Toward a 'World Literature' in French." Translated by Daniel Simon. *Contemporary French and Francophone Studies* 14, no. 1 (January 2010): 113–117. https://doi.org/10.1080/17409290903412755.
Barnes, Leslie. "Linda Lê, On Writing and Not Writing." *PORTAL: Journal of Multidisciplinary International Studies* 15, no. 1–2 (August 1, 2018): 20–30.
———. "Literature and the Outsider: An Interview with Linde Le.(Q & A) (Interview)." *World Literature Today* 82, no. 3 (May 1, 2008): 53–56.
Béaud, Stéphane and Philippe Guimard. *Affreux, riches et méchants? Un autre regard sur les Bleus*. Paris: La Découverte, 2014.
Bellil, Samira. *Dans l'enfer des tournantes*. Paris: Denoël, 2003. First published 2002 by Denoël (Paris). Page references are to the 2003 edition.
———. *Dans l'enfer des tournantes*. Lyon: Decitre, 2007.
———. *To Hell and Back: The Life of Samira Bellil*. Translated by Lucy R. McNair. Lincoln: University of Nebraska Press, 2008.
Bessora. *53 cm*. Paris: Le Serpent à Plumes, 1999.
———. *Cueillez-moi jolis Messieurs…* Paris: Gallimard, 2007.
———. *Et si Dieu me demande dites-Lui que je dors*. Paris: Gallimard, 2008.
———. "Unpublished Email Interview with the Author." May 16, 2019.
Beyala, Calixthe. *Amours sauvages*. Paris: Albin Michel, 1999.
———. *Femme nue, femme noire*. Paris: Albin Michel, 2003.
———. *Lettre d'une Afro-française à ses compatriotes*. Paris: Mango, 2000.
Blanchard, Emmanuel. "En 1998 comme en 2018, le discours d'une équipe de France 'Black-Blanc-Beur' reste un mythe." *Huffington Post*, June 21, 2018. https://www.huffingtonpost.fr/emmanuel-blanchard/en-1998-comme-en-2018-le-discours-dune-equipe-de-france-black-blanc-beur-reste-un-mythe_a_23462414/.
Blanchard, Pascal, Sonia Daugerm and David Dietz. *Les Bleus: une autre histoire de France (1996–2016)*. France: Wild Side Video, 2017.
Bouraoui, Nina. *Forbidden Vision*. Barrytown, NY: Station Hill Press, 1995.
———. *Garçon manqué*. Paris: Stock, 2000.
———. *La voyeuse interdite*. Paris: Gallimard, 1991.
———. *Tomboy*. Translated by Marjorie Attignol Salvodon and Jehanne-Marie Gavarini. Lincoln: University of Nebraska Press, 2007.
Britto, Karl Ashoka. *Disorientation: France, Vietnam, and the Ambivalence of Interculturality*. Hong Kong: Hong Kong University Press, 2004.
Bwesigye, Brian. "Is Afropolitanism Africa's New Single Story?" *Aster(ix)*, November 22, 2013. http://asterixjournal.com/afropolitanism-africas-new-single-story-reading-helon-habilas-review-need-new-names-brian-bwesigye/.
Carey, John. *The Faber Book of Utopias*. London: Faber and Faber, 1999.

Cazenave, Odile and Patricia Célérier. *Contemporary Francophone African Writers and the Burden of Commitment.* Charlottesville: University of Virginia Press, 2011.

Césaire, Aimé. *A Tempest: Based on Shakespeare's The Tempest: Adaptation for a Black Theatre.* Translated by Philip Crispin. London: Oberon Books, 2000.

———. *Une tempête: d'après "La Tempête" de Shakespeare: Adaptation pour un théâtre nègre.* Paris: Seuil, 1997. First published 1969 by Seuil (Paris).

Césaire, Suzanne. "Malaise d'une civilization (1942)." In *Le grand camouflage: écrits de dissidence (1941–1945)*, edited by Suzanne Césaire and Daniel Maximin. Paris: Seuil, 2009. Page references are to the 2009 edition.

———. "Malaise of a Civilization (1942)." In *The Great Camouflage: Writings of Dissent (1941–1945)*, edited by Suzanne Césaire and Daniel Maximin. Middletown, CT: Wesleyan University Press, 2012. Page references are to the 2012 edition.

Cevaer, F. and Calixthe Beyala. "An Interview with Beyala, Calixthe, a Novelist from Cameroon." *Rlc-Revue de Littérature Comparée* 67, no. 1 (1993): 161–164.

Chamoiseau, Patrick and Edouard Glissant. "Les murs." *L'Humanité*, September 4, 2007. https://www.humanite.fr/node/377104.

Chevillot, Frédérique and Tassadit Imache. "Beurette suis et beurette ne veux pas toujours être: entretien d'été avec Tassadit Imache." *The French Review* 71, no. 4 (1998): 632–644.

Chirac, Jacques. "Discours d'Orléans, 19 juin 1991." In *L'Obs*, "[Flashback] 'Le bruit et l'odeur', le tube de l'année 1991." March 25, 2011. https://www.nouvelobs.com/les-internets/20110325.OBS0255/flashback-le-bruit-et-l-odeur-le-tube-de-l-annee-1991.html.

Christian Bourgois éditeur. n.d.a. "Bibliothèque asiatique." Accessed January 14, 2019. https://www.christianbourgois-editeur.com/collection.php?page=1&IdCol=15.

———. "Calomnies." Design file, 1993. 742 BRG 154.5. Institut Mémoires de l'édition contemporaine.

———. "Cronos." Design file, 2010. SEL 5504.1. Institut Mémoires de l'édition contemporaine.

———. "In memoriam." Design file, 2007. SEL 4143.10. Institut Mémoires de l'édition contemporaine.

———. "Lame de fond." Design file, 2012. SEL 5596.1. Institut Mémoires de l'édition contemporaine.

———. "Les dits d'un idiot." Design file, 1995. SEL 4127.9. Institut Mémoires de l'édition contemporaine.

———. n.d.b. "Linda Lê." Accessed January 14, 2019. https://www.christianbourgois-editeur.com/fiche-auteur.php?Id=8.

Coverley, Merlin. *Utopia.* Harpenden: Oldcastle Books, 2010.

Davis, Derek H. "Editorial: Reacting to France's Ban: Headscarves and Other Religious Attire in American Public Schools." *Journal of Church and State* 46, no. 2 (2004): 221–235.

De Andrade, Oswald and Leslie Bary. "Cannibalist Manifesto." *Latin American Literary Review* 19, no. 38 (1991): 38–47.

De Meyer, Bernard. "La sage-femme, l'exilée et l'écrivain ou les bébés hybrides de Bessora." *French Studies in Southern Africa*, no. 36 (January 2006): 16–30.

Debord, Guy. *La société du spectacle*. Paris: Gallimard, 1967.

———. *The Society of the Spectacle*. Translated by Ken Knabb. London: Rebel Press, 2002.

Diome, Fatou. "Interview by Mouloud Achour." *Le Gros Journal*, Canal +, April 4, 2017. Video. https://www.youtube.com/watch?v=6Q5jbeoFzKc.

———. *La préférence nationale et autres nouvelles*. Paris: Présence africaine, 2001.

———. *Le ventre de l'Atlantique*. Paris: Anne Carrière, 2003.

———. *Le ventre de l'Atlantique*. Paris: Le Livre de Poche, 2005. Page references are to the 2003 edition.

———. *Marianne porte plainte!* Paris: Flammarion, 2017.

———. *The Belly of the Atlantic*. Translated by Lulu Norman and Ros Schwartz. London: Serpent's Tail, 2008.

Dubois, Laurent. *Soccer Empire: The World Cup and the Future of France*. Berkeley: University of California Press, 2010.

Éditions Albin Michel. "Amours Sauvages." Author's manuscript, 1999. ALB 2967.5. Institut Mémoires de l'édition contemporaine.

———. "Amours sauvages, Calixthe Beyala." Marketing flyer, 1999. 1719.5. Institut Mémoires de l'édition contemporaine.

———. n.d.a. "Calixthe Beyala. Amours sauvages." Accessed July 4, 2019. https://www.albin-michel.fr/ouvrages/amours-sauvages-9782226108180.

———. n.d.b. "Calixthe Beyala. Femme nue, femme noire." Accessed July 4, 2019. https://www.albin-michel.fr/ouvrages/femme-nue-femme-noire-9782226137906.

———. "Le petit prince de Belleville." Design file, 1994. 1233-13. Institut Mémoires de l'édition contemporaine.

———. "Maman a un amant." Design file, 1994. 1233-13. Institut Mémoires de l'édition contemporaine.

———. "Une œuvre originale et savoureuse: du caïman au piment et à la crème fraîche." Marketing flyer, 1999. 1719.5. Institut Mémoires de l'édition contemporaine.

Éditions Blanche. n.d. "Essais et documents." Accessed December 5, 2019. http://www.librairie-blanche.com/essais-documents.html.

Éditions de l'Aube. n.d.a. "Anna Moï." Accessed September 26, 2018. http://editionsdelaube.fr/auteurs/anna-moi/.

———. n.d.b. "Regard croisés." Accessed October 9, 2018. http://editionsdelaube.fr/nos-collections/regards-croises/.

Éditions Denoël. n.d.a. "Collection Impacts." Accessed December 4, 2019. http://www.denoel.fr/Catalogue/DENOEL/Impacts.

———. n.d.b. "Dans l'enfer des tournantes." Accessed January 1, 2019. http://www.denoel.fr/Catalogue/DENOEL/Impacts/Dans-l-enfer-des-tournantes.

———. n.d.c. "Je m'appelle Latifa." Accessed December 4, 2019. http://www.denoel.fr/Catalogue/DENOEL/Impacts/Je-m-appelle-Latifa.

———. n.d.d. "La mafia des cités." Accessed December 4, 2019. http://www.denoel.fr/Catalogue/DENOEL/Impacts/La-mafia-des-cites.

Éditions Fayard. n.d. "Faïza Guène- Millénium blues." Accessed December 4, 2019. https://www.fayard.fr/actualites/faiza-guene-millenium-blues.

Éditions Flammarion. n.d. "Fatou Diome. Marianne porte plainte!" Accessed January 15, 2018. https://editions.flammarion.com/Catalogue/cafe-voltaire/marianne-porte-plainte.

Éditions Gallimard. n.d.a. "Ananda Devi." Accessed June 5, 2019. http://www.gallimard.fr/Contributeurs/Ananda-Devi.

———. n.d.b. "Anna Moï. Espéranto, désespéranto." Accessed September 26, 2018. http://www.gallimard.fr/Catalogue/GALLIMARD/Hors-serie-Connaissance/Esperanto-desesperanto.

———. n.d.c. "Anna Moï. Le venin du papillon." Accessed May 7, 2019. http://www.gallimard.fr/Catalogue/GALLIMARD/Blanche/Le-venin-du-papillon.

———. n.d.d. "Anna Moï. Riz noir." Accessed September 26, 2018. http://www.gallimard.fr/Catalogue/GALLIMARD/Folio/Folio/Riz-noir.

———. n.d.e. "Collection Connaissance de l'Orient." Accessed May 7, 2019. http://www.gallimard.fr/Catalogue/GALLIMARD/Connaissance-de-l-Orient.

———. n.d.f. "Collection Connaissance de l'Orient, série vietnamienne." Accessed May 7, 2019. http://www.gallimard.fr/Catalogue/GALLIMARD/Connaissance-de-l-Orient/vietnamienne.

———. n.d.g. "Collection Continents Noirs." Accessed December 5, 2019. http://www.gallimard.fr/Catalogue/GALLIMARD/Continents-Noirs.

Éditions Léo Scheer. n.d. "La couleur dans les mains." Accessed December 6, 2019. http://leoscheer.com/spip.php?article2223.

Edwards, Natalie. *Shifting Subjects Plural Subjectivity in Contemporary Francophone Women's Autobiography*. Lanham, MD: University of Delaware Press, 2011.

Etoke, Nathalie. "Black Blanc Beur: Ma France à Moi." *Nouvelles Études Francophones* 24, no. 1 (2009): 157–171. JSTOR.

Fanon, Frantz. *Black Skin, White Masks*. Translated by Charles Lam Markmann. London: Pluto Press, 2008.

———. *Peau noire, masques blancs*. Paris: Seuil, 1952.

Fernando, Mayanthi. "Fadela Amara with Sylvia Zappi: Breaking the Silence: French Women's Voices from the Ghetto (Book Review)." *Journal of Middle East Women's Studies* (January 2009): 97–100.

Fulton, Dawn. *Signs of Dissent: Maryse Condé and Postcolonial Criticism*. Charlottesville: University of Virginia Press, 2008.

Gastaut, Yvan. *Le métissage par le foot: L'intégration, mais jusqu'où?* Paris: Éditions Autrement, 2008.

Genette, Gérard. *Paratexts: Thresholds of Interpretation*. Translated by Jane E. Lewin. Cambridge: Cambridge University Press, 1997.

———. *Seuils*. Paris: Seuil, 1987.

Gikandi, Simon. "Foreword: On Afropolitanism." In *Negotiating Afropolitanism: Essays on Borders and Spaces in Contemporary African Literature and Folklore*, edited by J. K. S. Makokha and Jennifer Wawrzinek, 9–11. Amsterdam: Rodopi, 2011.

Glissant, Édouard. "Open Letter to the French Minister of the Interior." Translated by Dayo Olopade. *Yale Global Online*, December 9, 2005. https://yaleglobal.yale.edu/content/open-letter-french-minister-interior.

Glissant, Édouard and Patrick Chamoiseau. *Quand les murs tombent: l'identité nationale hors-la-loi*. Paris: Galaade, 2007.

Guène, Faïza. *Millénium blues*. Paris: Fayard, 2018.

Hamdi, Nora. *Des poupées et des anges*. La Laune: Au Diable Vauvert, 2004.

———. *La couleur dans les mains*. Paris: Léo Scheer, 2011.

———. *La maquisarde*. Paris: Grasset, 2014.

———. *Plaqué or*. La Laune: Au Diable Vauvert, 2005.

———. *Trois étoiles*. La Laune: Au Diable Vauvert, 2002.

Hargreaves, Alec G. *Immigration and Identity in Beur Fiction: Voices from the North African Community in France*. Oxford: Berg, 1997.

———. "Perceptions of Ethnic Difference in Post-War France." In *Immigrant Narratives in Contemporary France*, edited by Susan Ireland and Patrice J. Proulx, 7–22. Westport, CT: Greenwood Press, 2001.

———. "Testimony, Co-Authorship, and Dispossession Among Women of Maghrebi Origin in France." *Research in African Literatures* 37, no. 1 (Spring 2006): 42–54.

Hennebert, Marion. "Unpublished Phone Interview with the Author." December 6, 2019.

Hitchcott, Nicki and Dominic Thomas. "Francophone Afropeans." In *Francophone Afropean Literatures*, edited by Nicki Hitchcott and Dominic Thomas. Liverpool: Liverpool University Press, 2014.

Hitchcott, Nicky. *Calixthe Beyala: Performances of Migration*. Liverpool: Liverpool University Press, 2007.

Huggan, Graham. *The Postcolonial Exotic: Marketing the Margins*. London: Routledge, 2006.

Huston, Nancy. *Professeurs de désespoir*. Arles: Actes Sud, 2004.

INA. "Interview du Président de la République, Jacques Chirac." *Institut National de l'Audiovisuel*, July 14, 1998. https://www.ina.fr/video/CAB98029177.

Ireland, Susan. "Bessora's Literary Ludics." *Dalhousie French Studies* 68 (2004): 7–16.

Jacob, Didier. "Les couleurs du succès." *L'Obs*, January 9, 2012. https://bibliobs.nouvelobs.com/actualites/20071219.BIB0508/les-couleurs-du-succes.html.

Kemp, Anna. "Freedom from Oneself: Artistry and the Postcolonial Woman Artist in Nina Bouraoui's *La Voyeuse interdite*." *French Forum* 38, no. 1/2 (Winter/Spring 2013): 237–250.

Kilcline, Cathal. *Sport and Society in Global France: Nations, Migrations, Corporations*. Liverpool: Liverpool University Press, 2019.

Kleppinger, Kathryn A. *Branding the "Beur" Author: Minority Writing and the Media in France, 1983–2013*. Liverpool: Liverpool University Press, 2019.

"La loi du 23 février 2005: texte et réactions." In *Cahiers d'histoire: Revue d'histoire critique*, 94–95, 2005. http://journals.openedition.org/chrhc/1077.

Lapeyronnie, Didier. "La banlieue comme théâtre colonial, ou la fracture coloniale dans les quartiers." In *La fracture coloniale. La société française au prisme de*

l'héritage colonial, edited by Nicolas Bancel, 209–218. Paris: La Découverte, 2005.
Lê, Linda. *Le complexe de Caliban*. Paris: Christian Bourgois, 2005.
———. *Voix*. Paris: Pocket, 1999.
Lê, Linda and Leslie Barnes. "Literature and the Outsider: An Interview with Linda Lê." *World Literature Today* 82, no. 3 (2008): 53–56.
Le Monde. n.d. "Sylvia Zappi." Accessed January 1, 2019. https://www.lemonde.fr/signataires/sylvia-zappi/.
Léonard, Marie des Neiges. "The Effects of Political Rhetoric on the Rise of Legitimized Racism in France: The Case of the 2005 French Riots." *Critical Sociology* 42, no. 7–8 (2016): 1087–1107. https://doi.org/10.1177/0896920515580175.
Leprince, Chloé. "'Black-blanc-beur': petite histoire d'un slogan ambigu." *France Culture*, July 13, 2018. https://www.franceculture.fr/sociologie/slogan-pejoratif-ou-cri-de-ralliement-dune-france-en-liesse-histoire-du-black-blanc-beur.
Lionnet, Françoise. *Autobiographical Voices: Race, Gender, Self-Portraiture*. Ithaca: Cornell University Press, 1989.
Loo, Hui Phang. *L'Imprudence*. Arles: Actes Sud, 2019.
Mango Éditions. n.d. "Accueil." Accessed December 5, 2019. https://www.mangoeditions.com//.
Mannoni, Octave. *Prospero and Caliban: The Psychology of Colonization*. New York: Praeger, 1964.
Marlier, Fanny. "Qui est Sylvia Zappi, la voix des banlieues au 'Monde'?" *Les Inrockuptibles*, May 16, 2016. https://www.lesinrocks.com/2016/05/16/actualite/actualite/sylvia-zappi-voix-banlieues-monde/.
Mbembe, Achille. "Afropolitanism." Translated by Laurent Chauvet. In *Africa Remix: Contemporary Art of a Continent*, edited by Simon Njami and Lucy Durán, 26–30. Ostfilden, Germany: Hatje Cantz, 2005.
McIlvanney, Siobhan. "Double Vision: The Role of the Visual and the Visionary in Nina Bouraoui's 'La voyeuse interdite (Forbidden Vision)'." *Research in African Literatures* 35, no. 4 (Winter 2004): 105–120.
Moï, Anna. *Espéranto, désespéranto: la francophonie sans les Français*. Paris: Gallimard, 2006.
———. "Francophonie sans Français." *Le Monde*, November 24, 2005. https://www.lemonde.fr/idees/article/2005/11/24/francophonie-sans-francais-par-anna-moi_713838_3232.html.
———. *L'écho des rizières*. La Tour d'Aigues: Éditions de l'Aube, 2001.
———. *Parfum de pagode*. La Tour d'Aigues: Éditions de l'Aube [Poche], 2004.
———. *Parfum de pagode*. La Tour d'Aigues: Éditions de l'Aube [Poche], 2007.
———. *Riz noir*. Paris: Gallimard, 2004.
———. *Riz noir*. Paris: Gallimard [Folio], 2006.
Mollier, Jean-Yves. *Édition, presse et pouvoir en France au XXème siècle*. Paris: Fayard, 2008.
———. "L'histoire de l'édition, une histoire à vocation globalisante." *Revue d'histoire moderne et contemporaine (1954-)* 43, no. 2 (1996): 329–348.

Murray, Brittany and Diane Perpich. *Taking French Feminism to the Streets: Fadela Amara and the Rise of Ni Putes Ni Soumises*. Urbana: University of Illinois Press, 2011.

Ndiaye, Pap. *La condition noire: essai sur une minorité française*. Paris: Calmann-Lévy, 2008.

Nguyen, Catherine H. "Vietnam by Removes: Storytelling and Postmemory in Minh Tran Huy." In *Post-Migratory Cultures in Postcolonial France*, edited Kathryn Kleppinger and Laura Reeck, 96–111. Liverpool: Liverpool University Press, 2018.

Nouvelles Éditions Place. n.d. "Collection poésie." Accessed January 14, 2019. https://www.nouvelleseditionsplace.com/collection-poesie/.

Oxford Dictionary of Literary Terms. n.d. "Griot." Accessed December 5, 2019. https://www.oxfordreference.com/view/10.1093/oi/authority.20110803095908752?rskey=9yIapb&result=13.

Pears, Pamela. *Front Cover Iconography and Algerian Women's Writing: Heuristic Implications of the Recto-Verso Effect*. Lanham, MD: Lexington Books, 2015.

Peras, Delphine. "Édition: la bataille des quatrièmes de couverture." *L'Express*, October 15, 2016. https://www.lexpress.fr/culture/livre/edition-la-bataille-des-quatriemes-de-couverture_1840238.html.

Présence Africaine Éditions. n.d. "La préférence nationale et autres nouvelles." Accessed December 5, 2019. http://www.presenceafricaine.com/romans-litterature-africaine-caraibes/383-la-preference-nationale-2708707221.html.

Puig, Stève. "'Qui fait la France?' New Configurations of Frenchness in Contemporary Urban Fiction." In *Reimagining North African Immigration: Identities in Flux in French Literature, Television, and Film*, edited Véronique Machelidon and Patrick Saveau, 17–30. Manchester: Manchester University Press, 2018.

Randall, Marylin. *Pragmatic Plagiarism: Authorship, Profit, and Power*. Toronto: University of Toronto Press, 2001.

Raspiengeas, Jean-Paul. "Anna Moï, la vigilante." *La Croix*, June 8, 2017. https://www.la-croix.com/Culture/Livres-et-idees/Anna-Moi-vigilante-2017-06-08-1200853335.

Reeck, Laura. "The World and the Mirror in Two Twenty-First Century Manifestoes: 'Pour une "littérature-monde" en français' and 'Qui fait la France?'" In *Transnational French Studies: Postcolonialism and Littérature-Monde*, edited by Alec Hargreaves, Charles Forsdick and David Murphy, 258–273. Liverpool: Liverpool University Press, 2010.

"Rencontre. Calixthe Beyala: l'éloge du métissage." *France Dimanche* (Montagne Centre), May 2, 1999. 1719.5. Institut Mémoires de l'édition contemporaine.

Ridon, Jean-Xavier. "*Littérature-monde*, or Redefining Exotic Literature?" In *Transnational French Studies: Postcolonialism and Littérature-Monde*, edited by Alec Hargreaves, Charles Forsdick and David Murphy, 258–273. Liverpool: Liverpool University Press, 2010.

Rix, Lucy. "Maintaining the State of Emergence/y in Aimé Césaire's *Une tempête*." In *The Tempest and its Travels*, edited by Peter Hulme and William Sherman. Philadelphia: University of Pennsylvania Press, 2000.

Rothstein, Edward. "Utopia and its Discontents." In *Visions of Utopia*, edited by Edward Rothstein, Herbert Muschamp and Martin E. Marty, 1–28. Oxford: Oxford University Press, 2003.

Saïd, Edward. *Orientalism*. 25th Anniversary Edition. New York: Vintage Books, 1994. First published 1979 by Vintage Books (New York). Page references are to the 1994 edition.

Sand, George. *The Devil's Pool and Other Stories*. Translated by E. H. Blackmore, A. M. Blackmore and Francine Giguère. Albany: SUNY Press, 2004.

Selao, Ching. *Le roman vietnamien francophone: Orientalisme, occidentalisme et hybridité*. Montréal: Les Presses de l'Université de Montréal, 2011.

Selasi, Taiye. "Bye-Bye Babar." *The LIP Magazine*, March 3, 2005. http://thelip.robertsharp.co.uk/?p=76.

———. "Taiye Selasi on Discovering Her Pride in Her African Roots." *The Guardian*, March 22, 2013. https://www.theguardian.com/books/2013/mar/22/taiye-selasi-afropolitan-memoir.

Sharpley-Whiting, T. Denean. *Black Venus: Sexualized Savages, Primal Fears, and Primitive Narratives in French*. Durham, NC: Duke University Press, 1999.

Spivak, Gayatri. "Subaltern Studies: Deconstructing Historiography." In *Selected Subaltern Studies*, edited by Ranajit Guha and Gayatri Spivak. New York: Oxford University Press, 1988.

Thomas, Dominic. *Africa and France: Postcolonial Cultures, Migration, and Racism*. Bloomington: Indiana University Press, 2013.

———. "New Writing for New Times: Faïza Guène, *banlieue* Writing, and the Post-Beur Generation." *Expressions maghrébines* 7, no. 1 (June 2008): 33–51.

Tvein, Marta. "The Afropolitan Must Go." *Africa Is a Country*, November 28, 2013. https://africasacountry.com/2013/11/the-afropolitan-must-go/.

Van Eeckhout, Laetitia. "Des historiens fustigent une loi prônant un enseignement positif de la colonisation." *Le Monde*, April 14, 2005. https://www.lemonde.fr/societe/article/2005/04/14/des-historiens-fustigent-une-loi-pronant-un-enseignement-positif-de-la-colonisation_638962_3224.html.

Vanoost, Marie. "Journalisme narratif: proposition de définition, entre narratologie et éthique." *Les Cahiers du Journalisme* 25 (Spring/Summer 2013): 140–160.

Vassallo, Helen. "Embodiement, Environment and the Reinvention of Self in Nina Bouraoui's Life-Writing." In *Women's Writing in Twenty-First-Century France: Life as Literature*, edited by Amaleena Damlé and Gill Rye, 141–153. Cardiff: University of Wales Press, 2013.

Viard, Jean. "Unpublished Phone Interview with the Author." August 28, 2019.

Waters, Julia. "From *Continents Noirs* to *Collection Blanche*: From Other to Same? The Case of Ananda Devi." *L'ici et l'ailleurs: Postcolonial Literatures of the Francophone Indian Ocean. E-France: An Online Journal of French Studies*, no. 2 (2008): 55–74.

Watts, Richard. *Packaging Post/Coloniality: The Manufacture of Literary Identity in the Francophone World*. Lanham, MD: Lexington Books, 2005.

———. "Translating Culture: Readings the Paratexts to Aimé Césaire's *Cahier d'un retour au pays natal*." *TTR: Traduction, Terminologie, Rédaction* 13, no. 2 (2000): 29–45. https://doi.org/10.7202/037410ar.

Yeager, Jack. *The Vietnamese Novel in French: A Literary Response to Colonialism, Vietnamese Literature in French*. Hanover, NH: University Press of New England publ. for University of New Hampshire, 1987.

Index

Afropean, 85–86
Afropolitan, 84–86, 92
Albin Michel, éditions, 31–39, 79–82, 88
Amara, Fadela, 45–50, 76
Angelo, Adrienne, 63–65
Anne Carrière, éditions, 110
Anyinefa, Koffi, 80
Arendt, Hannah, 15
Assouline, Pierre, 79, 89–90
Aube, éditions, 37–39, 119–20, 127–31, *131*, *132*
Au Diable Vauvert, éditions, 67, 70–74
Augé, Marc, 5
autobiography, 6–8, 50

Baartman, Saartjie, 94–96
banlieue, 1, 47–51, 53–57, 67–68, 70–72; riots, 118, 149, 156; victim, 8, 44, 46, 48, 50, 61, 68–69, 70–72
Barnes, Leslie, 148
Béaud, Stéphane, 13, 76
Bellil, Samira, 8, 44, 48, 50–59, *60*, 61, 72, 76
Bessora, 7, 9–10, 24–30, 39, 82, 91–101, 111–12
beur, 41–46, 48–49, 72, 87
Beyala, Calixthe, 9, 31, *32*, *33*, 34–37, 79, 82, 87–91
black, 83–84, 86, 87; literature, 9, 80, 86, 93, 105, 111–12

Blanchard, Pascal, and Sonia Dauger, 83
Bouraoui, Nina, 8, 61–67, 73–74, 76, 143
Britto, Karl Ashoka, 119
Bwesigye, Brian, 85

Carey, John, 14
Césaire, Aimé, 134, 145, 149–50, 152
Césaire, Suzanne, 147–48
cas Beyala, 2, 30, 79, 82
Chamoiseau Patrick, and Édouard Glissant, 60–61, 133, 156
Chevillot, Frédérique, 44–45
Chirac, Jacques, 16–17, 38, 115–16, 133–34
Christian Bourgois, éditions, 17, 36–37, 117–18, 140–44, 151–52
colonial, 15, 17–18, 20–21, 25–27, 37–38, 43, 62–63, 82–86, 106–8, 110–13, 120–22
Condé, Maryse, 7, 147, 156
Coverley, Merlin, 14

De Andrade, Oswaldo, 147
Decître, éditions, 59
De Meyer, Bernard, 84, 92
Denoël, éditions, 56–59
Devi, Ananda, 24–27, 98
Diome, Fatou, 2–3, 101–4, 106–10, 112
Dubois, Laurent, 23, 42, 107–9

Edwards, Natalie, 6
Etoke, Nathalie, 42
évoluée, 9, 81, 87, 93, 94, 112

Fanon, Frantz, 102–3
Français de souche, 15–16, 43, 57, 83, 100, 151
francophone, 3, 9–10, 17–19, 24–27, 80–81, 92–93, 116, 119–20, 128–29, 145–49, 157–59
Fulton, Dawn, 147

Gallimard, éditions, *60*, 64–65, 98, 119–20, 121–27, 132–35; Blanche, 24–28, 81, 98, 118, 143–44, 159; Continents noirs, 24–29, 97–99, 101
Gastaut, Yvan, 1, 10, 13
Genette, Gérard, 8, 18, 78
Gikandi, Simon, 85
griotte, 29, 91–92
Guène, Faïza, 50, 72–73

Hamdi, Nora, 8, 44, 61, 67–74, *75*, 76
Hargreaves, Alec, 42–43, 48, 50
Hennebert, Marion, 37–38, 121, 128, 130
Hitchcott, Nicki, 79, 85–86, 90
Huggan, Graham, 19
Huston, Nancy, 139–41

integration, 1, 9, 17, 34, 39, 51, 60, 62–63, 68, 76, 82, 133
intégrée, 44, 61–63, 66–67, 73–74
Ireland, Susan, 93

Kilcline, Cathal, 2

laïcité, 5, 24
Lapeyronnie, Didier, 53–55
Lê, Linda, 9, 17, 36–37, 39, 141–44, 146–52
Le Livre de Poche, éditions, 110
Léo Scheer, éditions, 67, 73–74, *75*
Le Pen, Jean-Marie, 5, 101

Lionnet, Françoise, 7
literary journalism, 46–48, 50, 52–53
literary patronage, 51–53
littérature-monde, 135–36, 157, 159
lois mémorielles, 133–34

Mbembe, Achille, 84–85
McIlvanney, Siobhán, 63
Moï, Anna, 37–38, 121–27, 135–37, 157–58
Mollier, Jean-Yves, 19–20, 21–23, 31, 38
More, Thomas, 14

NDiaye, Marie, 81
Ndiaye, Pap, 83–84, 86
neocolonial, 24, 34, 39, 53, 112, 125, 127, 129, 149, 155
Nguyen, Nathalie, 119
non-blanc, 1, 4, 20–21, 44, 90, 118, 129, 149, 152, 155–56

orientalism, 117–18

paratext, 18–21, 24–25, 27–31, 37–39, 44–45, 52, 61, 63–67, 70–74, 80, 86, 88, 93, 96–98, 104, 110–12, 117–18, 124–26, 142–44, 151–52
Pears, Pamela, 64–65
plagiarism, 4–5, 30–31, 79–80, 87–90, 112
postcolonial, 19, 66, 74, 121, 146–50
Présence africaine, éditions, 101, 104–5
publishing, 21, 23–24, 30–38, 57–61, 66–67, 70–74, 88, 93, 96–99, 118, 121–31, 141–44
Puig, Stève, 51

Rix, Lucy, 149
Rothstein, Edward, 14–15

Saïd, Edward, 117–18
Sarkozy, Nicolas, 5, 59–61, 133–34, 156

Selao, Ching, 115–16, 119, 128, 137–38
Selasi, Taiye, 84
Serpent à Plumes, editions, 29–30, 94, 96–99
Serpent's Tail, publisher, 110–11
Sharpley-Whiting, T. Denean, 94–96
Spivak, Gayatri, 96
stereotypes: gender, *31*–33, 37–38, 49–50, 57, 93–96; racial, 28, *31*–33, 43, 57, 80–81, 87, 91, 115–18
Stock, éditions, 65–66, 73, 143
Stoquart, Josée, 50–56, 68

Thomas, Dominic, 81, 85–86, 94
Thuram, Lilian, 1, 9, 82, 87, 105–7, 109
totalitarianism, 14–16

urban literature, 51

utopia, 2, 13–15, 46; "Black-Blanc-Beur," 2, 4–6, 13, 16–17, 24, 39, 83, 101, 105–6, 112, 133–34, 155

Vanoost, Marie, 47
Vassallo, Helen, 63
Viard, Jean, 37–38, 128–29

Waters, Julia, 24–27, 98
Watts, Richard, 8, 20–21, 26, 52, 63, 94, 98, 105, 142
World Cup (1998), 1, 13–14, 16, 23–24, 41–42

Yeager, Jack, 118, 120

Zidane, Zinedine, 1, 8, 41–43, 49–50, 66, 74, 87, 107

About the Author

Claire Mouflard is assistant professor of French and Francophone Studies at Hamilton College (Clinton, NY). She has published articles on the topics of immigration and migration in France, French and francophone literature and cinema, and the publishing industry in *Romance Notes*, *Women in French*, *Cinémas*, and *Humanities*.

www.ingramcontent.com/pod-product-compliance
Lightning Source LLC
Chambersburg PA
CBHW050907300426
44111CB00010B/1417